A Woman's Book of Money

A Guide to Financial Independence

A Woman's Book of Money

A GUIDE TO
FINANCIAL INDEPENDENCE

SYLVIA AUERBACH

DOLPHIN BOOKS

DOUBLEDAY & COMPANY, INC.

GARDEN CITY, NEW YORK

1976

A Dolphin Books Original
ISBN: 0-385-09883-9
Library of Congress Catalog Card Number 75-44952
Copyright © 1976 by Sylvia Auerbach
Printed in the United States of America
First Edition

Contents

A Woman's Book of Money

A Guide to Financial Independence

CHAPTER 1

Start Here for Some Financial Consciousness Raising

How do you spell independence? M-O-N-E-Y.

That's such a crass beginning for a book for women, isn't it? Women aren't accustomed to thinking that way, feeling that way, or above all talking that way. The shadow of the grasping gold digger haunts those of us in the not-to-be-trusted-because-we're-over-thirty generation. Those of us on the lower side of thirty are caught up in the desire to grasp life's true values—love, friendship, meaningful relationships. There's a pervasive feeling that to be concerned about money is materialistic—and therefore bad—and also unfeminine, and therefore worse.

For men, however, money is a natural masculine concern—not to mention a symbol of and a means to power.

Yet, whatever the attitudes we've learned, the real truth is that money has one common denominator for everyone: It represents freedom and independence.

Picture yourself in this scenario. You are married and have one child. Your main interests are ancient history, gourmet cooking, and stray dogs and cats. You know about women's liberation only from cartoons and snide remarks by television comedians. You are the shyest, most magnolia-and-orange-blossom, clinging-vine woman imaginable—and you just *know* that men know more about managing money than women, that women's place is in the home, and you wouldn't dream of having a credit card in your own name. You *always* run to your husband, your father, or in a pinch Uncle Joe when you want advice on how to spend the income from your million-dollar trust fund.

Here's a different scenario. You're divorced and you have a job that supports yourself and your small child. You have a master's degree in psychology, you're interested in politics, and your hobby is mountain climbing. You've been an ardent feminist since you first read Betty Friedan's *The Fem-*

inine Mystique in 1965. You were the first women's libber on your block and you've started about fifty consciousness-raising groups. You certainly don't need any advice on managing your money—you were actually much better at handling finances than your ex-husband—and you would love to have a credit card in your own name. There's only one problem: you don't have any money. In fact, with living costs so high and your pay so low, you're absolutely broke.

Who has more power? More independence?

If you have the slightest doubt, just ask yourself whether Ms. Heiress or Ms. Divorcée gets more invitations to open charge accounts, accept credit cards, invest her money.

Women's Handicaps in the Money Race

Managing money has always been an important ingredient in achieving success and independence. But women have always been handicapped in this money race by the idea, which they have too often accepted, that understanding money is beyond them. Just to test the validity of this idea, let's change the scene again.

Consider an emergency situation. You're the chief cook, maitre d', and bottle washer at your house (so what else is new?). You're suddenly called away. The man in your life has to take over, either to feed the children or to prepare meals for guests. You leave instructions that are, in your opinion, absolutely clear. The eggs for breakfast can be medium boiled, shirred, or served as eggs-in-a-basket. The fish for lunch is to be sautéed lightly. The baby's apples are to be puréed; the cabbage has to be parboiled for a few minutes before putting it into the soup; the beef should be braised.

You might as well have left a scroll written in Latin or Sanscrit. He hasn't the slightest idea of what you're talking about; he flubs the whole thing, and he feels confused, stupid, helpless, and dependent. (*And* the kitchen is a mess.) He knows it can be done because you do it all the time and do it well, yet he has failed though he really is a bright and charming fellow.

Why? Because he didn't know the language or the territory, he *couldn't* do well. If he hadn't felt so inadequate and if he had had a buddy to call, he might have gotten some help. But he was too embarrassed to show his ignorance—and besides, even if he hadn't been so bashful, who was there to ask? Whom would he have called and how could he have asked so many seemingly foolish questions?

I'm sure you both know and *feel* the point I'm making. Just as women are in control of a situation when they are prepared and know the language and the territory, so are men. And just as men are ill at ease and unprepared in a strange situation when they don't know the language or the territory, so are women.

Different Socializing: Men versus Women

This brings up the next question. Why don't we know more about money management? Because we haven't been trained, educated, or socialized to think we should. In fact, many of us have been taught there is something deliciously feminine about being ignorant. More about this later, but for the moment let's see some of the consequences of this kind of socialization at various stages in a woman's life.

(And though we all owe a debt to the women's liberation movement for raising our consciousness and pointing up the importance of becoming more independent, these new times are not an unmixed blessing. In some ways our problems have become more, not less, complicated because of women's liberation. The sexual revolution, the change in women's status, and the fact that women are now living longer don't necessarily mean they are enjoying life more.)

Let's start with the career girl. She has to support herself, in an era of rising prices, because it's expected that she will be independent, at least until some young man comes along and offers protection. And she expects it of herself. If she wants to compete with men she's supposed to compete on the same terms—but she still may have to get along on a lower salary or less-adequate training while she's fighting the battle for equality. (But supposedly understanding money is beyond her.)

Then along comes some nice man and marries her. This is the protection she's heard about—but she may have to wait four or more years to get it. They live in a world with a job market that demands degrees, so they decide that she will help him get a degree so that later she can retire and have babies, or she will help him get his degree first and then he will help her get hers. In either case she becomes the family's main breadwinner. But she's still supposed to be not-too-bright about money—after all this is only a temporary situation. And of course she has to protect his male ego by deferring to his superior knowledge, yet—ignorant though she is—she manages to get him through college or professional school.

Or maybe she is more liberated, decides against marriage and becomes that Cosmopolitan girl. She has all the right measurements, including a twelve-cubic-foot refrigerator full of some man's favorite snacks and drinks. Supposedly understanding money is beyond her, although she manages her money well enough to have a place so nice to come home to that he comes home to it (at her expense) instead of going to his own apartment in the singles complex.

Or let's consider the young marrieds whose marriage never gets old because the two of them decide to split. She finds that no-fault divorce means that through no fault of hers she is left with a child or children to support. Suddenly the man's world of judges and lawyers thinks she's *very smart* when it comes to understanding and managing money; she gets a pittance on which to support herself and take care of their children.

Worse off, very often, is the wife of fifteen, twenty, or even twenty-five years whose husband decides to trade her in for a newer, shinier model. She is thrown back on the job market when she has no skills, or skills that have become obsolete—her husband didn't want her to work, so she hasn't seen a shorthand pad or been near a typewriter in years, or she let her teaching certificate lapse, or she dropped out of college to get married. She learns about money the hard and bitter way: she can't use her charge accounts because they're in her married name; she moves from the spacious suburban house to the cramped city apartment; she stands a long time before the meat counter debating whether or not she can afford an occasional dinner of lamb chops or sirloin steak instead of scrambled eggs or hamburgers.

And finally, and the actuarial tables of insurance companies tell us this, most of us will outlive our men by seven to ten years. Then, at the very time when we are least equipped emotionally to make financial decisions, we will be faced with the necessity of making a multitude of such decisions. There will be all kinds and any number of men (and some women) around to help us make these decisions—but their advice won't necessarily be planned to protect us.

Men have a different kind of socialization. There is an assumption that of course men will be able to manage their money—they somehow or other acquire this knowledge along with deeper voices, hair on their chest, and their first paycheck. But stop and think about that a minute—do all the men that you know manage their money well? Of course not.

So it should come as no surprise to you—when you do stop to think about it—that all men are not experts at managing money. If they are very important men in real positions of power, they get stung by the millions. Just think of all the financial men who lost money when the Penn Central Railroad went bankrupt; when the Equity Funding Insurance company was selling phony insurance policies; or when the Home-Stake Production Company, a Tulsa oil-drilling outfit, promised large profits from oil production but drilled few wells and paid back little to such investors as the board chairmen of General Electric, Western Union, and Macy's among others. If they are less important, less powerful men, they will lose in the stock market or buy the wrong insurance or have trouble filling out their income tax form.

But one thing men do understand is the power of the purse string. They learn very early in life that he who controls the finances very often controls, although perhaps indirectly, just about everything else—or at least everything else he cares about and wants to control. There's much truth in those old folk sayings "He who pays the piper can call the tune," and (my favorite) "So long as he is rich, even a barbarian is attractive."

How to Play the Smart-about-money Game

Enter square one of the financial consciousness-raising game. You want to be a winner in life? You want to control your own destiny? Then—and at every stage in your life—you have to have some control over your finances, and you have to understand how to manage them. Only then can you be truly independent. This doesn't mean you have to do all the work yourself, or make all the decisions yourself.

It does mean—square two—that you have to take an interest in your own, or your family's or your husband's, financial affairs. It means you have to know how much your husband earns, what other sources of income you have, what provision he has made for continuing your income if he gets sick or reaches retirement age or dies. It means you have to know what benefits you get from your job and how to go about getting them—including a better job and a promotion and raise. It means you have to get equal pay for equal work. It means, in other words, that you have to educate yourself and assume some responsibility. Above all, it may mean—square three—that you have some money that you can call your own and get your hands on in an emergency.

It also means—square four—that you are going to get full value for your dollar, whether it's your own salary, a joint income, or money you inherited as a widow. It means you won't get cheated by lawyers, accountants, brokers, would-be partners, even sometimes, unfortunately, by relatives. It means you become an asset to yourself, not a liability.

You may think this is a tall order, one you're not capable of achieving. And I must tell you that I think you are wrong—you are actually smarter and more capable than you give yourself credit for, and that others give you credit for. Even as you are saying that you can't manage money, you are doing it—stretching your food dollars, meeting your rent or your mortgage payments, paying your daily expenses, occasionally buying something for your house, meeting your other bills—in short, managing. And at a time when inflation is making the job much more difficult.

Perhaps you can't manage your money as well as you would like, but you may be setting goals that are too high, perhaps comparing yourself to others who seem to manage better—but may have resources you don't know about. A rich uncle. A small inheritance. A different life style—hamburgers all the time when you like steak once in a while—so that, considering the life style you have chosen, you are managing as well or better.

This doesn't mean that you should rest on your hard-won merit badges. Not at all. For the fact is that, though women have managed very well on their share of the economic pie, the one thing we haven't done, at least until recently, is try to insure that we get a big-enough piece of the pie. From salaries to pensions to divorce settlements to child care to insurance to social security, etc., etc. We have not been getting our fair share—and it's time we did. But to do it we need to know more—which is one of the main purposes of this book. Money is power and so is knowledge. Together, they are a terrific combination. So let's start with some knowledge of where we are, and how we got there.

CHAPTER 2

The Score: Establishment 5, Women ½

Where to start? It's a difficult question, because no matter where we start to look at this question of equality we find inequality. So maybe the best place to start is where some progress has been made, just so we know there's hope—then into where women's work is still not done.

Giving women credit where credit was long overdue has been one of the success stories of the women's liberation movement. After many years of incorrectly taking it for granted that a wife's salary went to pay for tie pins, diamond pins, costume jewelry pins—but never diaper pins—banks and other businesses that give credit finally woke up. They permitted themselves to be dragged, kicking, groaning, balking, and muttering under their breath, into the twentieth century.

Don't think it was easy. It didn't come from bankers looking around them and noticing that most of the people who worked for them (and occasionally with them) were women. It didn't come from noticing that many of these women came to the bank from high school and college, and stayed right on, despite marriage and babies—or came back within a span of a few years. It didn't come from noticing that more and more women were staying single, getting divorced, or being widowed—and were therefore totally responsible for their own income, or were supporting dependents, partially or wholly, as single heads of families.

It didn't come from knowing that many families couldn't meet their mortgage payments, send their children to college, or maintain a decent standard of living without the income from a wife's job—a job that the wife had held for many years and intended to hold for many more.

It didn't come from recognizing that Title VII of the 1964 Civil Rights Act—the Title that prohibits job discrimination because of sex—was finally being implemented because women who had been discriminated against had taken their cases to the courts and won.

It should have—but it didn't. (No group gives up its power willingly.) Instead it came from very determined groups of women around the country who wrote letters, organized demonstrations, circulated petitions, held meetings, spoke to not-so-friendly or plainly hostile legislators: in short, women who applied pressure in an organized way. Finally, and at long last, discrimination in granting credit on the basis of sex or marital status is forbidden by law. Chalk up one-half point for our side.

We didn't do so well in the other areas that discriminate against women: marriage and divorce laws, especially when they apply to property rights; tax laws; pension plans; various kinds of insurance (health, disability, life, automobile); social security; and above all the special status of the greatest source of skilled unpaid labor in the country—the housewife.

(In all fairness, some of the laws that govern these areas also discriminate against men: The social security laws and pension are prime examples and we're sorry about that. However, since men have more power, more contacts, and more experience in fighting for their rights, I'm going to leave it up to them to wage and win their own battles—and concern myself only with women. Even before the millennium arrives there will certainly be many times when we'll cooperate with them to win equal justice all around. But right now my priority and yours is equal rights for women.)

I don't intend to disparage in any way the progress that has been made, because it's been enormous. Yet in each of the categories I've mentioned there is still a long way to go. Since women's groups and some sympathetic and fair-minded men in government, business, and academia are busy changing things, some of these injustices may be remedied by the time this book appears. (Don't hold your breath, however.) So, with this bit of caution in mind, here is how things stand.

Marriage

Marriage laws vary considerably from state to state, so what is applicable in one is not necessarily applicable in another. In Chapters 8 and 9 I'll tell you the things you should check off or check into before you enter into the state of matrimony. Let me here, just as an eye opener, tell you some of the laws that may apply in *your* state.

When you say "I do," you may also, though you don't know it, be saying I do consent to allowing my husband to choose where we shall live, and I am committed to abide by his choice. If I don't accept it he has the right to divorce me.

You may commit yourself to work in your home without pay for the services you give your husband. You may also be committing yourself to work in your husband's business without getting paid.

You may be expected to care for one of your husband's relatives without compensation—even if you give full-time nursing care and act as a housekeeper in both your own home and that of the ailing relative.

You may find that your husband has a greater right to your property than you have, including property you inherited from your family, if it has become part of your joint holdings.

You may find that if your husband pays for something such as stock, he doesn't have to declare the stock as part of your joint property—only the income is "joint."

Of course, if you live forever in wedded bliss, and it's just one sixty-year honeymoon, you couldn't care less about little ifs, ands, and buts.

Divorce

And if all goes well that is exactly the case. *But* if the two of you get divorced—and you have no separate income, or an inadequate income—these ifs, ands, and buts are going to loom very large indeed. Perhaps it couldn't happen to you but it has happened to other women, who:

1. Found their joint bank account was suddenly emptied.

2. Found the house they had bought from their combined salaries belonged only to the husband—since he had had the property registered in his name only.

3. Found themselves, like Dolores B., trying to support themselves and three children on a part-time secretary's salary ($60 a week) plus the $75 a week a judge had awarded for child care. (Dolores's rent alone was $225 a month, to say nothing of food, doctor bills, clothes, carfare, nursery school so she could work.)

4. Found themselves just about unemployable after being out of the work force fifteen years.

5. Found themselves only slightly better off with a low-level job that meant a very much reduced standard of living.

6. Found themselves, like Annette S., being forced to leave a job because there was no place to place a preschool toddler and so having to go on relief to stay at home and care for the toddler. And then being asked, "Why don't you go to work?"

I could go on, but it's not really necessary—you get the picture. We still have with us the weakest link in the divorce chain: the ability of husbands who want to evade their responsibility to find any number of ways to do it— from leaving the country to just being perpetually delinquent until their wives give up in disgust, because their nerves and their pocketbooks can't stand the strain of being perpetual bill collectors.

Nor has the concept of the no-fault divorce movement turned out quite as intended. In some cases, despite the best intentions of the women's lib movement, no-fault has served more to liberate the ex-husband than the ex-wife. Before, at least, the ex-husband was somewhat subject to the censure of the community since it was considered the man's job to provide for his wife and children. Now, with the concept of no-fault, ex-husbands are finding they have the freedom to evade their responsibilities to their ex-wives and children. In the meantime ex-wives are finding that through no fault of theirs they are latecomers to social security benefits, pension plans, health plans, and other benefits they had once anticipated sharing.

Benefits

Which brings up the question of pensions. Here again women are victimized—and as a result the 7.5 million widows and single women over sixty-five are just about the most poverty-stricken part of the population. In 1970 half had annual incomes of $1,888 or less. We are victimized in many different ways—and the fact that sometimes the victimization isn't intentional doesn't make life any easier. If we stay home to raise a family, we have fewer working years to get pension rights. If we move around the country with our husbands, as their careers demand, we lose the years of continuous employment that make us eligible to receive pensions. Ditto for working at part-time jobs.

Women are also discriminated against when it comes to their husband's pensions. It often comes as a shock that when the husband dies his pension dies with him. Even if he has tried to prevent this by taking less pension in exchange for a "survivors' benefit option," there are sometimes restrictive clauses that make it impossible for the widow to collect. She might not be able to collect, for instance, if he died while close to retirement age but still employed, or conversely if he died after he had retired. And as widows we only receive 82.5 per cent of our husband's social security benefits—though if our husband outlives us he is entitled to 100 per cent of the benefits. (The logic behind this is unfathomable.) At this rate a famous older woman like Whistler's mother would have had to pawn her rocking chair in order to stay alive.

"No-value" Labor

Nor is everything rosy with those of us who are still married. Unless we have income in our own name, through our jobs, or perhaps through inheritance, very often we have no security except that which our husband chooses to give us. A woman working at home, the "housewife" who is also purchasing agent, stand-by medical staff, chauffeur, gardener, healer of hurt psyches and skinned knees, still has no recognized value in the marketplace. As far as the gross national product is concerned (the sum of all goods and services produced), we just don't exist. And since we don't exist, we of course don't have social security, disability insurance, workmen's compensation, or pension rights. (To say nothing of no forty-hour week, weekends off, or guaranteed paid holidays.)

But is our work valuable? Does it have a market value? All we need do to prove that the answer is "yes" is to imagine what would happen if each of us now doing chores for our own family were suddenly to go across the street and do exactly the same chores for someone else's family. Immediately we'd get social security, and perhaps some other fringe benefits, like workmen's compensation, group health insurance, paid vacations, etc. (We can dream, can't we?) I can't see us all packing and moving—but this does illustrate how absurd it is that housewives aren't counted in as productive workers.

Taxes

The other inevitable besides death is taxes, and here women with children who work outside their homes and must pay for child care are losers. The way the law is set up, the more you earn the less you are allowed to deduct for child care. And there are all kinds of restrictions on whether you can file a single or a joint return, the number of days that must be worked, who can be hired to look after the child, and so on. In theory these rules apply to either spouse; in practice it is usually the wife who adjusts her working schedule to the demands of child-raising, so these rules generally affect her the most. What they do in effect is make it less profitable for a wife and mother to continue to work.

Insurance

We are still discriminated against in the area that affects us most directly—health benefits for pregnancies. We still can't get the kind of disability insurance that men can get, and we pay more for what we can get. (I'll go into much more detail on all these topics in the following chapters.)

These are the most glaring examples of how the laws have operated and are still operating to discriminate against women. But it isn't only laws that discriminate—it's also people and situations. And this is particularly true when it comes to the business, academic, and industrial world. Sometimes these more subtle forms of bias and pressure, including the pressures we put on ourselves, can be even more effective in teaching women their place—twenty paces behind our male counterparts, with head appropriately lowered so we can only see our little patch of turf and never realize what a big horizon there is, or could be.

CHAPTER 3

Power, Potency, and Poor Little Rich and Poor Girls

Why should a college graduate who mastered Mandarin Chinese well enough to teach it in college know so little about the family finances that she had to ask her husband—a highly paid television executive—if she can afford a new coat?

Why should a career girl who has been self-supporting since she was sixteen defer to her male colleagues' opinions on any and every financial topic at the lunch table?

Why should a working wife who contributes substantially to the family income as well as managing the household sign a joint income tax return—without even looking at her husband's salary?

Why should a widow who managed to feed, clothe, and make a pleasant home for her four children on her husband's often meager salary have to ask her sons how she should manage her now-comfortable income?

There is no intellectual reason—no reason at all. Each of these women is perfectly capable of understanding and managing her own, or even her family's, financial affairs. But somewhere along the way to adulthood, each has been brainwashed to believe she can't understand money or money management, or if she can understand it, maybe she shouldn't press the point because she might undermine the male ego.

No discussion of women and money can be considered apart from men's concepts of money. It is, in many ways, tied up with machismo, psychology, a man's estimate of his worth, even with his sexual prowess. Dr. Theodore Rubin, the noted psychiatrist, pointed out in a *Ladies' Home Journal* column that "people, especially men, regard the amount of money they earn as a measure of where they stand in relation to others. To them, a salary is synonymous with self-worth—and revealing that salary is revealing one's worth in society. The degree of secrecy about salaries is directly proportional to the extent to which the person measures his worth and general self-esteem by the money he earns. With such a man secrecy will increase as the self-esteem gets lower."

Dr. James A. Knight, professor of psychiatry and associate dean of the Tulane University School of Medicine, puts it another way. Money is an ego supplement, he notes, and points out further that "to some men, money is a symbol of their potency."

This, of course, is one subliminal reason that men don't tell their wives how much they make. In a way they are putting a price on themselves, and (though it may be a lot of money) if *they* are not happy about the price, they don't want to reveal it. This is also why widows who've been assured all during their married life, "You don't have to worry, you're well provided for," are sometimes shocked to find their estate much smaller than they had been led to believe.

The Advantages of Secrecy

And there are other more practical reasons, too. Madeline McWhinney, president of the First Women's Bank and Trust Company, tells of a union in Manhattan whose male members insist on getting paid in cash—despite a high crime rate in the area where they work—because they don't want their wives to know precisely how much they earn. And certainly this desire for secrecy isn't confined to men in the lower income brackets. Many men in the higher income brackets, particularly those who have their own business or professional practice and must declare their earnings for tax purposes, find that secrecy is the better part of valor.

Such secrecy enables them to at least fudge if not actually cheat on their income tax. It also enables them to pick up the tab for a female friend's dentist bill (so my dentist tells me); to send out two sets of Christmas gifts, one size six and one size twelve (so my favorite Saks Fifth Avenue salesgirl tells me); to dabble a bit in the stock market without having to reveal losses (so my broker tells me); and even—and more nobly—to help an elderly relative that a wife may not be particularly fond of.

Dependency Through the Ages

All of which points up something that, all through history, men have always realized, and fully exploited—money is power. Power, as I noted before, to control not only your own life, but also the lives of those dependent on you. Pick an age, from the earliest recorded history to recent times, and pick a culture in any part of the globe. You will find that women have had little control over money and therefore little control over their own lives.

One of the earliest legal codes is that of the Hammurabi about 1700 B.C., followed about six hundred years later by another body of laws from Assyrian scribes. Women were property of men, bought and sold. Though it was called "bride money" rather than the price, they were bought and sold from father to husband just the same. Whether the woman was Greek or Roman, Chinese or Japanese, Egyptian or Ethiopian, she was being passed on from hand to hand, with little to say in the matter. And this was true whether she was a peasant or a fine lady—her desirability was based not just on whether she could bear children and do women's work but also on how many head of cattle or purses of gold she brought with her.

In the Middle Ages the minstrels sang of noblewomen who had beauty of body and purity of soul. But the duke may have cherished the duchess-to-be more for the titles, lands, and power she was bringing with her.

This is not to say that during the ages some women haven't handled money. Some African tribeswomen were noted for their shrewd trading. Orthodox Jewish women were supposed to handle the family's finances so their men would be free to take care of the more important task of studying the Torah or holy book, so that God's messages would be clear. When the Crusaders went off to reclaim the Holy Land from the infidel Turk, they often left their estates in the hands of their wives, and many of them managed these large business enterprises very well. And there have always been a few heiresses who inherited fortunes and understood and used the money well—sometimes, in fact, using it as men do to control people, including men of course.

But even when the industrial revolution and changing modes of life over the centuries meant that women had some earning power on their own, the tradition persisted. Women were still brought up to conceive of themselves as mothers, nurturers, and helpmates—honorable roles but also dependent ones. And the sum of these perceptions, laws, customs, and attitudes meant that women have been almost completely dependent financially. This dependency has had a profound effect on how women think and deal with money. They have not only been deprived of their rights; they have also, as a result of this dependency, acquired certain attitudes and ways of thinking, starting very young and very early in the socialization process. So let's have a look at how that works.

How Women Are Socialized

According to Dr. Natalie Shainess, a feminist and noted psychoanalyst, the process starts in many and pervasive ways from the time the little girl, wise in the ways that children are wise, is observing and making judgments about the adult world—while seeming to be totally preoccupied making tunnels in the sandbox or piling up blocks into a castle. The little girl sees that Daddy is the decision maker in the family partly because he is the person who earns the money. She makes the connection—money is power. The little girl understands that her mother doesn't have any power, or perhaps very little power—and since her mother's opportunities to earn her own money are limited because she lacks training or experience, or is homebound and has no independent income from her services as homemaker, she is dependent on the approval and good will of the person who supports her.

Her mother may try to get around this dependency in a variety of ways—by wangling the money, offering or withholding sex, setting aside a little bit of the household money in an account that only she knows about. All of these actions influence the mother's concept of money and how to handle it. And of course the dependency influences how her husband feels about money and their financial relationship, and what the child perceives.

Consider, for instance, these excerpts from an article that appeared in *The New York Times Magazine*, which was based on a four-hour tape-recorded session with executives and professional men, husbands of women who were in a consciousness-raising group together. (Incidentally, many of the women were working, at good to excellent salaries.)

Engineer: "My wife also lets me take care of financial things—having been taught that a good wife lets her husband handle all of these so-called masculine functions. . . . I feel good about her becoming more independent. . . . on the other hand I think I feel very threatened. . . . at heart I like her being dependent on me. . . ."

Press agent: "In our capitalistic society who handles the money determines who's the boss."

Art Director (discussing an argument he and his wife had had about a ten-dollar table which she wanted to buy and he did not, because he didn't like it and also because they had a "covenant" that any purchase for their house should be jointly approved since it reflected the taste of both; she ordered it anyway though the salesperson had heard the argument, and he walked out of the store): "When we got home I didn't know how to vent my fury at her —(A) for breaking the covenant about agreement on household purchases, and (B) for effectively cutting my genitals off in front of a salesperson. She finally agreed it had been a castrating thing to do and, in fact, was contrary to the covenant. But she still seems to feel that it was also a money issue—and I know it was not that at all."

The little girl may then become accustomed to going to ask Daddy for money, and running the risk that she won't get it if he doesn't approve of some of her actions, or even if she thinks he doesn't or might not approve. In this way she develops a need for approval from the person in power, who is male, and this then translates into the need for male approval generally. By itself this might not be an undesirable trait, but it *is* undesirable if it means she doesn't develop self-esteem or confidence in her ability to make judgments or manage her own affairs. Nor it is a good idea if she grows up believing that the management of money is not one of her adult responsibilities.

In the best-selling and poignant book *Widow* (William Morrow, 1974), Lynne Caine discusses how shocked she was, as a young widow with two young children, to realize her husband had made no provision for the support of his family if something should happen to him. (He was uninsurable because he had been severely wounded in World War II.) Mrs. Caine says, on realizing that she had been left with two children to support and very little money:

> I wanted to hate Martin, but I couldn't. My conscience stood in the way. I had to ask myself, "Well, Lynne, what the hell did you do about it?" and that's the chiller. I had done nothing. . . . Martin and I had never discussed money. Just one of those unliberated things, I suppose, going back to the idea that little girls aren't good at math, a self-fulfilling prophecy that encourages financial incompetence. . . . I had never shared any of the real responsibilities of the household. My job? That was just running off to play. I "ran" the household just about the way a little girl plays house.

And so the little girl grows up with a more passive and dependent "role model." She may be given toys that encourage her to think of her biological role—dishes, stoves, dolls—while little boys are given toys that encourage them to think abstractly—blocks, puzzles. Boys are expected to learn to be "good providers" and therefore they are expected to learn about money. Fathers, at the dinner table, may talk about their business and expect the boys to listen; girls are not expected to pay attention.

At family parties the men and women separate—the men to discuss business and the women to talk "woman talk." Naturally, the boys can listen in on men. Again, boys absorb the fact that they are supposed to know about money, and the places and ways that money is acquired. Girls are more apt to learn that they should be attractive. If they do hear talk about money from the woman's viewpoint, it's more apt to be how to be a good shopper, find bargains, and be a good "manager," but only on the domestic scale. (Philip E. Hogin, an executive vice-president of Western Electric Company, was the first "executive-in-residence" at Bryn Mawr, an intellectual women's liberal arts college, in a program designed to acquaint women with business and vice versa. He says he was "appalled by the abysmal ignorance of the business world, even among girls whose fathers were businessmen."

And this "bargain" approach, in Dr. Shainess's opinion, can be a drawback. Women are bargain-oriented for several reasons: They are concerned with security, and therefore intent on saving, and of course a bargain does save money. But Madison Avenue also encourages women to get a bargain *and* win a compliment from a man.

Yet, the bargain syndrome can be a psychological approach that hinders women, because it encourages women to think in "cents-off" terms, to think small. Men, on the other hand, are taught that it's not the "cents-off" approach that brings financial independence, but rather the earning of dollars, the "make-a-buck" idea, that counts. Men are more encouraged to take a chance, to take risks. And because they have more confidence in their ability, because they have different training and different expectations for themselves, they are willing to take risks—with the understanding that they may make mistakes along the way—but that there is no other way to learn.

More Socialization Hazards

We have to realize too that there is learning in the kinds of jobs that men and women have. In the past women have gone primarily into the nurturing and service occupations: teaching, particularly at the lower levels; librarianship; nursing. These are not occupations where women were apt to learn more about money management. And the jobs that did involve financial planning, the higher level jobs, were mostly held by men, so again women were denied practical experience. This only reinforced their feeling that when it came to a decision involving large sums of money the subject was somehow or other beyond them. This in turn meant they never got any experience, which made them feel even more inadequate, particularly when their male counterparts in age and schooling were acquiring the knowledge and becoming the treasurers, comptrollers, accountants, financial planners.

And just as men have their subtle psychological feelings, "hang-ups" if you will, about money, so do women. Dr. Ella Lasky, who teaches the psychology of women at Manhattan Community College and also has a private practice, thinks that women have a defensive attitude toward money. Somehow or other, women believe that knowing about money is not a feminine attribute and therefore women shun knowing about it, since they don't want men to consider them unfeminine. And there is a certain logic to this view. Women are supposed to be more appealing if they are dependent—and having money implies independence.

When *New York* magazine took a survey of salaries in 1974, it made a special effort to get information about women's incomes. *New York* noted that feminists were:

> quick to aid the cause, but when it came to others—especially those who had moved up the ladder of success to an executive rung worthy of gold powder-room keys and impressive paychecks—the mood was less posi-

tive. One woman vice-president declined politely, expressing fear that exposure of her salary would "threaten, if not destroy" the egos of her male co-workers.

Of course, along with this game, and others that women have felt forced to play, goes a certain amount of loss of self-esteem. And this feeling of inferiority, this loss of self-esteem, sometimes means that women don't feel they can participate on an equal footing with the man or men in the family in the family decisions, particularly the decisions involving money. There is an interaction between the fact that economists and the world in general put such a low value on women's work at home and the fact that the women themselves do. Though they may put in a longer work week than their husbands, they very often have the feeling that "it's *his* money," and therefore the breadwinner, not the bread baker, is entitled to a bigger voice in financial decisions, though the family couldn't get along without both efforts.

I think that this loss of self-esteem and ability to handle money is an expanding process that works something like this. Boy and girl, both employed and both managing their own affairs, meet, greet, and sooner or later get married. In the beginning they may be on a par, or almost on a par when it comes to managing their comparatively simple affairs. But as they acquire car, furniture, installment loans, house, mortgages, insurance policies, perhaps some stocks and bonds, their financial affairs get more complicated.

At the same time they have also acquired a child or two and their paths have diverged. He has gone on to a more sophisticated world, which usually involves handling money—everything from paying his share of the check at lunch daily to juggling a department's budget. She, on the other hand, has retreated to a much more restrictive world, where she cashes checks at the supermarket, only occasionally juggles a lunch check on her few-and-far-between days "off," and gets to think in terms of the nickels, dimes, and quarters of the Cub Scout dues, or the annual dues of the parent-teacher association. Her vision of the world of money shrinks to a small-change size while her husband's expands.

Women's Fear of Success

Another hang-up of women in their relationships with men is their fear of success, based in part on their fear of competing with men because competition is unfeminine, and even success itself is unfeminine. What good is success and achievement if the price is no male companionship, no lover, no husband? And since success and achievement usually bring with them independence, many women choose not to succeed and not to be independent. And of course, since the power of the purse string is tied up so much with personal power and control, many women have consciously or unconsciously accepted the myth that financial planning, money management, is beyond them—a masculine realm they should not enter.

An outstanding example of this was given in a speech by Dr. Martha Kirkpatrick, assistant clinical professor of psychiatry at the University of California (Los Angeles) Medical School, at the 1974 annual meeting of the American Psychiatric Association. Dr. Kirkpatrick described the attitudes of some women psychiatrists who had formed a consciousness-raising group. Certainly these were not ordinary women. They had already shown a high degree of dedication in the pursuit of a career in a time when women faced many obstacles, from lack of financial support to outright hostility from their contemporaries. And their psychiatric training plus experience with patients had made them aware of psychic blocks. Yet, for these women, said Dr. Kirkpatrick:

The apprehension that professional power means loss of sexual power for a woman was seen to hobble their steps toward professional advancement and achievement. They experienced anxiety in situations where they felt themselves to be seen as openly competing with men—for position, for money, for the right to speak, for "room at the top." They needed to be more than ordinary women but were frightened by these same ambitious strivings which might lead them to struggle with men.

As the [consciousness-raising] group became more introspective, this theme was seen to strongly influence private relationships as well. Although the women provided one-third to one-half the income of their families, and at times much more, there was a tendency to retreat from managing the money—to deny that finances are an area which they could or should comprehend. Doctors are not known for great financial sophistication—women doctors tend to be doubly bound in ignorance in financial affairs. There was a strong tendency to believe wisdom was a sex-linked genetic trait despite whatever evidence to the contrary. The women had shied away from evaluating investment plans, insurance, wills, pension and profit-sharing plans, etc., despite use of their incomes in these plans. . . .

Surprising isn't it? And yet it shouldn't be. Old ideas die hard, and feelings and emotions and customs linger way beyond their useful life. For a variety of reasons (many based on false premises), money has been—until recently—strictly a masculine game. But socialization and old attitudes and misconceptions haven't been the only reason that males hung a "For men only" sign on the fence surrounding their greener money pastures. There have been good dollars-and-cents reasons as well. Before we begin to knock the fence down, let's take a look at some of the cold hard economic facts that have made it so profitable to keep women on the outside.

CHAPTER 4

Management's Biggest Bargain: Women

Just because some man almost knocked you down during the five o'clock exit from the office . . .

And just because you were the one to get up—in a bus full of men—to give your seat to a pregnant woman . . .

And just because on a rainy night, two men cheated you out of a cab by jostling you with their attaché cases—don't think chivalry is dead.

Chivalry is very much alive in, of all places, the business and industrial world. Legislators somewhat lacking in the faith that heaven would protect the working girl decided they would take over the job, in case heaven was occupied with other chores. The result was legislation that set limits on what loads women could lift or that kept them from having to work overtime, from working in places that might threaten their health or their morals, from endangering their health by having to continue to work while pregnant or too soon after childbirth.

Now, in theory this is very fine, and when many of the laws were enacted, either on the state or the federal level, they served a useful purpose. As Evelyn Dubrow, legislative representative, on behalf of the International Ladies' Garment Workers Union, AFL-CIO, testified during a Senate Subcommittee hearing on the Equal Rights Amendment (May 1970):

> From the time women began to enter the labor force in substantial numbers, their substantially weaker bargaining power made them the target of discriminatory practices. Substandard wages, inhuman working conditions, long hours, unsanitary factories, jobs that threatened health and safety—all of these were forced on women and minors by circumstances they could not control. They had no alternative—accept or starve. . . . Laws set minimum wages and maximum hours; they provided rest periods, sanitary facilities, ventilation, seating and limited work before and after childbirth.

And yet—and yet, despite the intentions, and without disputing the good will, many of these laws have worked not to help women but to discriminate against them. The laws have helped, along with some collaboration from management and unions, to keep some occupations almost entirely masculine. And conversely, women have been forced into female occupations that then became lower paying. (More of this later.)

Dr. Janice Fanning Madden, assistant professor of regional science at the illustrious Wharton (business) School of the University of Pennsylvania and Phi Beta Kappa economist, puts it this way: "The Government at all levels has officially recognized the female as a unique segment of the labor force. One of the forms this recognition has taken is the protective labor legislation for women. . . . These laws might be termed 'notorious' because, though they may have been written to protect females, they do not consider individual abilities and preferences and tend to discriminate as well as to protect, by limiting the job opportunities for females."

There are even cynics who say that it's no coincidence that some of these "protective" laws have served mainly to guard women against the possibility of earning the time-and-a-half or double pay that goes with overtime hours, or getting the larger tips that come from serving liquor at night in bars compared with serving coffee during the day in restaurants, or getting the higher earnings that come from being a telephone switchman instead of an operator.

Probably the outstanding proof that these laws have not been applied equally is the working conditions, hours, and wages of women who need the most protection—women who work on farms and domestic workers. Every year or so there is a documentary film or radio special about the fate of the migrant worker, including the women of course. They put in the longest hours, under the most backbreaking conditions, for the lowest pay and the least security. It's only recently, after bitter struggles to successfully organize a union, that they have had the beginnings of decent hours, wages, and working conditions. Though domestic workers (mostly women) have been somewhat better off, they came under the protection of federal law only in 1974 (by an amendment to the Fair Labor Standards Act), with a guaranteed minimum wage of $2.00 an hour and time and a half for overtime after forty hours. And these standards still apply only to day workers; so far there is no regulation of hours if the person lives in.

A New Look at Protection

There are two things we have to remember about these "protective" laws. First, times have changed. Equipment that used to require brute strength has been redesigned so that the strength now comes from electrical power or mechanical devices rather than someone's strong arm and brawny back. Second, the often unspoken but nevertheless potent argument that the better-paying jobs should be reserved for men because men were, after all, the family bread-winners, is becoming less and less true. More and more women are becoming heads of households—14 per cent of all American children under eighteen were being raised by their mothers alone in 1973, compared with only 8 per cent in 1960. There were, in fact, about 6.6 million families headed by women in 1973, up from 5.6 million in 1970—and the trend seems to be con-tinuing its upward movement.

Fortunately, these discriminatory laws are being challenged more and more frequently by women under Title VII of the 1964 Civil Rights Act, and the women are winning. One of the most well-known challengers was Lorena Weeks, an employee of the Southern Bell Telephone Company in Georgia, who wanted to earn the higher pay that switchmen got. (A switchman main-tains telephone equipment in central telephone facility buildings—the equip-ment that automatically switches calls to different exchanges.) Ms. Weeks couldn't apply for the job, partly on the grounds that the job called for lifting a thirty-one-pound fire extinguisher, prohibited for women by Georgia state law.

Like most of us who've ever had to move our office typewriter, or carry in a week's groceries from the trunk of the car, or pick up a child, Ms. Weeks had undoubtedly done her share of weight lifting in her life, and had managed to survive in good health. So she decided to fight the case as a question of dis-crimination because of sex. After several years of litigation she not only won the job but also got $31,000 to compensate for the wages she had lost during the time she wasn't allowed to be a switchman.

This illustrates what is one of the most important aspects of women's low earning power, an aspect as important as or perhaps even more important than equal pay for equal work. The basic issue is not equal pay, though that is important, but rather that women have either been shunted into or have chosen to go into occupations which are or which become primarily "female occupations." And once it is "woman's work" it has a lower pay scale. Sure it's very nice to have the pay of a woman vice-president brought up to the scale of a male vice-president when both are doing essentially the same job, but there just aren't that many vice-presidencies open. The space at the top is rather narrow—and, while everyone has a right to look up and aspire to the peak, most are not going to make it.

So, in terms of sheer numbers, it's necessary to worry about the women who are occupying the broad plane of the women's working world—the teachers, the secretaries, the administrative assistants, the hostesses, the receptionists, the nurses, the clerks, the waitresses, the librarians—and to be sure that they get not only equal pay but also equal opportunity. And if equal opportunity has been sidetracked or negated by laws that supposedly protect women, then some of those laws will have to be changed or modified.

Some Better Answers

Another reason for "protective" laws for women is the belief that they should not have to share the very real hazards that are part of some occupations—in the construction industries and mining, for instance, or some of the chemical industries. The answer to this, of course, is not that women alone should be protected from hazards—but that *no one*, male or female, should have to work under hazardous conditions, since everyone suffers. Just think of all the pictures you've seen of mine disasters, for instance—there are the wives and children waiting, tight-lipped, to find out what has happened to those who loved them and also supported them.

And if the work is so tiring that women need a place to rest for a moment —why shouldn't men too have a place to rest?

If women are protected by law against having to work overtime, so that they can, if they have to, get home to look after their children, the answer is not to discriminate against women by saying they can't work overtime, which (1) eliminates them from certain jobs that on occasion require overtime and (2) cuts them off from the time-and-a-half or double-time rates which, as men well know, are usually paid for overtime work.

Instead, as Susan C. Ross, a feminist lawyer and partner in a law firm that specializes in feminist litigations, points out (*The Rights of Women*, Avon Books, 1973), the real optimum solution for protecting the rights of children to have someone at home to look after them when school is out is to have new laws that would make overtime work voluntary. Then either a mother or a father, if needed at home, could choose to pass up overtime without being penalized. And both mother and father could choose to work overtime and get extra pay if the extra income were needed, for instance, to pay for a child's college tuition.

The fact is that protective laws have not protected women from an economic malady called *monopsony*. Janice Fanning Madden used monopsony to refer to "a labor market in which sex discrimination occurs. It is used in a liberal sense, analogous to 'imperfect competition.'"

"Perfect competition" would mean that everyone would know simultaneously about job opportunities and would be equally free to look for the job that offers maximum salary, best working conditions, most convenient location, and everything else that goes into making a job the best for an individual. Even for men, such conditions exist only in the economic textbooks. For women, the desire for such freedom of choice is often greeted with "are you kidding?"—which is another way of saying that monopsony is a particular form of *im*perfect competition that women suffer from.

Women's Approach to Jobs

Though things have changed somewhat with women's lib, we are still influenced by quite different factors than men are when we go job hunting. If we're married we don't look for jobs that will take us away from our husbands. If we have children we want a job close to home so we can be there to greet them after school. If there are relatives that need looking after, our job schedule has to allow for that too. And then we are always doing two jobs at once—our work on the job and our other job, running our households. So, like any good purchasing agent we like to be near our sources of supply, in order to do our homemaking job most efficiently. None of these factors are spelled out in just this way in the economic textbooks—but they have their collective impact on women's opportunities, and paychecks.

And employers don't need an economics textbook to tell them that the women in the labor pool they are going to draw on won't travel too far from home, even if they are offered more money, if it means they can't fulfill their domestic responsibilities. So there isn't the slightest reason for employers to raise salaries, improve working conditions, upgrade benefits, as long as they know they have a stable work force that isn't going to look elsewhere.

This isn't the only characteristic of the female labor market that affects us where it hurts—in our pocketbooks. It's also possible to structure a particular job so that, though no one says, "for men only," the job manages to exclude women. In the words of Dr. Madden: "If job requirements are structured so as to preclude part-time work, to require peak effort between the ages of twenty and thirty-five, or to require career continuity with one employer, that job will never be a female occupation." "Never" may be stating the case a bit too strongly, but it's certainly true that jobs can be set up so that it is very difficult for women to take them, or to succeed at them.

Here is a for-instance. Suppose that you are a banker. You honestly and personally don't believe in discriminating against women. Your bank has a written policy that says it won't discriminate. You believe in promotion from within.

You also have a training program that is open only to people in their twenties (twenty-nine is the absolute top age) and asks for a commitment of five years. You almost automatically eliminate women who have dropped out of the labor market to stay home with their young children and who don't go back to work until they are past thirty. Furthermore, since you give the best jobs to graduates of your training program, you eliminate women from becoming executives with your bank. But of course your stated policy is no sex discrimination.

Or you have only one kind of part-time job open at your bank—being a part-time teller. You set the wage for this so low that only someone who has another source of income or who can't go look elsewhere for a job because of other responsibilities can accept it. You don't promote from the ranks of your part-timers, because you have your executive training program. What a deal! You have a stable pool of intelligent, capable workers, who can't or aren't going to look elsewhere, who accept the fact that they aren't going to go very far at the bank, and who—since they have little choice—are going to work for a minimum wage. Women—management's biggest bargain.

And there are other ways—without breaking any laws—of keeping women in their place.

CHAPTER 5

Who Minds the Kids, and Other Put-downs

It's no longer chic, moral, or even polite to discriminate against women on jobs. It's not "in" to be a male chauvinist pig. But what really counts is that it's also no longer legal, or fattening to the profits of a company to discriminate. Corporations, government agencies, and colleges don't like the lawyers' fees and the bad publicity that result when they are sued for sex discrimination. (The law in question is the one we've mentioned before—Title VII of the Civil Rights Act of 1964, prohibiting job discrimination on the basis of color, race, sex, religion, or national origin, and administered by the Equal Employment Opportunity Commission, a federal agency.)

We saw in Chapter 4 how it's possible to discriminate by setting up a training program or a job in such a way that women are excluded in fact, if not law. It's also possible to have a law such as Title VII on the books and still discriminate. You can, for instance, have so few people responsible for monitoring the law's enforcement that no one knows what's happening. You can have long delays between the time a complaint is filed and the time any action is started to resolve the complaint. You can simply ignore the order and see that your friends get the jobs. And, as a matter of fact, investigations by the government's General Accounting Office have found that all these things have happened since the passage of the law. The result is that discrimination has continued both in government agencies and also in private companies that are supposedly being monitored by the EEOC. In fact, according to a report from the Civil Service Commission in May 1975, the EEOC has even failed to process quickly discrimination complaints from its own employees!

But there are still other ways of discriminating against women that aren't openly illegal or discriminatory—but that affect us just the same. In some ways they are almost worse, since there is no legal recourse and we can't point to them directly, which makes us wonder what's wrong with us.

Consider, for instance, the hiring patterns in the "old-boy" network: men in positions of power who hire people in their own image—a common phenomenon in any field. They like, or feel most comfortable with, people who have similar family backgrounds, or have gone to the same school, or have the same cultural biases or maybe similar political views, and—needless to say— who are of the same sex. And so that's who they hire—*men*, especially men who are so similar that they could be almost interchangeable.

The process actually starts long before hiring takes place. The professional schools—medicine, engineering, law, the ministry—have a long and well-documented history of limiting the number of female applicants. Now, with new laws and changing attitudes, more women are being admitted to the inner circle. But, once inside, they find that some are more equal than others. Women in medical school may have to sit through anatomy lectures that are illustrated with the kind of humor that is all right for high school boys or for the male locker room, but not for a serious class. Similarly, women in law school, in addition to having few if any female law professors, are still subject to hostility from male professors and fellow students. Little remarks like "What—you can cook too?" make it obvious that the men feel there is something unfeminine and unseemly about a woman law student. The stars of a graduating class, male and female, get many job offers—but the average woman student finds it much more difficult to get a job than the average male student.

Female enrollment in engineering schools and theological seminaries has been so minuscule that there is no real experience to draw on. However, in all these schools women often have to suffer the bias of professors, whether it's open antagonism or a subtler, perhaps unconscious bias. And since they are still a small (though growing) minority, they often have to endure the open or disguised hostility of male fellow students.

The same situation applies in craft unions where women are a rarity.

Needless to say, whether the hostility is open and realized or suppressed and concealed, it doesn't help the women on the spot to do their best work. Except for the unusual individual who thrives on the challenge and either doesn't seem to or really doesn't mind the pressure, most women feel the strain. It certainly doesn't help them do their best—and if the strain shows in their relationships, if they are peevish, or take offense when none was meant, or are pushed to the point of tears, then everyone immediately says, "Ah-hah, you see, women are emotional."

The Informal Barriers

Even when no discrimination is intended, the old-boy network can be a detriment, as any woman who has ever been shut out of the informal but influential administrative grapevine network can tell you. I can remember when it happened to me. At one point in my career I worked in the public relations department of a quasi-governmental agency. The department prided itself on the fact that it had hired me for the job (editing a daily news bulletin giving the highlights of the business and financial news bulletins of the day) that would ordinarily have gone to a man. I had all the necessary qualifications and I got equal pay and equal merit increases. (And I worked very hard.) There was just one problem. I was never invited to lunch with "the boys."

But it was at lunch that the department's affairs were talked about, wrangled over, and just generally discussed until disagreements were resolved and decisions were made. If my office hadn't been next door to a man with a loud and penetrating voice, who loved to rehash the lunch talk with a crony in a different department, I would never have known what was going on. It was, to say the least, disconcerting to find out over the transom what I would be responsible for—especially when I had no voice in the decision. I would have long debates with myself about how to approach my boss and tell him the decision I didn't know about wouldn't work well, or wouldn't work at all. It was an impossible situation and I felt like an idiot.

Finally I said that if they were going to talk about changes at lunch I wanted to go along. So one day they made the noble gesture and invited me to join them. We got into different lines at the company cafeteria, mine was longer, and when I went looking for them they had forgotten to save me a seat! So much for noble gestures.

(I was happy to be excluded from their morning coffee klatsch, since I had an early deadline and they didn't. Every morning as they sat around with the coffee and Danish or doughnuts, they would spend the time talking about—clothes. Honestly. My loud-voiced colleague in the next office was somewhat of a dandy—perhaps in compensation for his five-foot four-inch height—and they would discuss what he was wearing, whether they liked that tie with that shirt, how much the shirt cost, etc. *You know* how men are when they get together to talk about clothes!)

Two more examples. Consider Beth S., a systems analyst in a Chicago health organization. She still runs into customers who won't deal with a woman, so she has to have a man go along whom she has briefed. Then she tells the customer what should be done, while the man stays behind her and says, "She's right." And though she has been accepted by the men in her department as one of them, they say, by some chance *she* is always the person who gets the least desirable car for driving to customers' offices.

Or Doris S., a quite successful real estate broker. She works very, very hard, with innumerable wasted hours and trips until she finally manages to bring buyer and seller together. After many months the deal is at last consummated and everyone meets to exchange the necessary papers and monies. A lawyer, who hasn't been anywhere in evidence for all the months, turns up. He keeps Doris waiting while he takes care of all other business and all other details and then finally, almost as an afterthought, he takes Doris S.'s check and hands it to her with a grandiose "Here's your money, sweetheart," as if she had the most minor of minor roles.

These are the subtle forms of discrimination that are almost impossible to fight—something like punching a squooshy pillow, making a big dent, and then watching the pillow re-form until it's back to its original shape and all you've got is a tingling fist.

All the pressures aren't in the office either. Think of a man homeward bound. Whether he's sitting behind the wheel of his car or on a subway, bus, or train, he has visions of a cool drink or a scrumptious cocktail or maybe just the opportunity to flop in his favorite chair and relax after a hard day's work. A woman, on the other hand, has visions of running into the kitchen and turning on the roast even before she takes her coat off, or throwing a load of clothes into the washer, or sprinkling the clothes so they'll be ready for to-morrow night's ironing session.

When *McCall's* magazine (June 1974) surveyed its readership to get some idea of how working women, particularly working wives, were faring with their jobs, one of the things found was that "nine out of ten young working mothers and eight out of ten in the 35 to 50 year old group do not have any paid help at all in the house. They manage, it seems, with none-to-some-to-a-lot-of help from husbands, with some help from children, by ignoring a certain amount of dust and clutter and by *running themselves pretty ragged.*" This knowledge of her other responsibilities inevitably has an effect on her ambitions, plans, outlook, psyche, and energy.

The Demands of Home and Hearth

This knowledge of our additional responsibilities often makes us choose not the job we would like, not the job that offers the challenge and the re-sponsibilities that make it interesting, but the job that we can leave on time. Not the job that will contribute to our future, but one that's near the campus where our husbands are getting their advanced degrees—while we earn our P.H.T.s (Putting Husband Through)—less common these days but still very much with us.

And there is the still-prevalent attitude that it's the job of the working mother to make her arrangements for the care of her children, with little or no help from the Establishment, whether the Establishment is in industry, academia, or government. There are a few token day nurseries around the country run by enlightened employers. There are a few government-sponsored agencies. But the gulf between the need and the availability is about as deep as the Grand Canyon, and with as little likelihood of going away.

When an industry can't manage because it's been clobbered by something beyond its control—an oil embargo, or a national disaster of major proportions, or a shift in the climate that changes a whole food-supply pattern for years—government jumps in to do something. Even when the disaster can be attributed to circumstances that might have been in an industry's control if it had managed its affairs more carefully—the Penn Central Railroad, for instance, or Lockheed Aircraft Corporation or the Franklin National Bank—the government steps in to bail out the erring or careless or irresponsible management.

But so far government hasn't seen fit to help out the overworked and harassed wife and mother whose labor is making it possible for the nation's offices to run, stores to sell, restaurants to feed patrons, airlines to fly, and so on—to say nothing about how the fruits of this labor are adding to the gross national product and making it possible for American families to have one of the highest standards of living in the world.

The Single Woman's Problems

The single woman is also subject to special pressures that come from being a woman and being single, regardless of whether it is because she has never married or through divorce or widowhood. She is much more likely to be in a lower income bracket because she's been denied equal opportunity or she came into the job market late. And people in the lower income bracket are forced into different spending patterns than those better off. Typically, they must spend a larger proportion of their income for necessities, particularly food and housing. So what prices go up rapidly in periods of inflation? Food and housing. What choice does the single woman have? Practically speaking, none. She has to eat and she has to have a place to live.

Good-bye to such "luxuries" as books, an occasional concert, a much-needed vacation. Good-bye sometimes even to a needed visit to the doctor or the dentist, or to a night course that might help get a promotion. Hello to meatless and fishless dinners, secondhand furniture, shabby coats no longer warm, and worn-out shoes.

And finding satisfactory housing is made more complicated for a woman by her need to live in at least a comparatively safe neighborhood, even if that means long commuting time, cutting her off from friends and big-city cultural opportunities. Or she may have to live in a "studio" apartment, a fancy name for living in one room and learning the art of eating, sleeping, and relaxing without getting claustrophobic. And, adding financial insult to injury, small apartments are overpriced just because there is such a demand for them from single women.

Furthermore, it usually costs more to shop and cook for one, to say nothing of the almost out-of-sight prices for lunches in the local luncheonettes that cater to the working woman. Not for her the gracious service and well-balanced diet of the executive dining room.

In other words, in addition to the former legal discrimination against women, which still exists in some areas of our lives, there is economic discrimination that nobody particularly planned but that exists just the same. And it's no easier to accept just because both the rich and the poor (read single woman or woman alone) have an equal right to skip meals, live in crowded quarters, or forego medical care.

We know these things—both the out-and-out discrimination, and the discrimination that comes simply from having fewer opportunities, from being in a lower income bracket, from being excluded in a thousand careless or thoughtless ways just because the world has always been that way. Yet we can't go around forever being in a huff (even when it's justified), because it's too much of a drain on our psychic energy, energy better spent getting a bigger share of the financial pie that we helped to bake. Still, it's important that we become and remain aware of the obstacles that have been or still are in our paths and in the paths of our daughters, female friends, and colleagues. Why? Not only for simple justice, but also because—as we are increasingly recognizing—motivation is an important factor in success.

The Importance of Motivation

We've all known people with "drive" who succeeded where others might have failed, and we've recognized that this inner drive has helped them push themselves along. Now some scientific studies have confirmed not only that motivation is important but also that *achievement motivation* can be improved. A Harvard University psychologist, Dr. David McClelland, has shown in a series of experiments that, when people change the way they think about themselves and their surroundings, they can increase their achievement motivation and subsequently their achievements.

An article about Dr. McClelland and his experiments in the May 1975 *Reader's Digest* noted that there are several factors involved in achievement motivations: (1) having some "accomplishment feedback," i.e. succeeding bit by bit, so that you are encouraged by these minor triumphs to go on and achieve more; (2) having models of achievement, so you see it can be done because some individuals *are* doing it; (3) modifying self-image, so that you seek personal challenges and responsibilities and picture yourself as a person who must have success, responsibility, challenge, variety. When you think of yourself this way and believe it is possible to be this way, you "re-invent yourself" and develop the kind of achievement motivation that leads to success, according to Dr. McClelland.

How does this apply to us? I think we have to keep simmering on the back burner of our consciousness that there have been all kinds of legal, societal, open and subtle pressures on us to make us think we are less capable than men when it comes to handling our finances. We've had to fight and may still have to fight the old-boy network, government indifference, single responsibility for child care that should be shared responsibilities, the burden of having to fight the daily petty battles that consume so much of the energy of people straddling the poverty fence. All these things have in the past affected our self-image and our belief in the possibility of success. Now we are living in changing times, and as we change our image in these times, it's a sure thing that we will succeed.

CHAPTER 6

Paying the Price

You knew there had to be a catch to it—this question of independence—and you were right. It would be lovely if we could have things both ways: independence and the old "privileges" of being female. We could continue to have someone else deal with the stockbroker, argue with the bank, take out the insurance policy, balance the checkbook, worry about whether there will be enough money to pay for the meat and potatoes plus hopefully the croissants and caviar. That's what happens in romantic old gothic novels where our heroine suddenly finds herself with a tidy little inheritance, cleverly arranged so that she gets a generous monthly sum without ever having to worry about where it comes from or how she should manage it. (Inflation never rears its ugly head in gothic novels.)

But even in gothics there are catches—our heroine has to go and sweep the cobwebs out of the castle that was part of the package deal. And while she's sweeping, a few ghosts come around to annoy her and have to be exorcised.

There are also catches to being independent: some myths and old cobwebby ways of thinking about money and women's roles to be exorcised and a few local villains to be cut down to size.

Some of the myths are very old indeed, but still around, so let's exorcise them very quickly.

Myth #1: Women really own most of the wealth in the United States, and they shouldn't complain. Ever.

Fact: There was a time when women's names were on more than 50 per cent of the stock held by private owners in the United States. Nominally, they were the owners. However, frequently the stock had been put in their names by their husbands in order to avoid estate or income taxes, or to minimize the husband's liability in a business deal. Or husbands or fathers left stock to their wives or daughters, but it was administered by trust funds, over which the women often had very little control. (And notice that word *control*—that's the buzz word that's important.)

Above all, the fact that women's names were on the stock certificates didn't mean they personally got the income from the stock. They were, for the most part, owners in name only. The dividends were deposited to their husbands' accounts, or to a joint account, or to a trust fund. As a result the women learned nothing about what records to keep, when dividends were due, what brokers were doing or not doing—or most important, how much income there was.

Myth #2: Lots of women are lying around in redwood chaise longues on the patios near their swimming pools, nibbling on low-calorie snacks, while waiting for the mailman to bring their alimony checks. (At least the image has been updated—it used to be on satin chaise longues, nibbling on bonbons.)

Fact: Fewer and fewer divorcées are getting alimony, and even those who do are getting less and less. Even wives who get child support find that their payments taper off to almost nothing over a ten-year period.

Myth #3: Women take men's jobs and thereby contribute to the unemployment rate. This is an oldie that may come back from the grave during times of recession.

Fact: If every woman now working deserted her job and went home, many of the nation's offices, factories, banks, schools, libraries, stores, and hospitals would simply stop functioning. And all the king's horses and all the king's men, including all the men unemployed, couldn't possibly start things going again. As we saw in Chapter 4, women are concentrated in particular jobs in particular industries, and their jobs and skills are *not* interchangeable with men's jobs and skills. *Both* men and women are needed to keep the economy going, and both salaries are very often needed to keep a family going. To say nothing of the fact that women's unpaid work, in the home, is needed to keep the whole social fabric glued together.

So much for old myths. Now to take a broom and get after those cobwebs.

One of the biggest, fuzziest cobwebs is the idea that an understanding of money matters and money management is somehow or other in men's genes, so they instinctively understand a bank statement, a broker's stock sale confirmation, the stock market page, the national budget—even the waiter's handwriting on a restaurant check. Any time you find yourself thinking this, just remember the Franklin National Bank, which lost about $80 million before it finally had to be taken over by the European American Bank & Trust Company so that depositors wouldn't lose their money and the nation wouldn't lose faith in the whole banking structure. Or how about the collapse of a Wall Street investment fund, Takara Partners, which managed to lose huge amounts of money (how much isn't public knowledge—probably because the people involved are too embarrassed to admit the size of their losses) for such supposedly knowledgeable investors as G. Keith Funston, former president of the New York Stock Exchange, J. Richardson Dilworth, senior financial adviser to the Rockefeller family, and John L. Burns, former president of RCA.

Obviously men are just human—some are smart and some aren't; some get fooled and some don't. And some—despite expensive advisers, personal expertise, and being part of the "in" crowd on Wall Street, among bankers and in corporate boardrooms—are not above making tremendous, stupendous, colossal booboos, often, unfortunately, with other people's money.

So, one of the first lessons we have to learn is that everyone makes mistakes.

But even when these smart-money men make these tremendous, colossal goofs, no one hangs them, shoots them, or takes away their gold key to the executive men's room. Nor do people working near the offices where the "mistakes" occurred walk in the street because they're afraid of being hit by the bodies of men who've jumped out of windows after hearing the bad news—as happened during the 1929–33 Great Depression years. In fact, usually these men don't even get fired or demoted. And if they lose control of one mutual fund or valuable piece of real estate or family fortune, they often get control of another, after a decent period of eating brown-bag lunches, riding public transportation along with the rest of us ordinary mortals, and answering their own telephone calls.

Making Mistakes and Taking Risks

One of our first tasks as women, therefore, is to conquer our fear of making mistakes when it comes to handling money. We just have to accept the fact that yes, like everyone else, we're going to make mistakes. But so what? There is no other way to learn. (We might take a cue from Charles Evans, a wealthy construction company owner who, though presumably very sophisticated, invested the $250,000 minimum amount required in a mutual fund that was open to only forty investors. The fund managed to lose millions. Mr. Evans, who felt, along with the other investors, that he'd been had, said, "If you just lose $250,000 by itself, that's O.K. It's just part of the Wall Street game. You win some, you lose some. Sometimes you have a bad year. . . .")

That means we have to take the risk and learn by doing, whether it's balancing the checkbook, applying for a loan, filling out the income tax form, handling the family money for a given period of time, making some kind of

investment. And there is no substitute for doing it yourself—struggling with
the obscure prose, trying to remember how to add fractions (you haven't
done it since sixth grade), looking at the various plans or prospectuses given
you by an assortment of salesmen.

I'm not saying it will be easy—there will certainly be problems—but no
skill is easily acquired, and handling money is a skill. Nor am I saying that
you won't have some losses perhaps, but they may very well be less than the
losses you will suffer from ignorance. Part of the learning process will be evaluating the possible losses versus gains.

Consider the case of Dolores G., who knew nothing about property law
until she divorced her husband—and found that she and her two children, a
boy of ten and a girl of eight, couldn't stay on in the house they were living
in, because the deed was only in the husband's name. Instead of a view of a
gracious lawn from her lovely living room, with its wall-to-wall pale green car-
peting, fine furniture, and marble fireplace she is now living about a mile
away in a six-room house, badly in need of painting, with a view of the gasoline service station next door. At this point she knows a lot about property
law and divorce laws—but it's too late.

Or Evelyn P., who had counted on her husband's insurance policy to help
her be independent in her later years. She knew how much the policy would
pay, but that was about all she knew about their finances, although her husband frequently assured her, "Don't worry, honey, you'll be well provided
for." It was a shock after her husband's death to learn that their portfolio of
stocks was worth considerably less than she thought, because the stock
market had dropped. But worst of all, the insurance was only slightly more
than half of what she expected—her husband had borrowed against the cash
value and never paid back the loan.

She had to move to a much smaller apartment, start counting pennies almost literally as inflation bit into her income, and send to her son the piano
she loved to play, because it was impossible to get it into the only apartment
she could afford. And she is one of the lucky widows—a relative helped her
get a part-time clerical job that is very tedious but at least allows her a little
leeway on going to the movies, or buying gifts for her children and grandchildren, and saving a little bit each month for possible medical bills in the
future.

Or Melitta R., a Phi Beta Kappa single career woman with a health problem, who should be building her savings against the day when she might not
be able to work as hard as she does now. Yet all her money sits in a savings
account earning less interest than it could be earning in a carefully planned
investment portfolio—because she is "afraid she wouldn't understand how
the investment market works."

Problems to Be Faced

Are there obstacles in this money-learning course? Naturally. There are obstacles in any learning course—and they have to be faced.

The first obstacle is inertia; it's a particularly common symptom among married women. If your husband has always handled the money, it's just terribly tempting and so much easier to let him continue to do it. For one thing, it takes time to learn and time to do, and there are always more interesting things to do than balance a checkbook, or more interesting things to read than the instructions on filling out an income tax form. If you are serious about being independent, however, you will have to sacrifice some of these pleasures and some of the time—and also muster the desire and the energy to do and to learn.

If you consciously or unconsciously resist doing these things, you can't really complain or blame your spouse if you are ignorant about your family's financial affairs. It is an easier way out for the present—but remember that you may have regrets later—too much later to have much choice. You will be setting yourself up to pay a high price—dependence on the good will of lawyers, friends, relatives, maybe someday children who at that point in their lives are busy with their own children and ill-at-ease in the role of adviser to Mamma. All kinds of people will make decisions for you that you would be better off making for yourself. It's a terribly high price to pay—too high, I think.

But inertia isn't the only problem. A much bigger problem is the attitude of the "Establishment," whether the Establishment is a husband, a father, an executive sitting behind a desk in some corporation of a salesman with a portfolio. Even men who *in theory* accept women as equals sometimes find it hard, in practice, to give up old attitudes and control. These are problems that have to be dealt with on the road to independence.

CHAPTER 7

Keeping Your Cool While Asserting Your Rights

You've never thought too much about who handles the family finances. And though you've never really discussed it, somehow or other you've become keeper of the family bankbook and checking account. Maybe it's because your job is a little less time-consuming; or you're home all day with the kids, so (in theory anyway) you have more time. Or it's you who cashes the checks and does most of the family shopping, so it's only natural that you keep the books. Or maybe, just because women's lib is in the air, your husband likes the idea—it shows how fair-minded he is.

But then, something happens. The car breaks down and there's an unexpected repair bill. A few big weekends charged to your credit cards are forgotten—until the bills come in. Or little extras mount up: a small rent increase, a bigger food bill, some minor but unexpected medical bills. Or everyone you know decides to give birth or get married or have an anniversary—and all at once you have to be Santa Claus in July. Suddenly you are faced with a deficit where the bank balance used to be.

And then something else happens. The family controller of the currency gets nervous, and his first reaction is: Give back the checkbook; *I'll* handle the finances from now on.

Unless you want to abdicate your responsibility, *don't do it*. If you do, you are accepting the assumption that one person, *you*, is to blame for the financial crisis and the other person, your husband, will automatically be able to set things right. This simply doesn't conform to the facts—the reality of the situation—when two individuals are sharing their income and each is spending.

The better way is to suggest—in fact, insist—quietly, that neither of you discuss the question when both of you are angry and upset. Instead, agree to have a "financial committee" meeting at a peaceful time when tempers will be cool and energy levels will be high. Then, difficult though it may be, each of you analyze where things went wrong, what could or should have been done, and how the problem is to be dealt with in the future.

If you have never been a full partner in your financial decisions and have always let your husband make the decisions, you are going to be at a psychological disadvantage in such an arrangement. You may very well feel, whether your feeling is justified or unjustified, that you have indeed committed some major financial mayhem. If you're unaccustomed to keeping records, and it's not your thing anyway, you may have forgotten to enter something into the record. You may have been unrealistic about how much you could afford to spend on something. You may even have been extravagant. Or you may not have been or done any of these things.

For the purposes of your committee meeting it does not matter. As I've mentioned earlier, you have to accept the fact, if you're inexperienced, that you are going to make mistakes—but you will learn. Your husband has to accept this fact as well. Furthermore, don't overlook the possibility that the errors were his. He may have been the one who was careless or unrealistic or extravagant. Husbands too sometimes forget to enter a check in the checkbook, neglect paying a bill, or get carried away by a sale of tennis rackets or golf clubs or rock records.

The most important thing to remember is that if he helps you learn to manage money, he is no longer responsible for bearing the whole financial burden—and he'd be foolish indeed if he didn't see the advantages to himself. But, since we live in a society where money and masculinity are intertwined, he may not find it easy to accept a role as a sharer, not a bearer, of burdens. Which means that you are going to have to deal with this situation and decide on the best way, in your particular framework, to proceed. It's a very personal decision. Yet there are some ground rules you can follow if you want to have a productive discussion-argument that will lay the basis for a mutually shared, equal-partners financial arrangement.

1. Choose the battleground. Make it clear that you don't accept any of the myths such as that because you are a woman you don't understand about money, because you are a woman you're too emotional about money, because you are a woman you are of course extravagant, because you are a woman you should accept that the man of the family has ultimate control.

2. Keep the argument or the discussion to the issue: the plan that is needed, the budget that was in existence but didn't work, the error of judgment that has to be understood and guarded against irrespective of who made the mistake.

3. Emphasize that you will not settle for less than a joint decision, even if you, by working at home as mother, cook, household manager, are not con-

tributing *cash* dollars. You *are* contributing your services and they must weigh in the decision-making process.

4. Don't argue *ad hominem,* i.e. on a personal level with personal accusations. Avoid the emotional aspects of the argument and concentrate on the issues at hand—in other words, keep your cool.

Indulgent Fathers and Dependent Children

If you are a daughter (or a mother of daughters), you have a somewhat different problem. Life with father can be a tricky business when it comes to money matters. Many fathers like to indulge their children, especially their female children. I leave it to Freud and others to explain the psychological basis for this indulgence; let's just say here that it's a natural extension of a father's love and protective feelings—on the positive and admirable side. On the not-so-positive and negative side, it can also be an expression of a father's desire to control his children and an unconscious male chauvinism. If you are in such a situation, you may find that the indulgence, whether it gets you out of tight budget squeezes or permits luxuries you couldn't afford otherwise, is really not a favor if it keeps you from learning self-discipline, or keeps you dependent.

But this isn't the only aspect of the father-daughter money question. More insidious, because it's so much more subtle, is a father's unconscious exclusion of his daughter from the conversations, places, even attitudes that will help her acquire confidence and know-how about money matters. If you have that kind of father, you have to be understanding—he grew up in a generation that took it for granted that a woman's work was to find herself a husband to provide for her support, father her children, and take care of her through insurance and wills even beyond the grave. Even more to the point, he is still getting similar advice from bankers, insurance agents, lawyers, and many of the magazines he reads, whose editors seem to have been off on a Pacific island somewhere, talking only to the monkeys, for the past ten years.

Take a book published in 1974 by the very prestigious *Business Week* magazine, drawn from its pages, and titled *Business Week Guide to Personal Business.* Here are some typical excerpts:

> By age seven boys and girls begin to have different play interests. Most boys are greatly interested in racing cars, construction and science sets, work benches, and real tools. Now is the start of serious model building —planes, cars, boats. Girls' interest in house-keeping continues but now the toys are more sophisticated—like a sewing machine that really works.

From seven to nine, youngsters are interested in many board games (even chess). Boys want sports equipment that really works in a competitive game—and girls want elaborate doll wardrobes and realistic doll houses.

(Incidentally, the writer of the book, Joseph Wiltsee, offers no authority to back this statement.)

Wise parents will start emotional preparation for college in the high-school years—and before. The father has a special role to play. . . . The basic trouble is that the father, typically a business executive, often finds it hard to encourage his youngster to make his own decisions. . . . a lot of fathers can't let go.

(This, of course, applies to boys, since just about the entire book is written as if men had only sons, not daughters. But, if this is true of fathers' attitudes toward their sons, you can imagine how much more it applies to their daughters.)

On discussing estate planning:

When you contact a new lawyer, make sure your wife is along during your early conferences. But make it plain that, despite his liberality in counseling on a wide range of questions, the family attorney is in business, too. Mere chit-chat and verbal hand-holding on matters of little real consequence aren't part of the arrangement.

I must admit that this last quote is the one that riles me the most.

With advice like this, you can understand that a father will find it difficult to accept a daughter as someone capable of controlling her own destiny and her own finances. You will have to decide on the most tactful way of handling the situation, but no matter how you do it, you have to say—and *mean it*—that you want to learn how to handle your own money affairs and you will appreciate getting his help in learning.

If he really has money to spare, you might even suggest that he consider putting it in a fund for his retirement, or your mother's old age, so you can, as a family, always enjoy economic independence.

(It follows naturally from this that if you are a mother of daughters, even if you haven't quite made up your mind about your own financial role in the family, you can still back up your daughter.)

Standing Up to the Establishment

But the need to assert yourself doesn't exist only within the family circle. The same kind of situation will often arise when you are dealing with bankers, brokers, or credit managers. Old perceptions and old feelings die hard or not at all, and, despite the feminist movement, many men still cling to the old idea that women can't understand money matters. Depending on their experience, age, and personality, they will treat you in one of several ways:

1. Give you a pat on the head (occasionally even on the backside) and a "Don't worry about this, little girl; just let me handle it."

2. Make a halfhearted attempt at an explanation, but with no real substance since the assumption is: "You wouldn't understand it, but it's my duty so I'll humor you and at least make the effort."

3. Try to overwhelm you with a real snow job, full of as much financial jargon as possible, deliberately aimed over your head with a sort of "So you want to poach on men's territory, eh? Well, you don't belong here, and I'm going to prove it to you by making you so uncomfortable that you won't even try."

4. Give you an unwitting snow job. Joe Banker has been in the loan department of Fidelity Forever Bank since he won the mathematics prize at West Suburb High School thirty-eight years ago, then married a secretary at the bank, and settled in West Suburb. His entire life is centered around the bank and he simply doesn't know that most people aren't familiar with the terms he uses every day. He means well.

What should your reaction be? You have two aims: to learn, and to maintain your dignity, and the more important of these is to learn. It is not in any way demeaning to say you don't understand something and to ask to have it explained again. Admittedly none of us like to display our ignorance—but the price of never asking questions is to stay forever ignorant. That's too high a price to pay. Remember that you don't know these things because you haven't had the experience, not because you are stupid and certainly not because you are a woman. Remember too that many men have been in exactly the same position with exactly the same smattering of ignorance and have been, foolishly, too embarassed to ask. *You* aren't going to be that foolish.

There are going to be times however—especially with openly condescending or covertly hostile men—when it's going to be very hard to control your temper. Above all, don't accept a put-down. If you feel you can't change the situation, just say something like, "I'm disappointed. I thought you would be able to deal with me in an intelligent way. But you seem to be too busy or to have too much difficulty communicating with people. Thank you anyway, but I think I will have to go to the manager and ask for another appointment with another person who is more skilled in public and customer relations."

If you do walk out, calmly and collectedly (on the outside at least), take a moment to jot down a few notes on the specific remarks and attitudes and suggestions that annoy you. Then you will have some ammunition if you do talk to another officer in the company—for, in fact, you are not making an idle threat. You should indeed go over someone's head to a higher level of management, preferably the president, if you aren't pleased with your first interview.

Once you've taken the responsibility of fighting the good fight for your right to be accepted as a full-fledged, intelligent, responsible member of the money world, whether it's the domestic world or the business world, you have to assume some additional responsibilities. This doesn't mean that you have to do all the work or that you necessarily have to assume major responsibility. But you do have to assume your share. And though it's not an easy burden, it's not a dull one either, and there's great satisfaction in becoming master of your purse. Furthermore, it's easier to learn these things and fight these battles when you choose to, rather than having them forced on you at a time when you may be under great stress—when you've lost your job, or been turned down for a raise, or recently divorced or widowed. These are just about the worst of times, from a psychological and practical standpoint, to have to undertake new responsibilities.

CHAPTER 8

When a Girl Marries Should Her Troubles Begin?

When should you, as bride-to-be or newlywed, start providing for your economic future? The minute that the lyrics of the romantic songs you hear—you know, the ones that used to sound so stupid—suddenly make sense. In other words, the minute you realize you're in love and decide you want to make beautiful music and charge account payments together.

We all know today's rising divorce statistics, ending not with "and they lived happily ever after" but with they lived unhappily until the divorce courts did them part. But there's no need to look only at the minority report —after all there are still the two out of three who stay married and presumably happy enough. And remember too that the scare statistics on divorce, such as one divorce for every three marriages, are somewhat misleading. If we subtract teen-age elopements and the successive marriages of the divorce prone, at least 70 per cent of adult first marriages may last a lifetime. Yet even in this happily married context women suffer economic disadvantages: some inevitable and some preventable with planning. And it's the planning that I'm going to stress—because unless it comes early in the game, the game can be lost.

But first, let's take a look at the marriage contract, just to see where we stand. According to present laws and customs, which have been evolving since one of Eve's offspring hung a bearskin at the entrance of the cave she and her spouse had just pre-empted from the bear, marriage is a lifetime union, with each spouse granted certain legal rights under the terms of the contract. These rights do not, no matter how much a spouse may consider it essential, guarantee the privilege of sleeping late on Sunday morning, having little things fixed around the house as soon as they get broken, or always having a fresh supply of clean underwear. As attorney Harriet Pilpel points out, the "only rights husbands and wives have in relation to each other are those they can do something about legally." And these rights are, somewhat surprisingly, rather limited. They represent "the minimum framework of a marriage," and many of the relationships we take for granted in a marriage are enforced more by custom than by law.

However, one of the *enforceable* rights is that a husband must support his wife and children according to his financial ability. This is, according to *You and the Law* (Reader's Digest Association, 1971), "a legal obligation, affirmed both by the courts and by statutes. All fifty states have adopted the Uniform Reciprocal Enforcement of Support Act, which enables a wife to get a court order in the state where she lives directing her husband who has left the state to pay her money to support her and the children." (Collecting is another matter, which we'll go into in more detail in Chapter 10.)

Another of these enforceable legal rights is the right of domicile, i.e. to have your spouse live with you. In many states, if either spouse refuses, the other may be entitled to a divorce or a legal separation, or may forfeit the right of support. Usually it is the husband who decides where the couple will live, within reason. He cannot impulsively decide to set up housekeeping on an ice floe in the Arctic or on a deserted beach on the Pacific and expect his wife to cheerfully accompany him. But he does have the right of domicile, i.e. to choose where they shall live. Even if separate careers mean they have to live apart, the wife's domicile, i.e. the place that establishes such legal rights and obligations as voting, paying taxes, getting free tuition, welfare payments, is, in many states, where her husband has his legal address.

Another essential part of the marriage contract is the right to normal sexual intercourse, though not necessarily to conceive and bear children. According to Ms. Pilpel it is, in fact, the "purely sexual rather than the procreative aspect of intercourse which the law stresses most heavily." However, the law

> is not able to, and for the most part makes no attempt to enforce sexual obligations in marriage except in what might be termed the extreme cases of sexual maladjustment—impotence, "abnormal" sex practices, cruelty or refusal to have intercourse at all. In such cases, some states permit divorce and others separation. The cases involving sexual problems between man and wife are replete with references to the "right" of the husband to insist on the "duty" of the wife to "submit" to "reasonable" sexual intercourse. In broad terms, the word "reasonable" is interpreted to mean any time or frequency which is not injurious to the health of the wife. [*Your Marriage and the Law.*]

But we all know that there is much more to marriage than bed, board, and address, and these other rights and responsibilities are usually summed up more or less by the word "consortium," which one authority quoted by Ms.

Pilpel defines as the right to enjoy the person, affection, society and assistance of one's spouse. Ms. Pilpel goes on to say:

> As part of the rights of consortium, the husband is entitled to the services of his wife. If she works outside the home for strangers, she is usually entitled to her own earnings. But domestic services or assistance which she gives the husband are generally considered part of her wifely duties. The wife's services are so essential a part of what the law considers the husband entitled to as part of the marriage that it will not recognize any agreement between the spouses which provides that the husband is to pay for such services or society.

The Hard-cash Question

And it's right at this point that we begin to get to one of the most significant aspects of the still-existing financial inequality of women. It's not quite fair to say a wife is not paid for her services. If her husband is supporting her, this is a kind of pay. If she's "married well," as the women of an older generation used to say, she may be rendering her services and getting paid with penthouse apartments, two-acre homes with indoor and outdoor pools, and diamond-encrusted blue jeans. Much more likely, however, she is getting by, as most of us are, with a lot of help from the mortgage company, the low-cost–high-nutrition cookbook, and garden-dirt-encrusted blue jeans.

But she is not paid in coin of the realm, money, bread, call it what you will. And this can be very important financially and psychologically. She has no money that is all her own, that she has control over. She has no opportunity to buy stocks, consider a mutual fund, invest in land—in other words to do any of the things that men at least have the option of doing on their own, including taking risks and making mistakes.

Because men have these options, they think differently, concern themselves with their choices, make decisions. Not so for women—why concern yourself with independent decisions or choices when you have no way of carrying them out?

There may, of course, be cases in which no problems arise. Consider Joshua and Jane, who decide they are going to have an old-time conventional marriage—she wants to stay home, raise a brood, and follow him wherever his work takes him; so everything is fine. Their lives can proceed uneventfully through mortgages, childbirth, diapers, colleges, and retirement condominiums. Conversely, Elise and Elliott decide they don't want any children. She continues to practice law in Washington; he is a senior accountant for a Pennsylvania manufacturing company; they meet on weekends for thirty to forty honeymoon years; and she couldn't care less that her official domicile is Pennsylvania. That too is fine. The problems come up in the lives of the rest of us who are much more typical, and who have one dream at twenty, say, and quite a different reality at thirty, forty, or beyond.

For it's in these much more typical situations that women begin to lose the money game. Admittedly, we have probably left forever the time when a woman's main orientation is going to be toward her home and child-raising. But, since men still usually make higher salaries and have more opportunities, it's much more customary for the wife to follow her husband and the dictates of his job. She is the one who stays home, takes care of the infant and toddler, and weaves her life around the demands of husband, home, and children until the last child is in kindergarten. Then she suddenly realizes she is in her early or middle thirties, with more than half her life ahead of her, including about thirty years before she reaches retirement age, and it's time she think about what she is going to do with those thirty years.

But at that moment it's very, very late. She can't retrieve those years when other people were gaining experience, winning promotions, getting raises; she will lose even more time if she has to start getting the training and education needed to enter a professional field; she is too old for many executive training programs. She is even worse off if she gets divorced and finds she must not only support herself but also contribute substantially to the support of her children.

When to Plan a Career

So it's a whole new lifetime game plan, and women have to understand the options they must keep open, the problems involved, and the ultimate payoffs. A wife who wants to be a mother and, at some later time in her life, have an outside job has to plan her dual career with the same singlemindedness that a man has when he thinks about a plan for his life. A woman needs to have an awareness of the importance of time and the possibility of having to make choices always quietly simmering on the back burner of her consciousness.

Let's proceed from the premise that earning money is the name of the game—probably outside the house (possibly inside through special talents) on either a part-time or full-time basis. Then time and what urban planners call "access to services" (i.e. good shopping, transportation, repair shops, schools) are either allies or enemies. Minutes may seem unimportant, but if they add up to several hours or more per week spent commuting, or running errands—hours that could be spent acquiring or practicing the skills that could mean extra income, now or in future—minutes are supremely important.

And access to services means a lot more than having a handy shoe-repair man, laundromat, and drugstore. It means public transportation for children, so they aren't dependent on mother as chauffeur. It means being within commuting distance of schools and colleges that have schedules that accommodate women with household responsibilities and, equally important, offer a range of training so there is some choice among various kinds of careers. And even more than that it means living in a community or being near communities that offer some choice of jobs, so that a woman doesn't have to settle for a job she really doesn't like simply because nothing else is available.

But perhaps the most important problem of all is the question of child care. A wife and mother who also wants to have a job or career has to think in terms of being able to get some help with her child, which means she has to live somewhere accessible by public transportation. Research by correspondents of *Money* magazine for an article in the October 1974 issue (based on a chapter of my previous book, *Your Money: How to Make It Stretch*) showed that transportation for household help was a major problem of would-be working mothers around the country. Living on a bus line can make the difference between being able to get someone to look after a child or not—and consequently the difference between accepting or turning down a job offer.

There's a corollary to this problem of location and child care—the availability of nursery schools and day care centers, or, if none are available, the possibility of starting one. To do this one needs a good-size group of mothers or families to draw on and involve, comparative ease of transportation, the possibility of a building or space in a building, teachers, teachers' aides, food supplies. Yet consider the day care situation—the Day Care and Child Development Council of America estimates that in 1973 there were enough licensed day care centers to provide for 905,000 children, but about 6 million children needed some kind of day care, from all-day care for preschoolers to a place to go after school for children up to their teens. Then consider the generally lackadaisical, when not actually hostile, governmental attitude toward public subsidies of day care centers in the United States (despite the continually rising number of mothers working, including mothers with children under six). This means it is usually up to the mothers who want to work outside their home to get centers started and kept going. (I say mothers, but only because this book is addressed primarily to women. Fathers too are needed and do get involved.)

Vital: Choosing Where to Live

So one of the most important decisions a wife and mother, or potential mother, has to make is where to live—not in the usual terms of price, community, and attractiveness, but in terms of opportunities for a job, education, transportation, and child care. These factors should be considered too in evaluating house versus apartment.

Apartment living, in fact, has many advantages for working mothers, particularly mothers of preschool children: the possibility of finding mothers' helpers in the building, or sharing child care, or establishing nursery schools and day care centers—with no need to take infants or children out of doors in bad weather. And a bonus is the increasing availability of cooperatives and condominiums, which offer to apartment dwellers the tax advantages that were formerly available only to homeowners.

If the decision is a house, however, the same considerations should apply, particularly when there is a choice among several communities. Which offers the most potential in terms of educational opportunities, services, jobs? And since working mothers need all the help and friends they can get, the father's time has to be taken into consideration. A husband who spends hours commuting just doesn't have the time or energy to take responsibility for children or household chores.

The Job Choices

Which brings up the whole question of jobs. Here again it's important to have long-range goals in mind when it comes to the husband's choice of jobs —assuming there is a choice. (We'll get to situations in which there isn't a choice in a moment.) The possibilities for the wife have to be evaluated as well. There is certainly a trend toward doing this on the part of professional women, particularly young professional women—but it is only a trend. And these professional women make up a small percentage of all women. Other women are often too shortsighted, or too apt to underestimate their own talents and needs, to consider what their opportunities will be for earning money when their stay-at-time-with-the-children days are over. Then, when the time comes to job-hunt, women realize they have to adapt to what's available rather than what they would like. And very often they also have to adapt, as we saw in Chapter 4, to lower salaries. Thus they have to give up a slice of freedom—for that after all, is what money often represents.

What happens if there is no choice? In a sluggish economy this could very well be the case. If Jane Doe has chosen to stay home with baby Doe, somebody has to support the family—and the family has to go where the family breadwinner can earn the bread. Not a good situation, but a frequent reality. It doesn't have to be a hopelessly closed door, however. Even when you have no choice, and you must go where the job is, you still have some options. One is to try to develop new talents and new skills—to find resources that you never knew you had, until forced to discover them. The question is, how to go about the rediscovery process?

One excellent possibility is to go to a local college or government-sponsored employment service and arrange for an aptitude test, i.e. a test to evaluate your abilities. I say a college or government employment agency, though there also are private agencies that give aptitude tests, because the college or government agency will probably be considerably cheaper. With this profile of your talents you have a better picture of the scope of your skills—and, who knows, a new career may open up. At the very least you can start preparing by taking courses that will ultimately make a new career feasible.

Being a Smart Volunteer

Another possibility is to undertake some kind of volunteer work that, in addition to being useful, does more than just get you out of the house. Volunteer work should enable you to do well for yourself by doing good for others. The important thing is to choose the work as carefully as you would choose a job, so that you are furthering your own ambitions and opportunities.

There has been much controversy, since the women's lib movement began, about women being exploited when they do volunteer work. The anti-volunteer work thesis is that women should refuse to do volunteer work because such work should be paid for—society should be able to afford more hospital staff, more teaching aides, more visitors to old-age homes, and so on. Yes, society should—but at the moment society doesn't, and someone has to fill the gap in the meantime. And you may be able to launch yourself toward a job that pays.

Two things to keep in mind: First, have a definite goal before you volunteer. If you're interested in social work, ask to work in the social work department. Publicity—the publicity department. Technology? The laboratory. Accounting—the business office, and so on. Second, when you get into the department, make it your business to get to know the people in the field who wield the power, the administrators who make up the budget and the department heads or personnel people who do the hiring. You always have in the back of your mind that you're not just a volunteer, you are a goal-directed unpaid person who has a future paying job in mind.

So much for advance planning in its broad outlines. Now let's go on to some not-so-typical questions that are coming up in this ancient man-woman relationship.

CHAPTER 9

Some Quick Questions and Some Longish Answers on a Grab Bag of Problems: Marriage Contracts, Guilt Feelings, Feather-the-nest Eggs, and More

If you think you're the only one who hasn't satisfactorily solved all the problems of that admittedly delicate marriage/money question, be happy to know you are wrong. Each semester, during the course "Women and Money" that I teach at the New School for Social Research in New York City, some of the same questions come up again and again. The women who ask them are relieved to know that they are not alone with their doubts and their lack of information. Here are the questions most often asked. Perhaps you will find some answers you've been looking for.

Q: I would like to deal with my husband on an equal basis when it comes to money, but I feel funny about raising the idea. After all, he is the one who has that long daily commute and the hassle with his boss (who can be a real pain sometimes). He also often brings home work to do over the weekend. I am home looking after our children and our house. I want to be independent but I also want to be fair, and I feel guilty.

A: Stop putting down both yourself and the work that you do. *Neither* of you could exist without the contribution of the other. You too face a daily grind, the tyranny of subordinating your needs to those of your family—and you don't have to bring work home weekends; it's already there waiting for you. Your work is no less worthwhile because it doesn't have a dollars and cents sign on it; it is simply *different*.

Do you want to be really unfair? Then let your husband bear the whole burden—from paying all the bills to making all the money decisions. Add that on to his other responsibilities and you've got a good candidate for an early heart attack or stroke. If you become a partner in financial management because you know as much—maybe even more—about managing money, you lighten several loads. First, you make life easier for your husband when you relieve him of some of the paperwork involved in keeping track of the family's finances. Second, you ease a psychological burden—he doesn't have to have that nagging fear that his children's life would fall apart because you can't manage if something should happen to him. Third, since many fathers do have little time to spend with their children during the week, especially if they have a long commute, you are able to teach his children how to manage money, since *you* know something about it. What could be more fair than that?

Q: I am happily married but—and it's a big but—my husband doesn't accept women's lib when it comes to money. I am at home with our children and really have no separate money. Should I put some money aside from the household money my husband gives me? I rather hate to do it—it seems somewhat deceitful.

A: Of course you should. Yes, it does seem rather deceitful, but look at it this way. Your husband's attitude is a very old-fashioned one, based on the tradition that it is the man of the family who controls the purse strings. Another part of this tradition is that the woman does put something aside. Since he inherited this tradition from his own family, he probably also inherited the tradition that his mother had a little nest egg—no one knew exactly how big—from which she could draw for presents, occasional luxuries for herself, and a little bit of security for her old age. He almost takes it for granted that you are following this path.

(The most interesting example of this that I know of is Mrs. Q., who cleaned her own ten-room house but told her husband she had a one-day-a-week cleaning woman. He of course gave her money to pay the maid. This added up to a nice-size bank account as Mrs. Q. gave the "maid" raises and vacation money and paid the required federal tax.)

It is not the happiest situation when you have to do something like this—but we are a long way from true equality, and old traditions die hard. And in the meantime you have to face the reality that the marriage bond is not as strong as it used to be and you do have to think of your own future. After all, if the wife of the Shah of Iran, Empress Fara Diba, was willing to state publicly (in *The New York Times*, May 20, 1975) that she was putting aside some of her own money to have some security—she sold their first home for a million dollars—who are you to stand on ceremony?

Q: My boyfriend and I are thinking of writing a marriage contract. What are some of the financial arrangements that should be included?

A: The women's liberation movement has come up with several different versions of the marriage contract. Here, in nonlegalese terminology, are the main financial aspects of a marriage contract.

1. An inventory of assets before you get married.
2. A decision as to who owns what—including, if there are children from a previous marriage, what is their share.
3. A decision on who manages and controls property, both property that each owns separately and property owned jointly. This would include such things as bank accounts, stocks and bonds, mutual funds, insurance policies, cars, little houses in the country or at the beach, furniture, and so on.
4. A decision on how income is to be shared, no matter which partner it comes from—or if it comes from both.
5. Provisions for support of the children, not only during the marriage but afterward, should the marriage end in divorce.
6. Terms of a will, and rights of inheritance, for either spouse, and for children and/or in-laws and relatives of this marriage or of previous marriages.
7. A decision on how to divide your assets should you decide to split, which might be an agreed-upon formula on the division of property, debts, manner and amount of future payments. For instance, if one partner, usually the wife, gives up her career to stay at home with the children and then wants to go back to school to get new or further training, she might choose a lump-sum payment rather than a specified amount monthly, to cover the time it would take her to get trained and become self-supporting.
8. Provisions for "breach of contract." This might include, for instance, what would be done if either partner sacrifices or postpones getting a college degree in order to support the other partner's education—after which there is a divorce, so that the partner who paid the bills never gets her/his share of the contract, i.e. income after the degree is awarded.

In a landmark decision in New York State in 1975, acting justice Bentley Kassal ruled that Charles Morgan, a lawyer in a Wall Street law firm, earning $27,500 annually, had to pay his ex-wife $200 a week for alimony and child support. Ethelyn Morgan had given up her undergraduate studies to work as an executive secretary and data analyst to support Charles and herself while he went through the University of North Carolina's law school. The year after he got his degree they separated, and the following year Mrs. Morgan got a divorce and custody of their seven-year-old son on the grounds of abandonment.

In awarding the alimony and child support, Justice Kassal noted that Mrs.

Morgan could probably continue to be self-supporting by working at her present profession and could earn $10,000 a year, but that doing this would mean that she would have to abandon her ambition to be a doctor. He said, "In my opinion, the answer to this issue is that, under the circumstances, the wife is also entitled to equal treatment and a break, and should not be automatically relegated to a life of being a well-paid technician, laboring with a lifelong frustration as to what her future might have been as a doctor but for her marriage and motherhood." (At the time of the decision Mrs. Morgan was a premed student at Hunter College in New York City, and had achieved a 3.83 general average out of a possible 4.0.) Right on!

Q: Suppose we did write such a contract—would it really be legal?

A: Aha! You've asked the really significant question. There is one big problem with these contracts—at this writing they have not been tested in the courts and no one is quite sure how the courts would decide if a test case were tried before them. Furthermore, since marriage and divorce laws differ from state to state, what would be legal in one state might very well not be legal in another and there is no way of predicting what each state would decide.

Perhaps this is a good time to stop for a moment and explain what the law is. We probably all grow up with the idea that everything is neatly defined and then printed in books that look very impressive on lawyers' shelves. And we assume that—unless there is a crime involved, with the need for proving guilt, or a complicated set of circumstances with suits and countersuits—the law is fairly well defined. This is not the way it works at all. The true situation has been very well set forth by feminist lawyer Susan Ross in *The Rights of Women* (Avon Books, 1973).

Law then is not a preordained set of doctrines, applied rigidly and unswervingly in every situation. Rather law is molded from the arguments and decisions of thousands of persons. It is very much a human process, a game of trying to convince others—a judge, jury, an administrator, the lawyer for the other side—that your view of what the law requires is correct. The game of convincing others is carried out in a clearly defined forum with clearly defined ground rules but otherwise it is not really that different from trying to convince people in general that your position is correct and that they ought to act accordingly. Once women understand that law is a process of convincing others rather than formalized rules dropped down from on high, they will be able to use law as an instrument to create change.

In New York City a group of feminist women lawyers, banded together in a group called the Women's Law Center, looked into the marriage contracts as they might be judged in New York State. Though their findings are not necessarily applicable in other states, they give some idea of what might happen. Here are some of their conclusions:

The concept of marriage contracts is not a new one. For hundreds of years couples (usually wealthy ones) have entered into "pre-nuptial agreements" or "marriage settlements" before marriage. These contracts usually deal only with money matters and commonly are designed primarily for the protection of the woman. They are legally enforceable.

We cannot be sure how the courts will treat the "new" kind of marriage contract, however. . . .

The new marriage contract may also make provision for support and custody of children if a marital break-up should occur. Provisions concerning children are never binding on a court because a court has the duty to protect the children and make sure any such provisions are in the children's best interests. If the child support agreed upon is too low, the court can raise it; if the father is given custody under the agreement but the court thinks the children will be better off with the mother, it can order that custody be given to the mother (of course enforcement of this would be difficult if both the woman and the man agreed that the man should have custody, i.e., they hadn't changed their minds since signing the marriage contract).

In other words it's all very well to try to set legal limits, but when it comes to a human condition so delicate, so personal, so dependent on the individual temperaments involved, so whirled about at the moment by the tornadoes of change, the law cannot possibly supply definite answers to sometimes unanswerable questions. Therefore, in the long run, we have to rely on ourselves to work out these problems as expertly as possible. And we have to work within the confines of the present system while it is changing and while we work for its improvement. And under the system two things are necessary—a way of being self-reliant and independent and an understanding of some of the problems you might face. One of these problems could be divorce, so let's take a look at the financial problems of divorce for women.

CHAPTER 10

And So They Were—Divorced

No one gets married expecting to get divorced—though more and more of us know we have that option. And more and more of us are learning, often bitterly from the battle scars of friends and relatives, that the myth of the carefree divorcée is just that—a myth. Even in the enlightened state of California, where divorce is called "dissolution of marriage," and there are no plaintiffs and defendants but rather petitioners and respondents, the long corridor in the Los Angeles Courthouse where husbands, wives, and sometimes frightened and tearful children wait their turn in the divorce court has been called "heartbreak alley."

For no matter how amicable, how sane, how intelligent the former partners are, the process of divorce is a painful one. It is a failure in one of the most sensitive and deep-rooted of human relationships. And no matter how willing, even how anxious the participants are to pull out the roots, the process is traumatic.

And, because of our generally inferior economic position as women, the money side of the divorce can be one of the most traumatic aspects of this dissolution of the marriage—not only for the immediate shocks but also for the long-range effects.

If marriages are made in heaven, many a woman learns that divorces are made in hell. True, we have come a long, long mile since divorces were considered, to quote Thomas Parnell, "the public brand of shameful life." But that doesn't mean the problems of divorce are ended—in fact, in some ways they have been *accentuated* for us by new freedoms and new attitudes. Some of the traditional protection that women used to have has been eroded, while new attitudes have not benefited all women proportionately. Equality of the sexes has been confused with equality of opportunity and women have suffered, sometimes even when everyone's intentions were the best.

This should not be the case, and need not be if women are prepared—

which means knowing what they have to know in order to get the most equitable financial arrangement, which is, of course, the purpose of this chapter. I'm not talking here about the Rockefellers, the Niarchoses, the Taylor-Burtons, and other members of the no-debt jet set. I'm talking about the rest of us—the tourist class.

Divorce itself costs money. How much depends on how it is done. At one extreme is the couple who decide to part amicably and do all the legal work themselves. In some states they can manage to spend a lot of time and as little as about a hundred dollars in cash. At the other extreme is hatred so deep and irreconcilable that the case will go on for years and a battery of lawyers on both sides can retire early and rich from the proceeds. In between are the more average cases, where everyone starts out with good intentions, and costs are several thousand dollars. The plan is to do what is best for the children—if there are any—and to get "justice" for oneself.

But "justice" is very often not that familiar blindfolded female figure, weighing the evidence in the scales and being impartial because she judges only by that evidence in the scales, not by any biases that might result if she were able to see who stood before her. Alas, in real life and true-drab colors the reality is that women are very often, and unjustly, the financial victims of divorce settlements because of one, or any combination, or sometimes all of the following factors:

1. Husbands have been in the labor market for an unbroken period of time, acquiring skills, status, and increases in salary, professional fees, or income from their businesses, and so they have more money to live on after a divorce than their ex-wives.

2. Women who have been working, as we've seen before, are apt to be in lower-paying jobs. However, depending on her age and the circumstances of the marriage, a woman may not have worked at all. Then she is suddenly thrust on the job market with few or outdated skills—and the psychological handicap of feeling she is totally inept. If she is an older woman, and she usually is, she unquestionably runs into job discrimination because of her age.

3. Husbands have been in the business or professional world longer and have become more expert in managing financial matters, including in this case dealing with lawyers and accountants. If the husband has been the only or principal breadwinner, and *wants* to conceal part of his income, he either knows how to do it, has already been doing it, or can buy the expert advice that tells him how to do it.

4. Husbands may be aided and abetted in this by a variation of the old-buddy system. Their lawyers and accountants will probably be men who will empathize with husbands not only as clients but also as *men*. What may be even worse, the woman's lawyer may also be part of this old-buddy network.

The legal profession is not so big that its members don't know each other and count on having to work together some time on some future case, though they may be adversaries in this one.

5. The courts too may be part of the old-buddy system, since they are generally dominated by men, with male judges, who frequently have a conscious or unconscious bias against females. Thus the judge may empathize with the husband and, as a result, set ridiculously inadequate alimony and support payments.

(My friend Nina C. tells of sitting in court during the hearings on her divorce case and watching the judge, her husband's lawyer, and her lawyer joking together in the corridors during recesses and then going out to lunch together. She says she has never felt so lonely in her entire life. And this was a divorce started by her husband, who, after fifteen years of married life and two children decided he didn't like married life!)

6. A divorcée will learn—and it will contribute to her tremendous feeling of insecurity—that unless she has been married to her husband twenty years or more, *before the divorce*, she is not entitled to her widow's share of his Social Security payments.

7. Children are customarily left in the custody of their mother. This has many advantages for the mother from an emotional and psychological viewpoint—she is less likely to feel bereft and overwhelmed with loneliness, and her life continues to have some meaning and importance. (Myra S. spoke for many divorcées, I believe, when she said she would have done many foolish, foolish things if her children hadn't been there, needing her.) But there can be serious financial drawbacks. The judge who sets a low alimony figure isn't the one who has to see the kids go to school in worn sneakers in the winter because the alimony doesn't cover the cost of shoes at the old prices, let alone at new inflated prices.

8. Alimony, even inadequate alimony, isn't always easy to collect. True, a new law that went into effect in July 1975 establishes federal control in the search for husbands, ex-husbands, and fathers who have not lived up to their support responsibilities. (The law was much needed—several surveys had shown that more than half of fathers responsible for child support reneged on their court-ordered obligations, leaving many families no alternative but to go on welfare at taxpayers' expense.) The law has set up all kinds of machinery so that it will be effective: a "parent locator service," with financial bonuses to the states that help find errant parents; federal Social Security, Civil Service, and Treasury files open to the locator service; the help of the Internal Revenue Service in collecting the money—even the possibility of having wages garnisheed, i.e. a portion of the father's salary deducted before he gets it to pay for child support.

But the law can't solve the problem of who pays the bills during the search for the errant husband. The landlord, the grocer, and the doctor aren't going to defer being paid until Mr. Runaway has been found.

(And Mr. Runaway isn't always impoverished. One major league baseball player who earned $110,000 annually through his skill as an outfielder on the baseball circuit, was once sentenced to ninety days in jail in Los Angeles for skipping his alimony and child support payment.)

9. Women's liberation has not changed and probably cannot change some basic societal attitudes: Older men have their choice of younger women to marry; older women are more likely to remain single after a divorce, and the older they get, the greater their chances of not remarrying. The single man is considered an asset at a dinner party, an accepted figure by himself in the neighborhood bar, and—if he is reasonably affluent—a "good catch" in the matrimonial sea. A single older woman, on the other hand, is usually not even invited to dinner parties alone, is looked on as a threat by many wives (even sometimes those who consider their marriages secure), and is not considered a good matrimonial risk—unless she happens to be very wealthy.

10. And the woman with an independent income—either because she has a good job or because she got a good settlement from her husband—is often the prey of fortune-seeking men. Women real estate brokers sometimes warn divorcées to be careful and screen prospective male customers who say they want to see the house the divorcée is putting on the market. Some of the men haven't the least interest in buying a house but are interested in getting to know a divorcée who will soon have a substantial bank account as a result of the sale.

Consider the experience of my friend Miriam S. She's in her early forties, very attractive, and recently divorced. Her problem was getting back into some kind of social life—very difficult when you've been living in a typical suburban couple-land. So, like others in her somewhat leaky boat, she went to a nearby beach resort with a single clientele.

Did she meet men? Yes. Did she have a pleasant weekend and make some good social contacts? No. Mostly, she was invited—with few preliminaries— to share someone's bed. The general approach was: "Lucky you, be glad I'm asking you because in a few years I won't even bother." This approach bothered her, needless to say, but what bothered her even more was the not-so-gentle prying to find out not only what size her bra was but, more important, the size of her divorce settlement.

Sound dismal? Of course, and purposely so—it *is* dismal. Divorce is dismal, especially for the less solvent partner, the woman. But there's no need to make it worse than it is or to inflict unnecessary or uncalled-for hardships on yourself. You need to be prepared, and here are some of the things you need to know.

1. The divorce laws of your state. These vary widely and are important because they have a bearing on the financial settlement you are entitled to.

2. Your financial assets and liabilities. These too have a bearing on the ultimate settlement of your property. Many women who have been through a divorce say that before you talk to and hire a lawyer, it is as important—maybe more important—to talk to and hire an accountant if there is any doubt about your family assets and your husband's income. Why an accountant? Because a shrewd one can analyze a tax return and recognize where income has been understated.

3. The importance of paying a lawyer yourself. You need to be the one who controls the purse strings and can call the tune. Lawyers have financial responsibilities like everyone else and it is very difficult for a lawyer not to feel an obligation to the person who pays his fee. The natural question is, where are you going to get the money to do this? If you have some money of your own that you've been saving for a tearful day, you could be very well-advised to spend it on your lawyer. Remember that the divorce agreement is something you are going to live with for a long, long time and it's important that you have the best possible agreement. How close to or how far from "best" it is depends on the expertise of your lawyer. If you have no independent funds, your husband will be required to pay your lawyer, who can collect this fee when he arranges for temporary alimony and child support. If this is not possible, look into the possibility of help from a legal aid or legal services organization in your community. But you must make it clear to the lawyer that he is responsible to you, no matter who pays him.

Important: The Good Lawyer

This brings up one of the most important aspects of divorce—how to find and judge a lawyer. You want a lawyer who specializes in matrimonial law, a specialty that used to lack status in the profession but is now very much a good and lively field that has attracted feminist lawyers in particular. It's important to have a matrimonial lawyer, not only because he or she will be best able to look after your rights but also because the laws are changing as society adopts new attitudes toward marriage and divorce, and a lawyer must keep up with the field.

It's equally important to have a lawyer you are comfortable with, who will respect you as a person and empathize with you but at the same time not be afraid to differ with you when you may not see your best interest clearly. Even more important, she (or he) must consider your life not only during the divorce proceedings but also afterward. I'm thinking particularly of my friend Lynn, whose lawyer told her to quit her job on the grounds that she would get a better settlement from her husband if she were unemployed. It might have been good advice from a temporary monetary standpoint, but it was terrible advice to her as a person. She was in a field where jobs were scarce; she enjoyed her work; and most important of all, the job got her out into the world; gave her opportunities to make friends, and helped her readjust to her new single status. Fortunately, she didn't take this advice.

Women have to be aware and wary of the lawyer who is, wittingly or unwittingly, a male chauvinist. This kind of lawyer may even think he's being helpful when he says, "Don't you worry, I'll take care of everything." You can't trust your future to someone else—regardless of his motivation or good intention. You have to be in control, and this means getting from your lawyer an explanation of what he's planning and doing, and *why*.

This approach starts, of course, with the fee. Lawyers seem to disagree on this point, but responsible lawyers recognize that a client has the right to (1) a preliminary interview to see if the two will be compatible; (2) some idea of the kind of plan the lawyer will follow in representing the case; and (3) some indication of the approximate fee—approximate because unless it is absolutely routine (and few divorce cases are absolutely routine) it may be difficult for the lawyer to specify, down to the penny, what his fee will be. However, this doesn't mean he should have a free field; there has to be some kind of understanding.

Should you absolutely necessarily have a woman lawyer? Or to put it another way, does the fact that a lawyer is a woman guarantee that she will be best for you? Much as I like to support the feminist tradition just to offset the years of male chauvinism, a woman lawyer doesn't *guarantee* you anything. At the first marriage and divorce conference presented by the New York Chapter of the National Organization for Women one of the divorcées told how she had been ripped off by a woman lawyer who overcharged and underrepresented her; she then introduced her new lawyer, a man, with whom she was very pleased. (They have gone on to become not only client and lawyer but friends—the divorcée and her three-year-old daughter and the lawyer, his wife, and their two daughters.)

If possible, you *do* want a woman, simply because women should support each other and help each other. And it may be that a woman, just because she is a woman, will be more empathetic. But above all you want a good lawyer.

Finding a Good Lawyer

Where do you find her (or him)? Your first impulse will be to ask friends or relatives. This may or may not be a good idea, depending on the basis on which the friend or relative makes this judgment. Just because they were well served doesn't mean that you will be—your case may be different; you may not find the lawyer compatible; the friend or relative may be trying to do a favor for another friend or relative. Don't rule it out; just find out the reason for the recommendation.

A more likely source, probably, is a lawyer who, though he is in a different field, may be in a better position to judge another lawyer's competence. If neither of these sources is satisfactory, check with local feminist groups, such as a chapter of the National Organization for Women. Or a law school near you may have an alumnae chapter that can provide a list of women graduates who have gone into matrimonial work and have maintained their ties with the school.

There is also a national organization, the American Academy of Matrimonial Lawyers, 900 Lake Shore Drive, Chicago, Illinois 60611, with chapters in most major metropolitan areas. Though it works mostly with lawyers rather than with clients, it could be a source if you can't get a recommendation elsewhere. Check the telephone directory of the major city in your area under the listing American Academy of Matrimonial Lawyers. (It may be the number of the law firm of the current president, so don't be surprised if the phone is answered by an operator who reels off that list of ten names that law firms usually go under.) These chapters don't *recommend* lawyers, they simply refer them.

Another source is the local bar association. Here too there are no recommendations—very often lawyers are simply on an available list on a rotating basis, so you may or may not get the best possible person for you. And that is the most important criterion—who will be best for *you*. This is not one of the peaceful times in your life; you must find the lawyer compatible. No recommendation in the world is good enough to offset an instant clash of personalities.

Fees and Settlements

The next question, of course, is how much will it cost? Fees range— depending on the going rate where you live, and the skill and status of the lawyer—from $25 to $100 an hour, and from $100 to $500 a day for court appearance. On top of this, many lawyers insist on a retainer of between $1,000 and $2,000, payable on the first visit. An uncontested divorce can cost an average middle-income family about $2,500 to $4,000; one that is bitterly contested or gets complicated can cost much more—much, much more. From every standpoint, the less complicated the divorce, the less it will cost.

The agreement concerning fees should (1) be understood by *you*, (2) be understood by your husband if he is paying the bill, and (3) be put in writing.

What should your lawyer try to get for you? Something reasonable. That seems like an odd word to use at a time of trauma, when reasonableness is not the virtue uppermost on everyone's mind, but it is the *reasonable* disposition of assets that is the most likely to stand the test of time. Lawyers who specialize in matrimonial law point out that a financial agreement that is literally beyond the means of the husband or that he considers punitive or vengeful rather than realistic will be difficult to collect almost from the time it is awarded—and may become impossible to collect as time goes by. So with this in mind, here are the essential elements of a good settlement.

1. An even split of the assets acquired by the couple during the marriage, irrespective of who earned the income to acquire these assets. Such a division recognizes the fact that even though the man may have been bringing home the cash, the woman made her contribution through her services. This kind of division is almost automatic in states that have community property laws (one example of why you and your lawyer should be familiar with the laws of your state). House, furniture, and car are usually awarded to the spouse who maintains the home for the children.

If you are awarded your house as part of the divorce and there is a mortgage on it, check and see if you have mortgage insurance—insurance that guarantees that the mortgage will be paid in full should you die. It is usually available from your bank or mortgage company for a small fee. Also check whether there is any provision allowing you to omit a certain number of payments without having the mortgage foreclosed. Usually the bank or whoever holds your mortgage extends the period of the mortgage to allow for the missed payments. Such an arrangement is particularly important and helpful if you ever get sick, lose your job, or have some other kind of temporary financial setback.

2. Provisions for child support—carefully spelled out, since they vary greatly. Will they, for instance, include not only basic support—i.e. food, shelter, and clothing—but also medical bills, summer camps, tuition for college and graduate school? Summer camp might be not a luxury but a necessity if you are going back to outside work. And remember that child support ends—depending on state laws—when a child reaches a specified age,

customarily eighteen or twenty-one, though it may sometimes continue until the children have completed their education. It continues even if the wife remarries, unless the new husband adopts the child or children.

3. Alimony that will be, within the constraints of income, adequate for the wife's needs and in a form best suited to her future plans. You might, for instance, want a lump sum that would give you funds to retrain so you could qualify for a good job. The award should also consider the length of the marriage, and the wife's status and earning potential. There should be some provision for you if your alimony would stop when your former husband dies, if you will not be eligible for your own Social Security because you never worked outside your home. You should realize also that you are not eligible for your ex-husband's Social Security once you have been divorced, since you are no longer his widow, even if he never remarries, unless you were married more than twenty years before the divorce.

One solution to this problem is for the husband to have an insurance policy with his divorced wife as beneficiary. This is often a tax advantage to the husband. However, many lawyers think there should be a policy on the husband's life regardless of the tax situation—and also that the wife should be the owner of the policy and pay the premiums. In this way she can be sure that they are paid, so that the policy is kept up to date and she will have some income even if her husband dies.

4. An equitable tax agreement. But equity is not always easy to define, nor is it always possible to achieve. Yet some allowance has to be made for you as a wife if you have been penalized, as far as earning power goes, by staying at home with young children. The tax laws are tricky and intricate. (Alimony is tax deductible for your husband—but taxable for you, since it is income.) This is one area where you should check with your lawyer to make sure he knows the latest tax laws and has worked out the agreement that is most beneficial to you.

5. Some possibility of changing the agreement if the cost of living changes —something that again should be fair to both individuals involved. Remember that divorce costs money any way you do it, and the only sure way to cut down on this expense is to settle as much by out-of-court negotiation as possible. The more the two of you agree on what's equitable and the more you save on lawyer fees, the more you will have left to divide.

CHAPTER 11

I Guess You Could Say She's That Foolish Cosmopolitan Girl

Who hasn't envied her? There she is with her gorgeous hair, her perfect bosom, and that look that says, "I know something that you don't know." She invites you to take a peek at her "super" apartment, with her "super" wardrobe, before she's about to take off for a "super" vacation after giving one more smash party—so everyone can enjoy her latest records, admire her dog's new haircut ("expensive but worth it"), and covet the gold cuff links she gives her lover.

"When do you suppose I'll begin to feel guilty about the money I spend on clothes?" she asks. "On beaux (men deserve presents too!). . . . On trips. . . . Frankly I may not *ever* feel guilty. My favorite magazine says earning big and spending big on things you love are important 'perks' for a smart girl. I can go into tax-free municipals (or worry about the children's orthodontia!) later. . . ."

And there you are, grubbing away, worrying about putting money in the bank and what would happen if you got seriously sick and can you afford a budget minivacation and who will look after you in your old age. What *does* she know that you don't?

Since shyness and modesty are not two of the Cosmo girl's outstanding characteristics, let's take a frank look, a much closer look, at her life and life style. There are a few things she doesn't mention in those full-page ads that glorify her way of life (while pushing the products of the magazine's advertisers).

Consider the Cosmo girl's apartment, for instance. She's not always leaving it for glamorous vacations—and she doesn't always live in it alone. Who lives in it with her? A husband—but not hers. Someone else's husband or ex-husband. His wife or ex-wife may still be living in their lovely suburban house. In the meantime the Cosmo girl and her friends are, to quote one of them, "supporting impoverished men who in turn are supporting ex-wives in the manner to which the wives became accustomed, plus financing children in school and handling debts accrued while trying to maintain their own bachelor lives before they met my girl friends and me."

Divorce is a traumatic experience even when it is most amicable, and men too suffer emotional upsets afterward. So they run up what I call "recovery room" bills, which (depending on the individual) can be psychiatrists' bills, restaurant bills because they literally can't stand to eat dinner alone night after night, or bills at singles bars and spas and ski resorts while they go about finding themselves again.

I have no intention or wish to pass any moral judgments here. I just want to point out that very often it's the Cosmo girl, who, because she thinks she's sophisticated, foolishly accepts the responsibility for paying those bills without realizing what she's getting into.

Take Myrna S., for instance, a very pretty thirty-three-year-old with a fine figure and a beautiful, delicate complexion enhanced by her long reddish-brown hair. Myrna was divorced from her husband after a stormy marriage and now lives with her three young children in a four-and-a-half-room apartment. Since her husband has custody of her children over the weekend and never fails to take them, she has had ample opportunity to date other men. She met a man who was married but separated, and "took him in, fed him, and gave him money" until he got his divorce. At that point he decided he didn't want to marry her because he "didn't want to take responsibility for her children."

Or how about the part-time roommate—the man who likes to have his feet and his shoes in two worlds? He's unhappily married, he says, and he probably is. But he stays with his wife for the sake of his growing children ("What would my son think of me?"), his widowed or aging mother ("It would kill her if I split now"), his work ("You wouldn't believe, but even in this day and age my company is old fashioned, and it doesn't promote divorced men"), his political career ("I can't win in my district if I'm divorced").

Now these are old stories. Your grandmother heard them and so did your mother and mine. They all went to see the movies you might still catch sometime on the late late show, where the "back street" woman gave her all for love and endured the shame of being a mistress, the "other woman," because she couldn't give up the married man she loved. (Usually there wasn't a dry eye in the house at the end of the film.)

Now, in this day of women's liberation, things are different. But are they better? At least in the pre-women's lib day the man was expected to keep his mistress in fur coats and fine dresses, pay the rent, and support her in some kind of style. No more. *She* is supposed to settle her own charge account bills, provide for her old age, and not only pay her own rent but also be sure it's for an apartment large enough for him to find comfortable. He needs a place to keep his pajamas and a change of clothes and to watch his favorite program on color TV—and her salary should cover it.

Consider Peggy S. She met her lover on a cruise, fell in love with him almost at once, and didn't find out he was married until they had spent several weekends together. He was unhappily married and they discussed many times the fact that he was definitely going to get a divorce. Definitely. But it had to be postponed until his daughter got married. (He gave her a big wedding.) Then until his son graduated from high school and was sure of getting into college. (He got into a good, expensive college.) Then until his wife recovered from a serious illness. Then, then, then. After about five years, little arguments, big arguments, little scenes, Academy Award scenes, "final" farewells that somehow or other turned out to be not so final, Peggy has finally accepted what her friends knew all along, that Peter would never marry her.

When she got a raise and promotion, the extra money went into higher rent for a bigger apartment, because her one-and-a-half-room apartment was really too small for one and a half people. Peggy, an honors graduate of a prestige women's college, had considered herself much too intelligent and worldly wise to get caught in this kind of relationship—but there she is. She doesn't even have the consolation that women used to have—the solace of feeling put upon or being taken advantage of. She's liberated, isn't she? So now she's free to "have an affair," if you remember that quaint phrase, just like a man.

The Swinging Singles Scene

Somewhat better off, but only somewhat, is the swinging single in the singles complex. When she first moves in at age twenty-two, twenty-three, or younger, she thinks it's all fun and games and a good place to meet someone and probably eventually marry. She looks at the girls who are twenty-six and older and thinks (like drivers who know the accident statistics on a freeway but can never picture themselves in a wrecked car) that it will never happen to her. She enjoys being picked out of the crop and closes her eyes to her only slightly older sisters dangling unpicked on the vine.

Typically, while the bachelor or divorced man in the complex stocks his refrigerator with the makings of a smashing drinking party, her refrigerator contains the makings of good dinners, because she loves to cook and is proud of her skills as a gourmet cook. Besides, she earns several thousand less than the bachelors in the complex and can't afford to stock up on liquor.

His apartment is sparsely furnished—except his bedroom, which is all big bed and soft lights in anticipation of the nights he expects to spend in it with female companionship. She, however, has the nesting instinct common to women, and both likes and needs pleasant surroundings. Besides, she may consciously or unconsciously want to be seen in a framework of domesticity, so she does the whole apartment with taste and charm. The men do enjoy it.

She reads the Cosmo ads and for a while loves being the Cosmo girl. If she has a serious career in mind, and wants to pursue it, fine. (But then she doesn't belong in a singles complex, because she isn't going to have time for the social life that is one of the main reasons for the complex.)

What then are the ideal proportions of the Cosmo girl? It's certainly nice if she's not too far off from the 36-22-34 measurements of Miss America, but these aren't necessarily the proportions looked for. More important are the sizes of her paycheck, her apartment, and her bank account. Ideally she should know how to manage her finances well, so she won't make any demands on her boy friends or lovers. She should be a good hostess and cook so she can help the man fulfill his social obligations as well as being a good hostess on her own. She should have a comfortable apartment in a good safe neighborhood in case her lover has to go home to his own pad late at night. Her refrigerator should be well-stocked and have a large freezer compartment so she can come up with quick meals at the last minute, without too much fuss if she's had a hard day at the office. She should be a good conversationalist (but not too intellectual) and she should never mention (and preferably never *think* about) getting married.

Unfortunately, if she has marriage in mind, and at least a temporary dropping out of the nine-to-five routine, she doesn't know how the cards are stacked against her and her chances of being supported while she raises a family. There are usually at least twice and some reports say three times as many women living in the singles complexes as there are men. Even if not all of those over twenty-five are looking for husbands, the odds are still not in favor of the Ms. versus the Mr. Furthermore, the men over thirty who are living in the complexes are probably not looking for wives, either because they have been divorced and aren't anxious to return to the scenes of their former pain, or because, for a variety of reasons, they just aren't the marrying kind.

Now add another unfavorable fact of life. The men who are under thirty are probably looking for someone their age or younger. So once a Cosmo girl gets into her late twenties she very often drops into the category of also-rans. With her additional maturity she should be more attractive to and have more in common with an older man—but it doesn't work that way. Older men seem to be more interested in younger women, in part just because the younger ones are not yet interested in getting married, in part because an older man's attraction to a younger woman is a complex mixture of machismo, folklore about the sexual advantages to an older man of a younger partner, and other reasons known only to Masters and Johnson or to Freud.

What happens to the Cosmo girl when she "ages," i.e. gets on the upper side of twenty-five? People who've studied the singles scene say the Cosmo girl becomes a standby, someone who's around to provide a human security blanket when other, more desirable women aren't available, or a cushion on which to rest while recovering from an unhappy marriage and traumatic divorce, or an escape from the competitive dating scene. She may become a permanent refuge, if a man wants it that way, from being pursued or having to pursue, without the responsibilities of a legal commitment.

A Different Kind of Rip-off

But this rip-off by the members in good standing of the singles set (at least as far as they and their masculine colleagues are concerned) is not the only rip-off of the Cosmo girl. There's another kind that's more subtle, and in some ways more insidious. There are no single villains in this second rip-off—just all the mass media lumped together in their (very often successful) campaign to mold the Cosmo girl into one big fat checkbook that no one should ever bother to balance. Life is all fun, fun, fun, and spending, spending, spending—and don't worry about tomorrow. Later you can provide for a rainy or unemployed day; later you can take care of your children's teeth, and insurance for them if something should happen to you; later you can invest in something that will give you some security when you're older; but right now don't give it a thought.

I can't think of worse advice.

Manhattan, where I live, probably has more working women and career women than any other city in the United States. They were once described by seven extremely eligible New York bachelors in an interview in *The New York Times* as "interesting, intelligent, and diversified women." They are sought after. Yet Manhattan has large stratum of working women who probably would not be described in that way at all—never-marrieds and divorcées, living in cramped apartments, buying cheap cuts of meat, looking for free or inexpensive amusements in Manhattan. I don't know if they were Cosmopolitan girls but they certainly aren't now.

Does a woman really need this recently acquired "right" to support a man with little or no commitment on his part, except the emotional commitment he gives in good faith, and can just as easily take away in good faith? Is it really an advantage that he isn't even subject to community disapproval, though she may be—from dubious friends and relatives. Here is how one *Cosmopolitan* reader described her situation. After telling about three of her friends and herself who were supporting "alimony-poor" men, Ms. Hannah Frenweiler said:

> Here we are—*paying* for the company of the men we desire—and the world considers us losers and fools. "Drop him," friends advise blithely, but we, unmarried and world-weary at twenty-eight, know what's available out there—more poverty-stricken refugees from marriage who aren't as nice as the one we've *got*.
>
> I think well-meaning friends and relatives should begin to recognize that a woman supporting an impoverished (but desirable) man is not being foolish, but, on the contrary, may be *solving* her problem. She's saving a man from squalor, futility and in some cases alimony jail, but he's saving *her* from the singles' circuit (which she's *very* tired of) by giving her love, devotion and by making her *happy*.

It's no wonder that a survey by the Institute of Life Insurance, part of its continuing Monitoring of Public Attitudes series, showed that from 1972 to 1974, while public approval of women's liberation went to 56 per cent from 49 per cent, more men (61 per cent) than women (51 per cent) favored the women's movement in 1974.

What Price Happiness?

So where does all this leave the Cosmo girl? Or, what price "happiness"? Does she have to be out on a limb, clinging to it desperately? Not these days —not if she's smart. She's got options, and she's got choices. She can drop to the ground, which may not be as far away or as hard as it looks, and even if she gets bruised at least she knows where she is. Or she can climb back to a sturdier limb and then decide what to do.

What am I saying here? I am not an old sourpuss or misandrist (man-hater). I thoroughly agree with that old saying by Dr. Samuel Johnson that "marriage [or a relationship with someone] has many pains, but celibacy has no pleasures." *But,* and it is a *big but,* don't close your eyes and let things happen to you without knowing what's going on. It's all very well for the people who sell merchandise to try and sell it to you and do it with all the persuasiveness they know. That's the capitalist system in action. That doesn't mean that you have to buy. Why should you be "in" to everything expensive just because some designer, manufacturer, or resort owner says you should be? Discover how chic it can be to be "out." It can be more original, more daring, and, best of all, cheaper.

If you find yourself, for good and honest reasons, helping to support some man, at least don't do it blindly. Don't allow yourself to drift into a situation that starts with an occasional sleep-over and breakfast and ends up with a full-time, nonpaying roommate which is more than you had bargained for or can afford. And it's the afford part that we're dealing with here. (Whether you can "afford" it emotionally or psychologically is a subject for another book; that is a decision you will have to make on your own. And if you feel you can't afford it, by all means seek psychological help. In the long run it may turn out cheaper than supporting an affair.)

You Love Him But . . .

Let's say you are involved in a *literally* costly affair. Then, at the very least, do things to protect your financial future. Some suggestions:

1. Have your bank *automatically* deposit part of your paycheck in a savings account before you can put your hands on it.

2. *Never* sign over any property, coendorse a loan, or invest in your lover's enterprises without consulting a lawyer. And be sure it's *your* lawyer. Even where absolutely no fraud was intended, you can get caught in a business venture that is bad. You are in absolutely no position to make objective judgments, so leave it up to someone else who is not emotionally involved to make the judgment. If your lawyer says O.K., lend the man money if you must. The business may prosper and you'll both be rich—but be sure you ask for and get a signed legal document acknowledging the debt. If you can't bring yourself to ask, hide behind your lawyer, saying that of course *you* have faith but that you always abide by your lawyer's decision or that she/he won't keep you as a client unless you follow her/his advice.

3. Check on your car insurance policy to be sure you are in no danger of losing your coverage. Ms. Galen Kranz and Ms. Beverly Thompson both had difficulty keeping their car insurance despite excellent jobs, stable personalities, and fine driving records. Their insurance was canceled and, after a fight, reinstated (at higher rates) because they were living with men without, to quote the insurance investigator, "benefit of wedlock." Neither woman made any secret of her relationship. Both chose to sue, and at this writing the case is still pending. Nevertheless, be warned that there are companies that might consider this living arrangement cause enough to change your coverage. Check it out with your agent, and if you think there might be difficulty, consider switching to a company that has kept up with the twentieth century.

4. Worry, worry a lot, about your job security if your lover is in the same office. If things go wrong—company executives don't like the situation, or your lover changes his mind about you—guess who is going to get fired. Or

transferred. Or put into a situation so uncomfortable firing will look almost like a blessing. Not him. If you think it's better to change jobs, even if the moon is still casting a silvery light on your romance, do it while you have the choice—not when you are forced. At the very least make sure that your job benefits—pension, health, insurance, profit sharing—are transferable if you turn out to be transferable.

In other words, cherish your love but cherish equally your independence. In the world of the Cosmopolitan girl the keynote is impermanence. Ponder these words by one of New York City's most eligible bachelors, Marc Olden, author of adventure books. He admitted to mixed feelings about settling down—even though he had once lived with a woman for six years—and one of his reasons was the "infinite availability of interesting women . . . like grains of sand along the seashore." He added that there was no nice way of ending an affair. "That's like asking if there's a nice way to go get in and out of a dentist's chair, or a nice way to suffer through an Internal Revenue Service tax audit. It just can't be done."

So, if you think you might some day be just another grain of sand, remember that when you don't have your love to keep you warm a good substitute can be a cozy bank account and your independence.

CHAPTER 12

Part-time Jobs: Advantages, of Course, and Some Disadvantages Not Usually Mentioned

For a mother with young children and home responsibilities a part-time job is *the* answer to combining the pleasures of child-rearing, the demands of domesticity, the need for more income, *and* the opportunity to keep at least one foot firmly in the world beyond the crib and the playpen. That's what I would have written several years ago, and though I still think it's basically true I have a different perspective now—and I think the statement has to be amended.

These days I would say that for a family with young children a part-time job is the answer for *either* husband or wife, so that children have the benefit of a parent's supervision for at least part of the day—to say nothing of giving both parents the benefit of seeing their children more than evenings and weekends. After all there is no edict from the gods that says it's mother who has to work part time while father works full time. And there are many men who would relish the chance to be home during the week, balancing a power tool instead of a set of accounting books, or swapping stories with other fathers in the park instead of around the Xerox machine.

However, it still is more likely that the woman of the house will stay home while the children are very young, and then get back into the job market via the part-time route. So let's review briefly the well-known advantages of part-time work and then have a look at some of the problems that go along with the opportunities available.

The part-time job is usually nearer to home, so less time needs to be spent traveling. You can arrange hours that allow someone to see the young child off to school and be home to greet him when he returns. Time is available for doing the household chores. And you may have some flexibility of schedule so that a parent can watch the ball game when Daniel pitches for the winning team, or the school play in which Marc is at last playing the part of the king or Miriam has the most speaking parts. Time, time, time, to do all the little nitty-gritty things that provide the glue that holds the family together. For this a part-time job is great.

The Drawbacks of Part-time Work

But there are also drawbacks that have to be cited when discussing part-time work. Because part-timers aren't around when decisions are made, when committees meet, when questions need immediate answers, or when unexpected problems come up, in general they have little responsibility. As a result, their jobs are frequently tedious or dull or both. And not terribly well paid. In itself these things are bad enough—but there are other, more serious drawbacks.

One of the biggest drawbacks is benefits. Part-timers often don't share in such lovely little extras as paid holidays, vacations, bonuses, health insurance, retirement and pension plans. This makes the part-timer a big bargain for the company, but leaves her unprotected if she gets sick while on the job. What's worse, though not immediately apparent, is the situation when she gets older. If all goes well in her life and she is covered by her husband's health insurance and pension plan, she will be all right. But if things don't go well—if her husband is not covered or becomes disabled, or if they get divorced—having no fringe benefits can be a minor or even major disaster.

The Federal government has part-time jobs under many different classifications: intermittent, temporary, term, career-conditional. Each has its own rules governing benefits such as vacations, sick leave, insurance, and retirement. Some of the jobs, however, have no benefits—and the part-timer who isn't eligible loses out of course. When one of the legal holidays comes around, it's a vacation day for the full-timer, but a day's pay lost for the part-timer.

In the academic world there is a different but equally serious problem. Tenure, i.e. the right to have a job permanently after a certain number of probationary years, has always been a major goal for full-time faculty members. In this day of a shrinking student-age population and tight academic budgets, even many full-time people aren't being given tenure; for part-timers it is just about nonexistent. This means they are employed for this semester or academic year—but with no guarantees for the next or following years. Needless to say this leads to a fully justified feeling of great insecurity. (I have such a job, teaching at a local college—and every year I worry until my contract appears in the mail.)

Still another drawback is the possibility that a part-timer will have difficulty meeting the requirements for collecting unemployment insurance.

(At this writing the basis is twenty weeks of work in the previous fifty-two weeks, and earnings of at least $600.) Someone who can't meet these requirements could have long payless periods between jobs—a real pain in the pocketbook.

And yet another drawback—the question of raises. Unless she has a rare skill, a part-timer is very often considered expendable. What's worse, she may very well *be* expendable, with several dozen qualified (or, more likely, overqualified) women standing in line just waiting to get the job as soon as it's available. So raises may be either very minor or very infrequent or nonexistent.

What does this add up to for those of you who want to or can only have part-time jobs? Simply this: you are frequently exchanging present freedom for future insecurity. Furthermore, since you are just one in a long line of people waving your hand and yelling, "Hire me, hire me" (especially for that all-too-rare interesting opportunity), you have very little bargaining power. Still, it certainly pays to ask, when hired, what benefits go with the job, particularly if there are forms to fill out to become eligible for group benefits. Some do have benefits: either by law or because they don't cost the employer very much, because he gets a tax advantage by providing them, or because the benefits are part of a group package. If the job is newly created, it *certainly* doesn't hurt to ask, since the employer may not have thought of the question until you bring it up and may decide that at least some benefits should be offered. Nor does it hurt to aspire to raises—and work to get them—or to keep your eye on promotions and aspire to them and the goodies that go with them.

Some Personnel Problems

Which bring up some other problems in this gloomy (sorry about that) recital. You should be aware of them because they affect your long-term earning possibilities.

Part-timers are sometimes resented by people working full time, for a variety of reasons—some justified, some not; some preventable, some not. People longing for the clock to get around to five resent seeing someone leave at three or three-thirty, *even when they know the person is not making as much money as they are.* This resentment can show itself in petty ways on the job and make it more difficult for the part-timer to do a good job and to win raises, promotions, or even full-time status ultimately.

Even more serious, however, is the feeling that part-timers don't carry their fair share of a job. Supervisors sometimes have gripes about part-time schedules, saying they have to explain things twice, once to the full-timer and once to the part-timer. Or they may feel that a part-time job results in extra work for themselves when arrangements have to be made to cover for the part-timer. Most of this resentment is probably ill-placed, since many part-timers are actually more productive than full-timers. They run their errands, make their phone calls, see the dentist, and settle the dispute about when the rug is to be delivered on their own time, whereas full-timers usually have no choice but to do some of these chores on long lunch hours or on company time.

(Here is an instance where women can help each other, whether we're supervisors, full-timers, or part-timers. If there is a hassle we can go out of our way to set up some kind of system that will overcome problems that come up. It may be as simple as setting up a book of instructions or as complicated as holding regular, but informal, meetings to be sure everyone is briefed as to what's happening and what needs to be done.)

One particular kind of complaint, however, that may be quite legitimate can arise in the case of a part-timer with an executive job and responsibilities who has the help of a secretary or assistant. (This problem is apt to be peculiarly ironic, since both people involved will probably be women—at least until the time comes when men and women share this kind of arrangement.) What happens is this: As is usual with such jobs, the executive doesn't leave on the dot but rather when her work is finished. But her situation is complicated by the fact that she won't be in the next day, and therefore may not only have to stay late herself but also keep the assistant or secretary late. This can mean missed trains, canceled dinner engagements, broken dates, and so on. If it happens only very occasionally, it's accepted—but if it happens fairly regularly, it is resented.

Consider for instance Aileen G., who is a manager in one of the nation's most prestigious accounting firms. She had been full-time until the birth of her daughter, when the company was happy to have her switch to three days a week since she was too valuable to lose. Part of the secret of her value is that she doesn't keep clients waiting, and so if she doesn't finish a job by five o'clock and knows she won't be in the next day, she stays late to finish—and asks her assistant to stay also. Aileen isn't aware that her assistant, June (whom I interviewed separately), is resentful. June says, "If she wants to stay out the next day because she has a baby at home, O.K. But that's her problem, not mine. Why should I be penalized?"

The Long-range Outlook

Another problem for the part-timer is more long range. What happens to her promotion possibilities? The very fortunate or very exceptional woman will be eligible for promotion despite her part-time status. But she has to be *super*-superwoman, work in an exceptional situation, or have an exceptional boss—and sometimes none of these do the trick. An administrator in the New York office of the U. S. Department of Labor, in discussing Patricia M., who held an executive position as a part-time compliance officer, said, "The key is the person involved and here we have a very, very capable employee. The only disadvantage of the schedule is that we don't have her full time." However, when the question of promotion came up, he said it was "only fair to give preference to full-time employees of equal rank."

Patricia admits her part-time schedule hinders her chances of advancement and sometimes limits her assignments but says, "You do have to make compromises—mostly involving your children—but it's worth it."

Undoubtedly it is, but women who are making this compromise should at least be aware that they may regret their choice later. Take Beatrice D., for instance, an estate and tax planning lawyer with one of New York City's very prestigious law firms. She began her career with the firm in 1942, then took time off from 1947 to 1956 to have her three children. When her youngest was about two she came back to work part time, and has been on a some- times part-time, sometimes full-time schedule since, taking leaves of absence and vacation days to suit the needs and demands of her family.

Of course it's been pleasant, but as she looks back, Beatrice doesn't think she would do it the same way again. She now believes she would have been better off if she had continued to work part time while her children were in- fants and then assumed a full-time schedule as soon as possible—certainly as soon as the youngest was in nursery school. Her reason? By the time her youngest started high school, she had pretty well discharged her family re- sponsibilities. In terms of *time* in her law firm, given her training and ability, she should have been a full partner. Yet she was still and would continue to be in effect a junior partner, with salary and responsibilities about equivalent to those of the newer and younger partners in the firm. The men she had en- tered the firm with in 1942 (a good year for career women for a bad reason— World War II and the drafting of men into the army) had committed them- selves to a career; she had not. They achieved their potential; she did not.

There is a lesson here for women who want to have careers. Part-time jobs should be looked on as means to an end, not an end in themselves. They are bridges spanning the interval when family responsibilities make it difficult or impossible to hold full-time jobs. They may be a wedge into a new field. But they should always be considered in terms of a long-range plan that antici- pates where you want to be and what you want to be doing when you're a comparatively free agent.

For there's another reason, for us as women, to think today of tomorrow. In one sense Freud was right—apparently biology is destiny when it comes to age. Figures from the World Health Organization, United States population surveys, Social Security, and life insurance companies prove that women live longer not only in the United States (where supposedly we're pampered) but also in other countries in the world. This age advantage, say these statistics, can't be explained by environmental, occupational, or economic differences alone and seems to point to an innate biological or genetic superiority of women over men.

We have to be even more careful than men in planning our future—because we have a longer future. A husband will most likely have a wife to tend him in his old age—but who will tend her? That's why it's important to try to find the part-time job that will lead to full-time, productive, enjoyable work when family responsibilities make this possible.

Now the really big question: Where do you find such part-time jobs? It isn't easy, but, in the following chapter you'll find some helpful suggestions.

CHAPTER 13

The Question: Finding (or Creating) the Part-time Job

It's the big question—where do you find the interesting, well-paying, reasonably convenient part-time job that has excellent fringe benefits and will lead to future opportunities? How I wish I could answer that question with a nice long list of names and addresses of prospective employers that you could write to! But the truth is that usually you don't find such jobs. They have to be created, and sometimes are—for women who continue to do part time what they had been doing full time. These are the women who have sought-after skills to sell: the research chemist, the doctor, the dentist, the social worker, the accountant, the editor, the psychologist, the writer, the nurse. Some company or some institution wants them badly enough to accommodate to their schedule; or they have a profession that allows them to set their own hours and to be paid well enough to cover their expenses.

But you aren't all in the professions, or chemists, or editors, or public relations specialists, etc. Yet many of you who are working full time and would like to make the shift to part time have the possibility of creating your own job—if you plan. Plan, for instance, to become so valuable to your employer that he hates to lose you and therefore will accommodate to your new status. Plan to make some part of your job so essentially yours that there would be a big gap if you left, so your employer will be open to the idea that you stay on part time. Plan to establish a very personal relationship with the company's customers, so the company will worry about losing them if you leave. Plan to set up part of the job so it can be separated from the remainder and done part time.

Arlene G., for instance, an accountant with one of the country's major firms, planned her strategy along these lines when she first decided to get pregnant. She was fortunate to be working for one of the innovators in the company, and she made sure that she was an invaluable assistant to him. Then, when the time came for her to broach the subject of working part time, he knew her worth to the company and to himself, and also how well liked she was by the clients she served. He was willing to support her bid for being part time and to get the idea accepted by the company.

It's impossible for an outsider to tell you what part of your job can be lifted out—only you can judge. But here are some suggestions. Are there files that are difficult to maintain and important to the company? Perhaps you could take responsibility for supervising them and keeping them current. How about a customer mailing list that should be regularly updated? Some salesmen's records that need periodic review? Some research that no one has time for? A particular neighborhood in a social service agency's area that is usually not covered because it's so out of the way?

Some Sources for Jobs

If there is no part of your job that can be easily lifted out, look around where you are now working—whether it's an agency, bank, insurance company, or government office—for some service now lacking that you might be able to offer. In a variation of that old game, "What would you do if you had a million dollars" you might try, "What would you do that you can't do now if you had an intelligent assistant?" There are few executives of any organization who are completely satisfied with how much they accomplish with their present staff, few who wouldn't like to accomplish more if they had more personnel. If you can show them the possibility of changing these ambitions into reality, you *may* find yourself with a good part-time opportunity. There is no guarantee that this will work, but what can you lose by trying?

Consider the case of Simone F., a divorcée with two school-age children, who had majored in chemistry in college but had dropped out in her junior year. She decided she wanted to get a job in the research center of a hospital near her home. She went to the library of the hospital, found out who was on the staff and what kind of research was being done. Then she chose a man who was doing work that she knew something about because of her background, went to see him, and asked if he needed a part-time assistant. She had prepared a résumé that showed how her background qualified her to understand his work enough to help him in the lab, research the literature for him, and edit and type his papers intelligently. He had a grant that allowed him to hire part-time staff, and in about a month he had rearranged his budget so that she had a twenty-hour-a-week job.

Another possibility is the department that has to stay late on Friday night, or work over the weekend or on holidays. No fun for you either, of course, but since part of your aim for this part-time job is to get out of the house and get experience, this may be your opportunity to do it. Also, if you want to save on child care costs, the oddball hours mean that your husband will be at home to take over the child care.

Still another possibility, if you've exhausted all the potential at your own job, is to look around at suppliers of goods and/or services to your company. You might have a special appeal to them just because you know the problems of *their* customer, your employer. Similarly inquire among your company's customers to see if they have any openings. They will be interested in you because you know the ins and outs of your company—who really can expedite an order, or who is the vice-president to get through to if someone wants to sell a new idea—in other words, who has the clout. This is certainly not an idea that I dreamed up. Retired army generals in charge of Pentagon purchasing have been hired by army suppliers and contractors for years—who knows better how a department works, who orders what, etc. than someone who has actually been involved?

Problems in Selling Yourself

Next comes the selling job, with *you* as the product. One of the first things you have to do is deal with the question of status. Let's say the only part-time opening is a job without much status. The prospective employer, particularly if you've had a higher-status, full-time job hesitates to offer you such a job. Yet, he or she would like to—and you can foresee the possibilities in the job.

You can see what's on the employer's mind. If you are more qualified or have more skills than the job calls for, he's afraid you are going to get bored or tired and quit as soon as something better comes along. This is a legitimate worry on his/her part and you have to answer it. (You know you aren't going to quit because there aren't that many part-time job opportunities, but you are not going to say that, of course.) The important thing is to answer his unspoken objection in a way which is logical and acceptable. You are the one who has to bring up the subject and deal with it. Say—*and mean it or don't say it*—that you understand the work is at a somewhat lower level than you've been accustomed to, but you don't mind for several reasons:

1. You believe in that old-fashioned work ethic that no honest work is beneath any person. (That's what my father always used to say—a very healthy attitude, I think. If your father didn't say it, you can quote mine.)

2. You look on the job as an opportunity to learn more about the business and possibly to give the job more value (not status) by doing it well.

3. You have a long-range outlook, you are planning to return to work full time some day, and you look on this job and this company as a place to learn while doing a good job—and to prepare yourself, perhaps, even to fill a vital, full-time spot in the company when you and the company are ready for each other.

Once that is out of the way, you have to deal with something else that is on the employer's mind—the question of fringe benefits. (Here I am going to be a bit contradictory, but only because life itself is often contradictory—with that inevitable clash between hope and reality, between what we'd like to get and what we actually can get.) The fringe benefits are important, and, as I said before, you aim to get them. But you also have to recognize that employers worry that such benefits will cost more for a part-timer than for a full-timer. You have to point out that they can be prorated so you cost no more. For instance, if you work only three days a week he is required to pay only three fifths of the benefits—only three days of vacation, or sick leave, or whatever. The one exception to this may be medical insurance, which is different. Costs for medical insurance do go up on a per employee, per component (i.e. what's covered) basis, and an employer might not want to pick up this extra bill.

One way to overcome this objection is to specify that you do not want to be covered by the health insurance (if you have coverage through your husband), or to say you will forego some parts of the coverage, or you will accept limited coverage, i.e. only for yourself, rather than for yourself and members of your family. In other words, if this might be a potential obstacle to getting a part-time job because it would add to the expense of hiring you, there are ways to cut this expense. If you are well prepared to discuss this, you add to the good impression you make by anticipating the problem and pointing out how it can be solved—without damage to you or the prospective employer.

Volunteer Work: Yes or No?

If there are no part-time jobs available on a paying basis in a field in which you're interested, should you do volunteer work? Feminists say no. Women should get paid for their work; they've been exploited too long. And a good case can be made for this.

On the other hand, you can sit at home in noble isolation, consoling yourself that you are fighting the good fight, advancing the cause of women everywhere, showing "them" you won't be taken advantage of—and where does it get you? Nowhere. As long as the job market is "soft" and as long as there is work to be done and, *most important of all*, as long as you have something to gain from doing volunteer work on a part-time basis, I think it's an option that should be considered. The point is to make the process work for you. That means go into any volunteer work with the attitude, what's in it for me? In other words, do well for yourself while doing good.

Pamela A., for example, wanted very much to get some kind of part-time work in her field, physiological psychology. But there were absolutely no paying part-time jobs on the college campus near her home. So she volunteered to work in the psychology lab at the college, helping someone do his research, and she did work, conscientiously, for about a year. Then she heard of a job through a friend of a friend she had met in the lab. She applied, got an excellent recommendation from the researcher she was working with (who was sorry to see her go but felt she deserved the opportunity), and has been happily working and getting paid ever since. If she hadn't volunteered, she would never have heard of the job, nor would she have had such a pertinent recommendation.

Pick the field you are interested in and the kind of work you want to do and go and look for volunteer spots in that field. If you're interested in the medical field, inquire at local hospitals—but get down to the precise area that you are interested in. If clinical work is your interest, find out about that; if mental health is a field that you'd like to enter, ask about mental health facilities attached to a hospital. If it's administration that appeals to you, ask about working in the fund raising campaign.

Whatever you do, keep your own interests and long-range goals in mind. Be sure you get to know the people who have the power, who handle money and jobs, so that your work is appreciated and when jobs open up you will be in line for them. You will have to learn to be your own publicity agent, to be sure that you are getting proper credit for what you do—especially if you introduce any innovative ideas.

Keep some kind of diary of your contributions of ideas and suggestions, so that when you are ready to move to paid employment you will have acquired a good résumé that will help you get a paying job. This is a plan that has worked well for many women, including women in the feminist movement who have gone on, after running volunteer workshops and campaigns, to paying jobs doing exactly what they had done as volunteers.

And one final point: Be selective about the agency you're doing volunteer work for. You are giving a real gift—your time and talent. Be sure the agency is well run, not only from an administrative standpoint, but also from a financial standpoint. There have been too many instances of agencies which served more as middle-class welfare projects for their professional staff than as genuine social agencies. This is not to say that they don't do some good—but the "some" may be very small in relation to the funds and effort expended. When you're considering whether a place will offer you opportunity, check into its financial report and its rating with the Better Business Bureau to be sure you aren't becoming part of something that is not itself meeting professional standards.

CHAPTER 14

"Job Politics" Is the Name of the Game: Learning How to Play

To hear about office politics from husband, lover, or friend is one thing. To experience it is something else. And that something else is shock—almost unbelieving shock when you learn, the hard way, that when Leo Durocher correctly and wisely said that nice guys finish last, he also meant nice gals.

Women are brought up to be nice, cooperative, passive, to stay clear of trouble—and above all not to initiate fights. Aggressiveness is "unfeminine," "unmannerly," and not part of the nurturing role. Little girls grow up thinking they should not be combative and assume that other children, particularly other female children, are the same.

Though the situation is changing somewhat, until now little girls didn't usually hear their mothers at the dinner table talk about getting "shafted" by the guy at the next desk, or about losing a contract through dirty dealing by a competitor, or about the absolute necessity for "playing the game" or "doing unto others before others do unto you."

(This is not to say that there aren't chicanery, dirty doings, and nasty dealings going on in women's clubs, sororities, and organizations, but there are differences. The stakes are much lower—people's egos may be on the line, but not their livelihood. And women are less apt to talk about it at the dinner table. For one thing their husbands may not know the people involved or just may not be interested. Another and more important reason is that the children may know very well the person involved, and see her at the play ground or in the car pool or in the schoolyard, and little pitchers not only have big ears, they also have big mouths.)

As girls grow up, this socialization to be gentle and noncombative continues in the kind of vocations they have been going into—the service-to-others and nurturing fields of teaching, social work, nursing, librarianship.

Compare this with the socialization of boys, who are expected to fight, who learn in the schoolyard that there are dirty fighters, and who grow up expecting to have to compete, even if they don't particularly like the idea. They also expect to find aggressiveness and foul play and are more apt to be surprised by someone who plays fair than by someone who doesn't. Add to this the more traditional vocations of men, jobs in business and industry, with the assumption that there will be competition and it will be rough. Men know, almost with a gut knowledge, that they are going to have to learn to adapt to and play the game of office politics, whether the office is in a union hiring hall, a hospital complex, the executive suite, or City Hall itself.

Job Politics

Actually the phrase "office politics" is too narrow—it really should be "job politics." Because, no matter what field or kind of work is involved, politics is involved—if you define politics as people trying to hold on to what they've got and get more of the same. Job politics involves status and all the perquisites that come with status—promotions, raises, out-of-town trips to exotic places, stock options, etc., etc.—plus the things that money can buy—the big house, the well-stocked freezer and liquor cabinet, the first-class vacation. When you think of it this way, you understand why it's not a game; it's a serious business and that's how serious people play it.

There are people, men as well as women, with illusion that only in big business, complete with carpeted floors and executive suites, are the swords drawn or unsheathed. So they opt for government or institutional jobs, or go to work in the groves of academe, thinking they've found a refuge. Then they find that the daggers are just as pointed, just as quickly unsheathed, and just as quickly used. The only difference may be the delicacy with which the deed is done. People in government do it more slowly and circuitously, with everything in triplicate (it's the bureaucratic influence). People in academia do it with more finesse—they have a long tradition of courtesy and gentility to uphold. But it really doesn't matter how the dagger is wielded—the result, for the person on the receiving end, is just as deadly.

Therefore, be advised: The people you work with, no matter where you work and whether they are male, female, or undecided, are sometimes going to be untrustworthy, mean, conniving, hypocritical, any combination of these, or all of them. If you are young, they are going to try to take advantage of your youth, expecting that you are overtrusting and naïve. If you are older, they are going to try to take advantage of your age, expecting that you're suffering from hardening of the arteries of ambition, if not of your actual arteries. (And remember that to someone in her/his twenties anyone past thirty-five, say, qualifies as old.) If you have just returned to the job market, they are going to try to take advantage of your newness, regardless of your age.

In other words they are going to act like people who do nasty things, sometimes because they are just plain nasty, but just as often because they are driven by inner demons, or terribly scared, or terribly insecure, and therefore following the law of the jungle, which is first of all, and instinctively, survival.

So what kind of things can happen? Here are some case histories. Kathe H. was hired, on the basis of her training as a nurse and a child care specialist, to be the head of a new division of a long-established social work agency dealing with unmarried mothers. When she was offered the job, she was told in glowing terms (of course, everything starts out glowing—the worm comes later) the plans for the new division and the size of the budget and staff she would have to work with. Nobody told her that the figures were on paper only—and that the actual budget was only half of what was projected. So what happened? She expected to fulfill her duties and use her training by supervising nurses' aides; instead she had to supervise the carpenters, electricians, and other workmen who were just beginning to set up the rooms in which the babies were to be kept.

Then came the board meeting and the complaints that the division wasn't caring for the number of babies it was supposed to. The head of the agency put all the blame on Kathe, saying she was inefficient and disorganized. No mention that the babies' area was still being built, that half the supportive jobs were unfilled, and that Kathe had become a foreman, not a child care supervisor. Kathe received a copy of the minutes of the meeting and almost fell off the rickety chair she was using at her makeshift desk. Needless to say, she never got the opportunity to present her side of the situation to the board—who dealt only with the administrator.

Or consider Donna L., who worked for a mail order house in the complaint department—about which there had been many complaints, since it was behind in its work. Donna was asked to lunch by one of her colleagues who hadn't been terribly friendly before. They began to talk about the work and some of the things that might be done to upgrade the department. Donna had thought about the problems quite a bit and talked about her ideas. Her colleague just sat there quietly, occasionally dropping in an "ummm" and a "hmmm" or an "I don't think that would work—it's not practical."

How surprised Donna was, at the next staff meeting, to hear those same "unworkable" and "impractical" ideas presented by guess-who, as if you didn't know. And if you think Ms. Guess-who was embarrassed when, flushed with the compliments she got from their boss, she brushed passed Donna (still sitting at the conference table slightly open-mouthed and stunned), think again. The Guess-who's of the world have an astonishing ability to convince themselves that the ideas they have filched from others are really their own. (Psychologists have a word for the ability—it's known as a variety of cognitive dissonance, which roughly translated from psychological jargon, means the ability to convince yourself of something you want to be convinced of, whether or not it conforms to reality.)

Then there was Sophie A., a secretary but would-be editor, whose boss knew she was a facile writer. He asked her if she would mind looking over a procedures manual he had just written for new employees, "just to see if she had any suggestions." She read it, realized it was badly organized and badly written. She told him tactfully it needed "a little work," and then stayed late every night for a week reorganizing and rewriting it while keeping some of the original tone so it still read as if it came from him. (It wasn't easy. Though he's in his early thirties, his mind is still wearing high-button shoes and celluloid collars and his writing sounds it.)

At the next staff meeting he was complimented on the manual, mentioned that Sophie had checked it for "accuracy," offered his thanks—but said not a word about her editing and rewriting. When the head of the department said she shouldn't have been asked to do anything on it, since she had other work, her boss said she had volunteered.

Then an editorial job opened up. Guess who got nominated for the job. Sophie? Are you kidding? Her boss nominated his best buddy and daily lunch companion. (Sophie's only consolation was that this same buddy was busy going around the department undermining her boss, since they both aspired to the same promotion.)

Or perhaps you have had this experience. You share a gripe session with your colleagues and all agree that something has to be done. You decide collectively on a plan of action and each of you agrees to raise a different issue. You pride yourself on being articulate and at the next meeting you get the discussion started with the first complaint. You wait for the others to speak out as agreed on, you look around, you wait some more—while everyone suddenly gets very busy lighting cigarettes, taking notes, studying the wood-grain patterns in the table, contemplating the specks of dust on the light fixtures. You become not the office spokesman but the office sorehead.

How to React

I could go on but I won't. If you need more case histories, just ask your friends. The question is, what to do about it? First, you have to recognize that the problem is there. When people are not under pressure they can be very nice; in an emergency they can be magnificent. But when their job security and all that it means are at stake, watch out, especially if the job also represents a big chunk of their social life, status, and their feeling of self-esteem.

Second, wear your daggerproof vest at all times. And I mean at all times—from the executive dining room, if you get to eat in it, to the ladies' room.

Third, develop a built-in warning buzzer, something like the buzzer in cars that warns when you're exceeding your speed limit. This little buzzer should go off every time you are about to say something that will leave you in an exposed condition—something that can be misinterpreted, used to down-grade you, or "adapted" (I might even say "stolen" if I wanted to be nasty) by someone else to give him/her an advantage without giving you proper credit.

Does this mean that you should become a year-round Scrooge type, bitter and cynical? Not at all. It just means that you recognize reality before reality comes and hits you over the head.

Beware especially of the amateur psychologists who are always probing your motives, your reactions, your psyche. You criticize an aspect of the job; they ignore your factual criticism and respond with a personal attack on you, using some set phrase such as "You're not very adaptable, are you?" "You don't take criticism well, do you?" "You're not able to deal with this are you?" or, a variation of this ploy, "You're not able to deal with this in a mature way, are you?" When this situation arises, your little buzzer should be buzzing loud and clear: Stop. Don't rise to the bait. Don't answer the personal accusation. Stick to the facts. Return to the facts. Deflect the personal part with some phrase like "We can talk about me another time, but in the meantime let's talk about this," or "That's my problem, but it's not the issue at hand," or "I hadn't noticed that," or "I'll take that up with my shrink, but in the meantime. . ." or "I'll mention this to my group therapy meeting, but in the meantime. . . ."

The very fact that you are prepared to cope with such situations means that you may not have to. When you follow this approach consistently, your opposition soon learns there is no point in continuing the tactic because it doesn't work.

This pays off in several ways: You become tougher and much less vulnerable, always an advantage in the competitive world; you no longer waste valuable energy and time responding to the attack on a personal level; you save the psychic energy required to overcome the bewilderment and anger that raises your adrenalin level, makes your palms sweat and your heart pound, and sends you back to your desk or home at night exhausted. Best of all, you spare yourself the agony of reviewing over and over what you said, or the brilliant put-downs you should have thought of but didn't. It's a great hook to get off of.

Needed: An Old-Girl Network

Learning how to play job politics personally isn't the only answer, however. As women we also have to learn to work with and for each other; we need to create an "old-girl" network similar to the old-boy network men have. No matter where we work—corporation office, bank, insurance company, college, retail store—we owe it to ourselves and to each other to keep alert to any and all job and promotion possibilities and insure that women have their fair chance at them. Here are some of the things we can do:

1. Use our influence to have working schedules set up that will make it easier for women to work, if they have home responsibilities. After all, secretaries to male executives have been covering for their late arrivals, long lunch hours, and early Friday afternoon departures for years—why should we do any less for a colleague who has to come in a little bit late because the school bus was late, or her baby sitter didn't come in on time?

(I will never forget the look of gratitude I got from a fairly new secretary who apologized profusely for having come in late one morning because her daughter had a cold and couldn't go to school and it took some time until an aunt could come over and stay with her. As a working mother how I empathized! And I told her so, and said I knew how guilty she felt and that we would arrange to have her work covered if she had to stay home the next day. She became one of the best, most conscientious secretaries in the department, always willing to help others; so from a managerial viewpoint it paid off also.)

2. Meet informally, but regularly, to discuss women's problems in the company and what can be done about them. When there are concrete suggestions, present them to management as a group, so that there is group rather than individual responsibility.

3. Have work consciousness-raising sessions, to explain the workings of various departments and how women can train themselves to be eligible for the jobs in those departments. During these sessions offer each other support in our efforts to overcome male prejudice, handle difficult situations, and qualify for promotions.

4. Pass on the same information that men pass on to each other: Which departments are getting funds and which aren't. Who is heading for a promotion and who is on his way out. Who is more open-minded and who should be avoided like the plague. Where opportunities are expanding and where they are declining. When it's a good time to be visible, ask for a raise, or suggest a new way of doing something—and when the powers that be are in a foul mood, harassed, or under pressure and will automatically say no.

For years women have passed on these valuable tidbits of information to male colleagues, salesmen, and other men clever enough to fish for it by means of flattery, wheedling, cajolery, and just plain eavesdropping. It's about time that women—who are very often in a real position to know, since they type so many minutes of meetings, handle correspondence, take phone calls—use their knowledge to help each other. I am *not* suggesting that confidential information be passed along or that women betray the trust they've earned by being discreet (despite all those nasty, antiwoman jokes that say women can't keep a secret). I am simply saying that information from the grapevine (which, you can be sure, never appears in the company's slick "ZYX Company Employees' Weekly Reader—News of Your Company and Ours") can be infinitely valuable and we should have equal, or better yet, first crack at it via our own grapevine, the old-girl network.

How to Succeed at Picking Up the Check

I used to laugh at cartoons picturing women fumbling over restaurant checks. Then, when I had my consciousness raised, I stopped laughing and started feeling somewhat sad and chagrined instead. For as I observed my friends and colleagues—even those who had been in the business world some time, had traveled on their own, and were not unsophisticated—I couldn't help seeing that there is a certain amount of truth in the joke. Women *are* often awkward when it comes to picking up the check.

Why is this so? In part, it's a logical outgrowth of the dating game, with women being taken out and treated by men. Naturally, men get lots of practice paying the check, figuring out what the tip should be, and just generally being at ease in the situation. Waiters, as part of the picture, customarily hand the check to the men in the group.

In part it's also the pattern of women's versus men's lunch hour. Men very commonly have informal lunch "clubs," comprising the same group eating together every day. They either have an unofficial treasurer, who picks up the check, adds the tip, and tells each person what he owes, or they are very casual about dividing the check equally among the members of the "club." They know from previous experience that, though Joe may have two martinis one day after a particularly grueling session with his boss while everyone else settles for a beer, in the long run everything evens out, and so no one worries about getting stuck.

Also, because men earn more, they are more likely to have credit cards, particularly the so-called T and E (travel and entertainment) cards such as American Express and Diners Club, most commonly used in restaurants. This makes it very easy for them to sign the bill and settle with the group later. Even more important, just because they did (and still do) earn more, they don't worry as much about a quarter here and fifty cents there.

Women have a quite different lunch pattern. Though they do get together with friends and colleagues at work, it is more casual and less regular. Women are much more likely than men to spend their lunch hour doing "woman's work" such as shopping for gifts, replenishing their linen closet during a sale, picking up something for dessert for dinner that evening, buying panty hose for their daughters or underwear for their sons. Since they are less likely to be able to "trade off" lunch expenses, they are more apt to be money conscious. Because of past discrimination against women when it came to issuing credit cards, plus the lower salaries that made them ineligible, there may be no one in the group who has a credit card so she can sign for the check and then let everyone settle. And, because they still do earn less, they *have* to be money conscious; those quarters here and fifty cents there do make a difference.

Add to this the fact that many men still have the gut feeling, though they may not believe it intellectually, that they should pay the check. Add also the natural confusion that arises when, even though a woman is taking a man to lunch, the waiter automatically gives the check to the man, who is then in a dilemma whether he should ignore it, pass it over to the woman, or reach for it in the anticipation that she will say, "No, it's my treat"—and you have a damn awkward situation. Awkward, but not impossible.

Let's get rid of the small problem first—the casual lunch with female friends or colleagues. It's comparatively simple to avoid any hassle by either asking the waitress for separate checks or deciding in advance that one person will be the "treasurer" and pay the bill and everyone else will settle with her later. An alternative, when you have a group that eats together regularly, is to agree in advance on a set amount that everyone puts into the kitty. Anything left over goes into a general fund that the group can use at its pleasure. I once worked in an export company where this was done, and the surplus from the kitty went to pay for Christmas presents for underprivileged children. Another group in the same company used its kitty to pay for occasional trips to the theater. (We weren't that much more noble—the other group met during the year to dress dolls for an annual Christmas party they gave for girls in a local orphanage; the boys were taken care of by a men's group.)

Now let's get to the bigger problem—handling the check for business lunches, particularly business lunches where you want to appear urbane. The first thing is to get yourself a credit card, which will, of course, facilitate paying the check. The fee for the card preferably should be paid by your company, but if need be, pay the fee yourself. There are also some other ways of easy payment (particularly if you're like my friend Susan N., who doesn't want to own a credit card—no matter who pays the annual dues).

One possibility is always to take your guests to the same restaurant and make yourself known to the captain. Then it's easy enough to arrange in advance to have the waiter bring the check to you, or to have a charge account so that you only have to sign the check. Alternatively, find out if your company has charge accounts at certain restaurants, used by other people in the company, and be sure that you too are given this privilege.

You also want to learn the proper routine for paying at any restaurant so that you can do it effortlessly and smoothly. The first thing you have to do is *get* the check, which means you have to let the waiter know that you are the one who is paying. This is easily done if, when you are ordering the last course, whether it's dessert or just coffee, quietly but firmly you say to the waiter, "May I have the check please," which gives him his cue. After this (and now I'm really getting down to the fine nitty-gritty) you must observe the little ritual that check-paying consists of.

First the waiter brings you the check. After you've scanned it and added the tip, you sign the bill on the back so the waiter has a signature to compare with that on your credit card. Then you lay the credit card on the bill; he takes it away, runs it through the credit-card machine, and returns with the three-part credit form—one part for the restaurant, one part for the credit company, and one part for you as your receipt (to be saved for your accounting department or for tax purposes). You check to be sure he's written down the correct amount, then sign it, and take the receipt he hands to you.

It's really not a complicated procedure, yet when I began to take people out to business lunches I found that I was very awkward—simply because I had never paid attention to the process. I will never forget the time I took to lunch a psychiatrist who was helping me with my first book, and I forgot to add the tip onto the bill. The waiter came running after me, announcing the fact very indignantly and very loudly. I was mortified! I decided I wasn't going to get caught in that bind again, and when I told my husband, he not only coached me on the proper procedure but also volunteered to be my guinea pig. I literally practiced with him until I could do the whole thing just about automatically. I recommend this, i.e. getting practice with husbands, boy friends, lovers, until you too can pay the check with complete urbanity.

One final word—don't handicap yourself with an overstuffed pocketbook, so that you have to fumble. If you must carry around many things, prime yourself ahead of time by being sure your wallet and credit card are easily accessible.

CHAPTER 15

Getting Your Just Rewards—or, Promoting Yourself into Promotions

Whether you aim to advance one desk closer to the executive suite or you'd prefer a private office in the executive suite itself, you must have a plan in order to fulfill your ambitions. Hard work is one of the first requisites, of course, but hard work alone is not enough. We all know the hard-working female who is the backbone of many offices but has never earned the job status, the recognition, and most of all the salary she deserves because she didn't know how to find her way through the corporate maze.

The maze is more complex now, since the economy of the whole world is in a more difficult stage. The beneficial effects of the women's liberation movement, making it easier for women to advance, have been partially offset by the recession of the past few years. We are going to have to compete more effectively, and to do this we have to know how to go about it. Fortunately, it is a skill that can be learned.

The actions called for will vary considerably, depending on the kind of job you have and your aspirations. But there are some general guidelines that you can tuck into your desk drawer—and that will serve you well, no matter where you are.

The first thing to learn is the shape of the maze that you're in or—to put it a more businesslike way—what is the corporate or management structure of the company, group, institution, whatever it is that you're working for. Is it centralized or decentralized—i.e. do orders come down from the top and have to be carried out by the subordinates below, or do the various divisions have a good bit of autonomy in making their own decisions? Why do you have to know this? Because promotions are given by the people in power, and you have to know where the power is.

There is no point in knocking yourself out, as my friend Paula S. did, staying late, meeting deadlines, doing the job of two people when she had to—for an editor who had absolutely no power. He couldn't help her get a promotion, even if he had thought about it, because the company was just waiting until he got to the compulsory retirement age, at which point they let him go. Then a new editor came in from the outside and reorganized the department. The reorganization meant bringing in new people, since the department under Mr. B. had pretty much stood still, not losing money but not making any real gains either. Poor Paula. She didn't understand this, and she worked terribly hard. But when Mr. B. retired, she didn't get the promotion she had hoped for—because she had acquired the aura of stodginess that went with her boss.

So, *lesson number one*—find out who has power, and try to arrange to work for the person, or the department that has the power. How do you go about this? Formally and informally, since that's how power is often arranged. To see the formal structure and the lines of responsibility, get hold of a copy of the various organization charts of your employer. This gives you some idea of the structure of the organization—who is at the top; which departments are on the same line, meaning they are (at least in theory) of equal importance, and which departments are only branches of others; what person (or what title if there are no names on the chart) heads the department, and who is responsible to whom.

To add some insight to this picture, get hold of your company's annual report. (I am using company here as the catch-all word covering the many places you might work: a business, a bank, a social agency, a school, a branch of the government, or whatever.) A careful reading of the annual report will give you a good picture of the variety of the company's products or services, its financial standing (always put in the most favorable light), its officers, its progress—all wrapped up in the image that the company wants to project to the outside world. Very often one of the most interesting aspects of these annual reports, particularly for social agencies, is the list of names of the members of the board of directors—this often gives you some idea of the direction the agency is taking, or where the various aims and directives are coming from.

But you're not only interested in what your company has to say about itself —you're much more interested in what outsiders say and think about the company. For this kind of information you turn to outside sources such as:

1. Stock reports from Standard & Poor's Corporation, which give financial background on companies that are listed on the New York Stock Exchange, the American Stock Exchange, or the over-the-counter market.

2. Articles about your company that have appeared in the trade press. It is very often fascinating to learn about your company from articles that have appeared in magazines written for people in the field, which is what I mean

by the "trade" press. Just about every field has its own magazine or news-letter, to keep the insiders up to date on what's happening—and it's a source you should know about. (You may sometimes be surprised at some of the so-called "facts" about your company that may be quite different from what you consider to be the true picture.)

3. If your company has a library and a librarian, cultivate him or her and be sure that you are put on the routing list for the publications that deal with company problems. Ask the librarian to keep you posted on new material that comes in that is pertinent.

4. Follow the news of your field in the daily papers, of course, plus some of the national papers such as the *Wall Street Journal* and *The New York Times*, particularly the Sunday edition, which often has in-depth coverage of medicine, science, education, labor.

5. Even if you're not a union member, try to get a look at union news-papers in your field. They will often have material that you can't get else-where.

So much for sources of information and background to make you, and keep you, informed about your own industry. On the basis of this informa-tion you can plan a better strategy for getting ahead. *Anyone* interested in getting ahead has to plan a course of action; women have some special re-quirements just because they are women. I've touched on them before, but I'd like to repeat them, just to set the framework within which we operate.

Careers are a combination of planning and luck—of being prepared and being in the right place at the right time. And, despite all our brave talk to the contrary, again biology is in some ways destiny. No man has to consider how maternity leave and breast feeding would fit into his job schedule or for how long a time he will be out of the job market to stay at home and care for an infant. Furthermore, biology is still destiny until we reach the millennium in which ability is the only criterion for any job. In the meantime women still have to adapt to the world in which we find ourselves at the moment, and this world presents problems for us.

Steps to Success

I've already discussed the first step, which is to get as much information about the company you're working for as possible and keep that information current, so you always know where you stand. The second step is to recognize that you are going to have to play the game of job politics, even if you find it distasteful. The third step starts with an unbiased, objective, soul-searching self-analysis so that you know your strengths, weaknesses, abilities, and inter-ests. On the basis of this analysis you decide quite specifically what kind of a career you want to pursue. Then you establish your course of action with specific goals, minor and major, along the way and how you expect to achieve these goals. Your plan would include the additional training or education you need, the salaries you should achieve, the various kinds of responsibilities you want, the kinds of projects you want to undertake, and where you hope finally to land.

Obviously this kind of plan cannot be inflexible—it should serve only as a guideline and be subject to periodic review. But you must have some kind of orientation, some kind of blueprint, some kind of personal road map if you want to get ahead. Though this is true for men, it is particularly true for women, since, because they do take time out for family responsibilities, they usually have a shorter time period in which to achieve their goals. And so they have less time to "waste" or to drift if they are going to have successful careers.

When I say successful careers, I don't necessarily mean successful in the eyes of the world—president of this, or chief operating officer of that. I mean successful in your own terms—which might include becoming president (why not?) but might also have a quite different goal that would mean success for you: manager of a division, or part of a research team, or head of a department, or executive secretary, or chief copywriter, or whatever you choose. The important thing is that you don't sit and wait for things to happen, or drift along thinking next year you're going to get organized. If you are going to achieve anything at all, you have to exercise some kind of control.

True, other factors will be at work over which you have little or no control. The state of the economy on every level, from the world itself down to the community in which you live; the state of the particular company you're working for; even the state of the very small pond you are swimming in at the moment. But you do have some control over your own plans and preparation, and not to exert this control is to *cheat yourself of your own potential.*

The Spotlight on You

And, in order not to cheat yourself, you have to *learn* how to show your talents—very often a combination of keeping your foot out of your mouth on some occasions, avoiding playing footsie on others, and putting your best foot forward on still others. This ability to show talent, to be aggressive when need be, is one area in which women have been backward. It comes, of course, from their traditionally supportive role, being the woman *behind* the man on the political platform, at the executive desk, sitting in the principal's office. (And men have been happy to get this support—why not?)

Actually, there is nothing wrong with a supportive role as such. It is only wrong when it serves to keep you from getting the promotion or the raise that you deserve on the basis of the work that you are doing. If you are hiding your light under someone else's bushel basket and he is getting all the apples, here are some concrete steps you can take to end this situation. They are a consensus of advice from successful businessmen and women.

1. Visibility is the key. Don't let your ideas, recommendations, or reports result in credit to anyone but you. If your ideas are going to be presented orally, make sure that *you* are the one who presents them. If you think you won't get a chance to present them, or the credit, keep them to yourself until you do.

A corollary to this, incidentally, is that after a while you learn to give yourself credit where credit is due without having to think about it. Let someone mention informally that he (or she) thought of something, and without even priming yourself you'll automatically say, "Oh, I remember I was the first one to suggest that; it was at the last staff meeting, wasn't it?" The first few times you do this you may have a few fast heartbeats or sweaty palms, but soon you'll have absolutely no reaction except a tiny glow of satisfaction for becoming so adept at job politics.

2. Learn to check on what kind of acknowledgment you are going to get when you contribute in writing to reports, bulletins, recommendations, newsletters, or any other form of written or published communication that is not part of your regular work. If it's an article that's going to be published somewhere, see that your name is on the by-line. If it can't be on the by-line, see that you get a mention somewhere: "Parts of this report were based on ideas contributed by," or "research done by," or "the author wants to thank," or whatever. The first time you suggest this, it may not be possible, especially if it has been a fairly common practice to ignore contributors, but keep at it until you do get credit.

Keep two points in mind: (1) it pays to speak up for yourself and therefore you *must* do so; and (2) sometimes it's not conniving on the part of a boss that leads to lack of recognition—it's just that the person never thought about giving you credit. This isn't always the case, of course; the policy can just as easily be deliberately calculated to keep you in the background in order to get credit where it isn't due. My friend Clare worked for an editor, a fine Southern gentleman, who cheerfully took credit for every innovation she introduced in the business bulletins she edited. There were absolutely no available channels for her to get her work known, and, after trying unsuccessfully to arrange a meeting with her boss's boss as a last resort, she finally went looking for and found a better job. But this is a drastic and not always a possible or desirable alternative.

As Clare looks back now, she says she realizes she didn't do enough to get credit for herself or to get promoted—since she really liked the company and would have preferred to stay with the job. What might she have done? Experienced management consultants say the way to play the job-politics game is to draw attention to yourself. If you have a boss who isn't anxious to see that you get ahead, you have to do some things on your own—not going over his head, which is frowned on, but going around him.

How can you go about this? One of the best ways is to speak up and present new ideas at meetings, as if the idea has just occurred to you at that moment—but of course it hasn't. You are prepared. You have anticipated what might come up at the meeting and *have done your homework* on the topic. You have ready facts and figures that will bolster whatever it is that you are going to suggest "spontaneously." You should, says one past master of this game, literally rehearse your spontaneous remarks. Close the door and practice in front of a mirror. Or do it while you're putting your makeup on in the morning. Try to think of what questions and objections might be raised and prepare yourself to answer them. Put yourself in the shoes of the person or persons who will ask the questions and guess how you would act, what you would say and do, if you were that person. Then, slipping back into your own pumps, answer yourself. Above all, have a good case and be prepared to defend it.

What happens if, despite the fact that you do have a good case, you realize along the way that you can't win this time. Don't argue; it doesn't pay to win the argument and lose future opportunities. Instead, concede with consummate grace before anyone even realizes you have lost—and you'll be in a better position to win the next time.

In addition to speaking up at meetings, there are other ways to become known. Consider doing what Terri K. does as one example. She works for one of the "big eight" (the eight largest and most prestigious accounting firms in the country). Terri makes it a point to go to all the company's social functions, and since women are still a minority in her company, she is very much in evidence. She gets to meet the officers in the company, and when some special opportunity comes up, they think of her. For instance, I got acquainted with her when I needed a woman accountant to speak to a class I taught on money management at the Women's Center of Barnard College; I called her employers and they recommended her as a speaker. Since their company is interested in building its public image by being of service to the community (and thereby getting customers), they were very pleased that she agreed to take the assignment. "Be on hand and on view," Terri says, "and you'll be asked to do things." And you'll have something to recommend you when salary increases and promotions are being given out.

How else can you get visibility?

Volunteer for jobs that will bring you in touch with the people in power, the executives, in your company. Be on the committees that arrange the meetings, that discuss employee-employer differences, that plan company newsletters, that set up the Christmas party and the annual charity fund drive and the office picnic. Your object is always to stand out from the crowd, to be known as someone who has a little bit extra to offer.

Get your name in print. Offer to do stories about employees with unusual hobbies, to review a book that's of interest to company employees, or perhaps to write about your own hobby for the company newsletter. If you have a certain amount of writing talent, so much the better. If you don't, get all the facts, write them up in a brief workmanlike way and ask the editor's help in making the article better. And don't confine your writing to in-house publications. If you are participating in something interesting in your company, even if you're not the person in charge of the project, suggest writing about it for one of the magazines that serves your field. Then contact the editor of the magazine either by phone or by a letter on company stationary, suggesting your idea. If it's pertinent, the editor may be very willing, not only to help you come up with a good story, but also to help you write it so it reads well.

Speak up on all occasions. If you find yourself tongue-tied even at the lunch table, get some training. Take a public-speaking course, so you get the practice you need. Or buy a tape recorder, listen to yourself, and learn that way. (Should you ask your company to pay for the course, if they have a policy of reimbursing employees who take courses for self-improvement? Maybe, but maybe not. If you think they will approve, you should—but if you don't want to alert your boss that you are planning to compete more effectively, you may prefer to keep quiet, pay your own way, and then surprise everyone. In this case, check with the Internal Revenue Service to see if it can be considered a tax-deductible expense.)

Spotting the Power Sources

What if you feel you can't make it solely on your own, since your company tends to be run by groups or committees? Then your job is to learn all you can about the office political setup and try to affiliate yourself with the group that is upward bound. How do you identify such a group? One way is the company budget: Obviously the departments that get increases in their budget, or don't get their budget cut while other departments are slashed, are the departments with power that are going places. The heads of those departments are the people you should cultivate, and those are the departments you should aim for a transfer to, if you're thinking of transferring.

You will run into problems. Some are the standard problems of anyone who wants to get ahead: competition, lack of opportunity within the company, the industry, or even the economy itself. But there are also problems what you will face particularly as a woman—and you might as well know about them so you will be prepared to cope.

I pointed out earlier that women are still often excluded from the old-boy network and it's not the kind of discrimination that can be legislated against. Women can't *insist* that people invite them to lunch, or out on the golf course; they can't hang around Joe's Place and *expect* to be invited to join the group. They have to develop some alternate strategies—in addition to having an old-girl network. And the old-girl network is not enough to offset the disadvantages of missing the company information, opportunities, and power struggles that take place during these informal get-togethers. Here are some alternate strategies:

Not invited to lunch with the men who are the same rank as you in the pecking order? Try to find one man in the group who might be sympathetic to your problem, or who owes you a favor, and get him to invite you to join the group at least one day a week. Find some topic that would be of interest to the group and tell them you'd like to discuss it—but since there's no time for the discussion during regular business hours, suggest lunch. If that doesn't work or isn't possible, do you have a friend who works in a field that might be interesting to the lunch group? Ask if you can bring him/her to lunch with the group some day.

In other words, try to break down the barriers, but in a way that won't be resented. Then come prepared to contribute your bit of sparkling conversation, news, even office gossip to the lunch table. And have your antennae out so you pick up the unspoken but very real etiquette of the group: no smoking, or everyone has a drink before lunch, or no one has a drink before lunch, or everyone has coffee or tea. This is not a sell-out of feminism, at least not in my opinion; it is simply an extension of the psychology of getting along with any new group. The exact same advice would apply to a man faced with the same problem.

Not part of the informal, get-together-for-a-drink-before-we-go-home group? And you perceive, quite correctly, that it would be misunderstood if you went solo to Joe's Bar. (Besides, you'd feel very uncomfortable.) Find a co-worker or several co-workers, preferably some in the same dilemma, and go together. More natural, less conspicuous, easier all around. Depending on the group, you may find it possible to become a part of it or you may *not*. But it's worth a try. If there is a certain amount of resentment, you may find the group breaking up rather than admitting women. If so, save your sympathy. Any group that is so purely sexist probably acts as a pressure group, either consciously or unconsciously, to discriminate against women—and should be broken up.

However, there is one aspect of this that you must take into consideration —the men in the group may not worry about their own machismo, but rather about their wives' reactions. He tells her he has to stop off after work for a quick drink with "the boys," and someone else (her best "friend") says, "By the way, Marge, who was that woman Harry was with last night at Joe's Bar around five-thirty?" Nor is this problem confined to occasional after-work drinks. Policemen's wives objected strongly and publicly to having their husbands teamed with women police officers; accounting firms have found that wives of male accountants object to having their husbands sent on out-of-town assignments with female accountants; men who would like to do business with female saleswomen, which entails having lunch or dinner with the women, hesitate to do so because of what their wives would think.

What can be done about this? The long-range solution is to have women realize that whenever they react this way, as wives, they are jeopardizing their own chances to hold jobs because they are cutting down on women's opportunities. The short-range solution is to attempt to include the anxious wives in the business lunches or dinners to reassure them that such get-togethers are indeed business affairs. If you are married and have a spouse who is willing, your spouse and you can both take them to dinner, a technique used successfully by some of the top saleswomen in the business world. The out-of-town trips are not so easily handled; very often management has to intervene. One solution has been for management to make sure that the wives and the travelers meet at some social function in the hopes that the wife will be reassured. (If you happen to be a former model and beauty queen, presently divorced, with no children, this is not apt to work. In many cases, however, it is a successful tactic.)

CHAPTER 16

The Salary Question—or, How to Get More Bread, Meat, Chick-peas, Caviar, Etc.

O.K., everyone used to "know" that women didn't "have" to work, and only worked for "pin money." This was correct if by *pin* you meant such under-pinnings of life as the mortgage payments, college tuition, medical bills, new chairs to replace those with broken springs, and other such "luxuries."

I have never understood why it was considered noble of people like Nelson Rockefeller, George Plimpton, the DuPonts, the Kennedys to work when they didn't "have" to. Nobody ever said they worked for pin money—though of course it would have been diamond-studded pins—and their work was valued and taken seriously. However, when women worked for things that raised their family's standard of living, including television sets, washing machines, vacations, this was thought of as working for pin money and therefore was not to be taken seriously.

Now it is generally accepted that women work for any and all the reasons men do, and in this sense they "have" to, just as men "have" to. And there is also general acceptance that women should be paid the same scale as men for the same job. It's not only the law of the land; it's being more and more accepted among people who *set* salaries. The catch for everyone, *but especially for women,* is finding out what price tag a job has—not an easy task.

Why is this somewhat more difficult for women? Because they have less experience in the job market; because they have less of an old-boy network to rely on; because they are sometimes going into newly created jobs; because they have less skill at negotiating a salary, particularly a raise in salary; because they are more apt to be offered the lower end of a salary range. So here-with some ideas and suggestions for becoming an old pro in the high-stake game of salary negotiation.

First, because it bears on the case, what determines a particular salary? As in many other aspects of the world of high and low finance, there are broad factors at work over which you have little or no control, and specific factors which affect your salary when you get or change jobs.

A quick look at the broad factors first. On a very broad basis salaries are determined by the state of the economy, the location of the job (state, city, town, or suburb), the industry, the company, whether the job is controlled by union scales or civil service classifications. You either have no control or very little over these factors. But there are other factors, much narrower ones, where you do have some choice if not some control. And the more you know about these, the more control you have. So let's take a look at some of the possibilities when you are negotiating for a job.

The vital thing to appreciate is that there can be a range of possible salaries for a particular job. Whether you get the figure at the bottom, the middle, or the top of the range depends on a variety of factors.

The first thing to find out is the going rate for the particular job you're interested in. How do you find out? There are many published sources; here is a representative sample:

Publications of the Bureau of Labor Statistics of the U. S. Department of Labor, including the *Occupational Outlook Handbook*, published biannually, the *Occupational Outlook Quarterly*, to keep information in the *Handbook* current, and the *Monthly Labor Review*, which publishes special surveys of the labor force several times a year. These are available at your public library or at a regional office of the Bureau. (To find the address look in your phone directory under U. S. Government, and then under Labor, or write to the Bureau of Labor Statistics, U. S. Department of Labor, Washington, D.C. 20212.)

Annual office salary surveys, published by the Administrative Management Society, Willow Grove, Pa. 19090.

The annual survey of executive salaries published by *Business Week* magazine in the first issue in May.

In just about every field there is some kind of survey of salary structures. For instance, there is an annual survey by job, industry, and region in the electronic data processing field published by Auerbach Associates Inc., 121 North Broad Street, Philadelphia, Pa. 19107. (No relation, incidentally.) Either on your own, or with a little help from your friendly librarian, you can get a pretty good picture of the going rates.

Now you want to get even more specific and so you begin to look closer to home. You start with the classified ad section, which will give you some idea of the rates for the job you are after. I say "some idea" because if the ad is placed by an employment agency it is most likely to list the top of the range to attract applicants. But that's useful to know—it's the top of the range that you're aiming for.

You should also consider all the professional sources and people you know. Interested in the health field? Ask your doctor, especially if he has some affiliation with a hospital. And while you're at it, ask his nurse or secretary, who may know more than he/she does. Accounting? The law? Real estate? Business? Wherever you know people in the particular field you are interested in, ask them what they know about the salary scales.

Here is a very specific way in which women can help each other, through their old-girl network. And it is a reciprocal thing; you will respond in kind when your friends or relatives or friends' friends ask you, and they know this, which gives them an added incentive to be helpful.

Of course, since people hate to reveal how much they earn, you won't be able to call up and say, "Listen, Jean, how much do you make?" or, "Would you mind asking Tom how much he makes?" Not at all. Nor do you necessarily have to reveal that you are looking for a job. It's just as easy to say, "A friend of mine has been offered a job at XYZ Company (or Agency or School or whatever), and she's wondering what salary she should ask for. I was wondering what your advice would be."

Getting Inside Information

This technique is a source of information when you are approaching a company from the outside. But how about within a company where you are already working, when you are thinking of asking for a different job or are being offered a promotion and the salary hasn't been specified? How can you find out what the salary range is? Here again is a way in which women can help each other. And here too is where you will really run into the problem of people wanting to be secretive—for a variety of reasons, ranging from not wanting to reveal how little they make, because they're somewhat ashamed, to not wanting to reveal how much, because they're afraid of the flak from their colleagues, particularly their male colleagues. (And a bit of the prefeminist protective attitude toward men; it would, to quote one woman executive, "threaten if not destroy" the egos of her male co-workers.)

How can you get around this? Here are some ways that women have done it. They all have one thing in common—a certain amount of organization was needed, i.e. some kind of group already existed or was formed in order to be able to implement the following suggestions. Where a group did exist, whether for consciousness raising or social purposes, this group was the basis for taking action. Where there is no such group, someone will have to organize it—but it can be done informally and can exist only long enough to serve its purpose unless the group decides it should last longer. Anyway, here is what different groups have done:

1. Invited someone who had left the department permanently to stay home with a baby, and who knew salaries, to come and tell the group what she knew.

2. Invited someone who had gone on to a similar job in a different company but at a much better salary to come and tell her salary and what she estimated was the salary scale of her new company. And, in this particular case, to tell how she got the salary. When she applied for her new job, she simply went in and told them what she thought she was worth as an executive secretary. Then, somewhat to her surprise, they gave her what she asked for.

3. Took a survey of what people in various departments earned and then passed the information around anonymously. (This was done in a tightly knit group that had already begun an organizing campaign to form an independent union just for that one company.) Obviously, where a group and group leaders already exist, this kind of plan is easier to carry out. But why couldn't several women just get together on an informal basis and plan a survey that would provide guidelines on salaries? The survey could look something like this:

Job title
(Secretary, Administrator, Supervisor, Junior Executive, etc.)

Responsibilities
(For example, all secretarial work for one boss; or expediting customer orders; or supervising filing department.)

Length of time
1) less than one year
2) two to four years
3) five years or more
4) ten years or more

Present salary range
1) less than $10,000
2) $10,000–$13,000
3) $13,000–$16,000
4) more than $16,000

As you can see, the questionnaire is worded in a rather general way, so that people's anonymity is respected, if that's the organizing group's decision and aim. In a smaller company it may be necessary to take especial care to make the questionnaire as general as possible to avoid pinpointing jobs.

The advantages of this approach are obvious. No one has to show his salary "face" personally, thereby opening up a whole can of very wormy worms. (What! Jane's only been here a year, she's a senior representative just like me, and she makes $1,000 more. . . . What! Suzy makes $19,000 a year and said she couldn't afford a $2.50 contribution to send flowers to Margie's mother. . . . What! Annette only makes $10,000! Where does she get off telling me how to run my department!) Yet everyone gets some idea of the ranges possible within a given job classification and therefore the possibilities, depending on one's bargaining power. And one of the most important aspects of bargaining is knowing what the possibilities are.

The Need for Objectivity

Now, a few well-chosen words of caution here. Look on these figures as interesting, informative, useful—but not as the only base from which to bargain. In the past one of women's troubles has been their narrow approach, comparing their salaries to what other *women* in the company get. This is *not* the right approach. What is? An *objective* one, i.e. what does the job entail? At what level is it in the structure of the company and what are the responsibilities involved? These facts should be what determines the salary attached to a job, not who has been doing it.

Taking this approach means that management can no longer get away with paying women less simply because women have traditionally held certain jobs in the company, and certain wage scales (always lower, naturally) have been attached to those jobs. Then, when raises were given they started from a lower base and the actual dollar salaries didn't match salaries paid to men for jobs with *comparable* (not identical) status and responsibility. Equal pay laws weren't applicable in many of these cases, since the jobs weren't identical, and someone claiming discrimination would have had a difficult time proving her case.

In the past women have succumbed to a subtle and dangerous kind of flattery: "Look, you're the highest-paid woman on our staff," to their detriment. No more.

My friend Celia B. went along with this attitude for many hard-working years. Then she decided that enough was not enough but too much. She went in and insisted quietly (which is her style) but firmly that on the basis of her performance, not her sex, she had earned her good salary and the right to have a formal announcement of her title and her authority. No more cajoling people to get the work out because she "looked out for them," or "was really nice," or would see that they got off early when they had personal business.

Some of the top executives in the firm (a major investing company) stuck their dinosaur heads in their *Wall Street Journals* and said, "But if we give her the title and the salary we'll have to do it in other divisions for other women. Never!" But, Celia says, there were enough men in the company to overrule the dinosaurs, because they either were unprejudiced, were afraid she would quit (she was prepared to—an absolute prerequisite for taking a stand), or were worried that the firm could be prosecuted by the Equal Employment Opportunity Commission. Her job and salary are now securely based on the objective criteria of the work and the responsibility involved. And that's the only basis all of us should agree to.

We don't want special privileges, but we do aim to be the fairly treated sex.

CHAPTER 17

How to Bargain

Let's say you have been offered a job and you have some idea of the salary range. How do you go about getting the best possible deal? Let's take a look at the various factors involved and how to handle them. (It's not going to be easy.)

First, a look at the other side of the desk, so you can understand some of an employer's motivations. What makes an employer decide to hire you and not the other applicants? He makes a judgment that attempts to integrate several factors on the state of the market from *his* viewpoint:

1. Are there lots of applicants to select from or just a few? What kind of response did he get from his ad—fifty excellent prospects or two, neither of whom was very good?

2. How urgent is his need? Is he desperate because someone has quit, work is piling up, and orders are unfilled—or can he take his time?

3. What level of skill is involved? Is it a highly skilled, very specialized kind of job that involves lots of training, so that it will be a big pain if you don't work out, or is it a job where you could be replaced fairly easily? In other words, could he fire you in a month with no great loss if it didn't work?

4. How close do you come to fitting his image of the ideal candidate, in terms of past experience, age, education, background, salary requirements?

5. How does he react to you? (And all kind of things go into this—his background, training, prejudices, preferences, maybe even how he feels that day.) Obviously, if the pool of applicants for the particular job is small, if you come fairly close to fitting the picture he's got in his mind in terms of experience, if your personalities seem to mesh well, if he needs someone quickly and doesn't want or doesn't have the time to look extensively, you are going to get the job offer. Then comes the question of salary negotiation. And this is the delicate part.

Assuming a situation where there is some leeway on the employer's part, and assuming he's not desperate, he will want to *offer* you something toward the lower end of the range, if not the lowest point itself. It's to his advantage to pay you the lowest salary possible within a range that you will find acceptable. You, of course, don't have to accept the offer—but you have to judge how good the cards are that you hold, so you know if you can or should negotiate and try for something more, and if so, how much more.

Let's assume that you are now working, and you plan to do the smart thing, which is hold on to your present job until you find another. Curious creatures that we humans are, we always want what someone else has, and this applies to employers too. So, if you are working, you are in a much stronger bargaining position. If you don't have a permanent full-time job, try to take some kind of temporary work, both to show you're employable and to keep up your morale and faith in yourself while you are job hunting.

The starting point for any salary negotiation is usually your present salary if you're employed, or your most recent salary if you're unemployed. This is the figure that employers look at when estimating how much bargaining they are going to have to do and from what base. Unfortunately, as we all know, this base is loaded against women, except perhaps for those who have recently come into the job market with skills that are very much in demand. Most women have had lower salaries than men in the past, so that, when there is a range of possibilities, women are offered the lower end of the range.

There is no foolproof way around this fact of life. The way to handle the problem, when you are negotiating and discussing your most recent or current job, is to emphasize your accomplishments and responsibilities rather than what you earned. It will be very difficult, in fact almost impossible, to say, without appearing to be making excuses for yourself, that you would have been paid more had you been a man. What you can say, however, is that you are leaving because you are frozen into a table of organization that puts a limit on your salary, which is quite true. When you come into a different company you come in at a different level—and hopefully this level is based on the new equal-pay-for-equal-work ethic rather than the old women-automatically-get-less syndrome.

One thing to remember since you want to appear in your best, i.e. most financially valuable light: whenever you state your present salary, you mention all the benefits that make your salary look as high as possible. If you are due for a raise you mention that. Remember too that you avoid making specific demands so that you don't back yourself into a corner and have to lose face if you can't win these demands.

Checking Salaries: Is It Done?

Is it safe to—shall we say—"stretch" your present salary a bit? In other words, to add on a thousand or, better yet, several thousand to the actual figure? Will your prospective employer check on you? Some application forms even have some clause like "Any false information on this form will be grounds for dismissal." In practice most firms probably won't check on you if you are now working, because they would be defeating their own purpose. If they want to hire you away from another company, you and they are dealing with each other in confidence, and they would betray that confidence by doing any checking.

Furthermore, they would have to call your immediate supervisor or the personnel department of your company in order to get really accurate verification—and many companies have a policy of not giving out such information over the phone, especially in these days of affirmative action, equal opportunity, and nonsexist hiring policies. So you are probably safe if you exaggerate within reasonable limits, though there is some risk involved. If they really want to, they can check after you've been hired, but if you've worked out well there would be little reason to do this. And if things haven't gone well, they can find some other excuse to fire you if they don't use this one.

If you're not working, it's a different question. Then it is possible to call and check, with no harm done. Which only points up again the wisdom, if you can manage it, of not quitting until you've gotten another job, no matter how unhappy you are. The fact that you are planning a change and are actually looking, even if it's a strain and it is, will help you endure your present misery.

However, and you might as well recognize this, it is possible for a prospective employer to get a true picture of your earnings by asking to see a payroll stub or a copy of your income tax form or W-2 form, or even by using an outside agency to check on what you have said. These are all unlikely possibilities. The more likely one is that he will know fairly well what salaries are paid in a given industry, and if you go too far out of line he will doubt your figure—and this will add to his reluctance to hire you.

The Market Place

Now let's consider three basic and different hiring situations and the best way of negotiating in each of them.

First situation: You're a seller in a buyer's market. Though your qualifications are good and the interview goes well, there seem to be many, many qualified applicants and you feel you don't have much bargaining power. If asked, you state realistically what you think you are worth and add that one of the reasons you are making a change is that you want an increase that will help you achieve a higher standard of living after taxes. You emphasize what you can bring to a job.

Most employers will respect your appraisal of yourself, if it's fairly accurate, even if they can't offer, at least immediately, the salary you are asking for. Very few will rule you out just because you have asked for a higher figure than they are willing to pay, if that higher figure is within what they consider a reasonable range, say a few thousand. (If they offer $12,000 and you are looking for $25,000, you're looking in the wrong ball park, obviously.) Furthermore, if you do accept the job at the lower figure, because you believe it offers future opportunities, they like the feeling they've gotten a bargain, and that you thought enough of the company to accept the offer.

What you can do, in this situation, is ask that you be given a salary review within a given period of time, say three to six months, after you have proved your worth. And that at that time you be given a raise that will bring you up to or near the original salary you were looking for. There are two other possibilities: a bonus, not particularly advantageous, since it may be a one-time-only arrangement; or increased benefits, which are more difficult to arrange and not easily transferable to a different job.

Second situation: You as a seller and the prospective employer as a buyer are about evenly matched. Your aim is, as always, to get the maximum salary; the company's aim is to get you at the lowest possible salary that you will accept. This is an improvement over number one, since you do have a more equal bargaining position. How much better it is depends on your appraisal of the situation—and that's difficult to judge. If there is such a thing as "feminine" intuition, and you think you have it, use it. Try to judge how good an impression you have made and how much the company wants you, as compared to the other candidates for the job. If you think you are very much in the running, you will naturally try to get the maximum and be less willing to compromise.

Again, if at all possible, don't mention the question of salary; let the interviewer bring it up. In this kind of job situation, where the employer doesn't think he has all the cards and he's anxious to get the best individual, he probably has some kind of leeway on salary figures, and can go up if he has to in order to get just the right person. How far up? Let's say the bottom figure for the job is $12,000 and the maximum is $15,000, set by the fact that once you go much over this figure you're running into the salary bracket of employees with a higher rank. The employer has to set the salary figure lower than this

$15,000; if he doesn't, he risks having the people in the upper ranks discover the higher salary paid to someone in a lower rank. They would immediately begin negotiations to have their base level raised, to continue the distinctions between the two levels. So, from about $1,000 to $2,500 maximum is negotiable.

How much can you get? I wish I could offer some rules that would guarantee the maximum but it's not possible. Your chances are best if you are superbly well prepared for the interview: You are looking your best. Your résumé, which you've brought with you, is succinct, aimed at showing what you accomplished for your previous employer, and an absolute model of neatness and clarity (having several copies so they can go to several executives isn't a bad idea). You've done your homework so you have some idea of what the company is doing and how you can contribute. And lady luck has saved a smile for you that day. Yes, luck does enter into it. If you're lucky you apply the day the person you'll be working for has decided he needs a vacation—but he's got to hire someone and train her before he goes away. He's then psychologically tuned to making a quick and favorable decision.

Let's assume a favorable situation when the question of salary comes up—but a figure is mentioned that is below what you anticipated. You bargain, saying that you had in mind something higher—about $2,500 higher in fact. And you bargain rather firmly, emphasizing that you feel you will contribute that much to the company—in other words, that you are really worth that much. If you are really the right person, and the situation is right, you have a good chance of getting what you ask for. Even if the employer can only offer somewhat less than the figure you ask for, at least you are getting more than you would have received if you had done no bargaining. Though there is, admittedly, an element of risk involved, if you are fairly evenly matched, buyer and seller, it's worth taking that risk in order to maximize your starting salary. It's always possible to come down if there are other aspects of the job that particularly appeal to you: the opportunities for advancement, the particular work you'll be doing, the field you are in.

Third situation: You're in the driver's seat. You are the perfect person for the job or you come close to it. If this is the situation, you don't need much advice. The only danger may be that you don't realize how well you fit into the scheme of things, and, because you are very impressed with the interviewer, the opportunity, the office you'll work in, the people you'll work with, or any combination of these factors, you settle for less than the maximum possible. How maddening it is, after you've started a job, to find out how really valuable you are and how easy it would have been to have started at a higher salary—if you had only known.

So, when you feel everything is right and you are being offered less than you think the job might pay, ask for the maximum, and hold out for it as long as you think is reasonable. At the very least, don't accept the offered salary without bargaining for more—and don't accept on the spot. Emphasize that you are offering quality—most employers recognize this when they have the right person. Your chances of getting the top of the range are good, and the risk you run is comparatively small.

Remember that when you're in this situation, especially if you're in an upper bracket job, there are fringe benefits and perquisites that often go with the job. They should be spelled out, not at the initial interview, when you are still trying to make the impression that will get you the job, but at a confirming interview. The package may include, for instance, car expenses, moving expenses, a stock option plan, an executive health plan (different from hospitalization), even a financial planning service. Be sure that you understand the details of these things before you make your final commitment.

Women are really just beginning to move into the salary bracket that includes such "perks," and it's important that they know what they are and are not getting. Some examples: Insurance plans—do they cover your spouse on a nondiscriminatory basis; i.e., is he protected in the same way as the wives of executives holding comparable positions? Moving expenses—will the company pay the cost of moving your furniture only, or will they pay for all the expenses that arise from the move: hauling your furniture, plus any hotel or motel costs you may incur during the moving, double rent that you may have to pay if you can't time your leases so that they don't overlap, plane trips back home while you're getting settled?

Money is the name of the game, and salaries at all levels are the chips. The game is somewhat like poker in that it's not only the cards you hold that make a winner but also how you play them. Let's hope you'll have a good hand and this chapter will help you play it well.

CHAPTER 18

Your Own Business—At Last! Or Alas?

What woman hasn't, at one time or another, dreamed of being her own boss? If we're out in the working world, we often feel we've had it with the mouse maze: the rigid schedule, the flak from colleagues, the lack of appreciation from the boss, the unreasonable demands of customers, the oddball questions from all the oddball strangers who always seem to get put onto our extension. If we're working at home, we've had it with the whole spectrum of domestic doldrums, from diapers and dishpan to dogs and detergents. Yet we doubt that we want to change this set of at-home demands for the comparably onerous demands of the business-world bind.

If we're older, with diminishing home responsibilities, but accustomed to being the major-domo in our household, we're aware of the many skills it takes to run a household successfully. Understandably, the idea of doing dull, routine work at a dull, routine job that pays a dull, routine salary and doesn't use any of our skills isn't very appealing. We have, after all, already served our apprenticeship as a scullery maid.

So what is the common thought that unites all of us, regardless of which world we're in? The thought of being our own boss, of being in a business where the effort we put forth is to our benefit, the customers are our customers, we don't have to talk to the oddballs, we can set the schedule to suit our convenience—ah, sweet dreams. And sweet smell of success? Maybe—but maybe not, unless we have the right approach. Because I write about business and financial management I frequently discuss the problems of small businesses with successful executives who advise would-be small businessmen and women. They report conversations something like this:

S: I've designed wall decorations for so many of my friends, I'm thinking now of going into the business. I'd like to open a little store and sell the things that go into the decorations—you know, the pictures, flowers, antique items, all the things I use. But I wouldn't only sell the things—anybody can do that. Mainly I'd sell my artistic services in putting them together. What do you think of the idea?

Adviser: It sounds like a possibility. Have you thought of starting from your own home? Then you wouldn't have to make much of an investment until you see what the possibilities are.

S: Oh, but the whole idea is to get out of the house. If I'm home and they know it, the customers will be calling me up all the time and bothering me with their stupid questions. You know what it's like to deal with the public. This way, if I'm in a store, they'll only call during store hours, and I won't have to spend much time with them. I'd rather concentrate on being artistic.

R: I really want to have a little travel agency. I've always booked our own travels—you know we've been just about everywhere around the world—and I've always enjoyed making the arrangements. It's a lot of fun and I'd like to do it for other people.

Adviser: Do you have any experience? Have you ever worked for a travel agency?

R: Oh no. I suppose I could try to get a job with one of the local agencies, but they keep such terrible hours. I only want to work from ten to four, so I can still get in my daily tennis game.

B: I've always loved books and I've always wanted to open a little bookstore. I think it would be so satisfying to work in a place where I was surrounded by books all day. I love to read and I could read so many of the books when the store wasn't busy and tell customers what was good and what wasn't.

Adviser: Have you ever worked in a bookstore? How much do know about store layout, ordering, inventory control, and all the other little nitty-gritty details?

B: Oh, but I really don't like that part of the business, so I plan to hire someone to take care of all that.

These are extreme examples, but alas they are authentic. They are typical of the unrealistic attitude of many people (men and women) who think that being in your own business is the solution to the problems of the workaday world: long or inconvenient hours, having to do dull, routine, nitty-gritty jobs, catering to people's whims (though of course when you are the customer they don't seem like whims). Unfortunately, it ain't necessarily so. It also isn't necessarily true that you will have to work very long hours, cater to customers' tiniest and most unreasonable whims, and pay strict attention to all the nitty-gritty details from how many paper clips are on hand to how well the post office is delivering the mail. But your chances of having to do all these things are higher on the probability scale than your chances of succeeding at working from ten to four, with agreeable customers only, while someone you've hired does all the unpacking of boxes, checking of shelves, paying of bills, etc.

Think of some of the individuals who sell you their services—the hairdresser who does your hair, the shoemaker who fixes your shoes, the cleaner who gets out the spots from your favorite dress, the watchmaker who fixes your watch. All of them are probably in small businesses. Or think of some of the little stores you shop in—the boutique where you go for unusual gifts, the dress store that stocks the kind of sweaters you like, the plant store that sells you a bouquet for your hostess and a little plant to fill the empty spot on your kitchen window sill. They too are usually small businesses.

Then think of your expectations about them. You expect they are going to be there in the morning before you go to work so you can drop off your repairs, and open when you are on your way home from work so you can pick up your finished work. You expect them to be there on Saturday or several late nights, so you can do your shopping or get beautiful on your time off. And because they are usually neighborhood shops, with a very personal relationship with their customers, you expect that they will go out of their way to please you—even when you (in your heart of hearts) know you may be taking slight advantage of them. So much for the hours.

And sometimes when you're in their shops you may catch a glimpse of the backroom, where, while the part-time salesclerk and you confer about which is more becoming, the peach or the blue blouse, the owner is busy unpacking big cardboard cartons, or looking harassed as she goes over the bills, or in a tone of quiet desperation pleading with a supplier to send her order which is already a week overdue. (Small shopkeepers don't have a lot of clout with big manufacturers. Very often their small orders would scarcely be missed.)

And when times aren't good, who is it who has difficulty riding out the recession? The small business owner, who doesn't have a long line of bank credit, who doesn't have a lot of capital so that she can afford to lose money week after week until business picks up again. (One of the first signs of the recession in my neighborhood of Manhattan was a sprouting of "going out of business" signs and empty stores.) Of course the small businesswoman doesn't have unemployment compensation to fall back on, since she hasn't been paid a wage.

Next logical question—why do so many people operate small businesses? Why indeed, since their eighty-hour week, moderate to low pay (often, in fact, substandard), and poor working conditions would make them eligible for any union organizer? Because they still believe in the old ideas and ideals that have characterized pioneers everywhere—but particularly pioneers in the United States. They are individualistic, willing to take risks, highly motivated, and convinced that this is still the land of opportunity and they will succeed.

So, if you would like to become a member of this very important part of our economy—a part which is more open to women now than it ever has been—you have to start not by looking at your banker but by looking in your mirror. You have to be a sort of modern Snow White saying, "Mirror, mirror on the wall—who's the most ambitious of them all?" And then you have to ask yourself some very difficult questions that call for some very honest answers.

The Difficult Questions

Are you prepared to work the eighty-, ninety-, even hundred-hour week— perhaps for several years? This will mean a drastic revision downward of your social life. Are you willing to do everything from handling the difficult customers to balancing the books to opening the packages to—you guessed it— sweeping the floors? Do you have the stamina to survive the days, weeks, even months, when there is nothing but discouragement from morning to night? The college girl you hired as a part-timer gets a better job elsewhere and doesn't let you know until the very day she was supposed to start—and you were counting on her, of course. Your major supplier has a strike on his hands and doesn't know when he'll be able to ship anything, which means all your orders are going to be late. The bank says it's not sure if it will be able to extend a loan, and even if it can, it's not likely to be able to lend you as much as you need. Furthermore, you're probably going to have to pay more taxes than you had estimated. And so on and so on, for worrisome days and sleepless nights.

Even if you're prepared to make these sacrifices, how about your family, your spouse? Will you be able to provide for their care with these other demands on your time? This is much more a problem for married women than for married men—because a married man has a wife at home to look after house and children while he gets a business going, but a married woman usually doesn't have this option.

And finally, but often the most crucial part of it all, do you have the money to invest? And it has to be money that you can *afford to lose*, since there is no guarantee of success.

Is it a frightening picture? Yes. And there's more fright to come, so grip the arms of your chair, never mind that your knuckles are showing, and take a few deep breaths to brace yourself for the next part.

Let's say you have the motivation, the stamina, either no dependents or a domestic situation that won't interfere—maybe even a mate who will be helpful—and a way of raising some capital. What are the odds against you? Unfortunately, they've always been fairly high, and the downturn in the economy in 1974 didn't help. The scoreboard for the success of new businesses, as reflected in the continuous record of new-business failures maintained by the business reporting firm of Dun & Bradstreet, is not likely to inspire confidence in the fainthearted. (Dun & Bradstreet's tabulations exclude professionals, such as doctors, lawyers, and accountants, and very small one-man/woman services, but they can still be regarded as indicative of the general trend.)

Most companies manage to survive during the first year, but the rate of failure begins to go up after that to a peak in the third year. In a pattern that's been fairly typical for the decade of the sixties and into the seventies, about 55 per cent of new businesses fail by the end of five years. Those that survive through the first five years then have a better chance; from the sixth to the tenth year the annual failure rate has been about 22 per cent; above ten years the comparable figure is 10 per cent. The recent recession hurt small businesses more than big ones; in 1974 there were about 10,000 failures —the largest number since 1971, when there were more than 10,000. Total dollar liabilities were about three billion dollars, a record high.

Why this rather dismal showing? On the basis of its reports and on information from the creditors who suffered from the failures along with the owners, Dun & Bradstreet concluded that fraud, neglect, disaster, and "reasons unknown" account for a small percentage of the unsuccessfuls. About 92 per cent of the difficulty is attributed to general mismanagement—a broad term that includes about 50 per cent incompetence and then an almost even mix of lack of experience in the kind of business opened, lack of experience as a manager, lack of "balanced experience," i.e. experience not well rounded in sales, finance, purchasing, and production on the part of the individual in case of a proprietorship, or of two or more partners or officers constituting a management unit.

Add to these some hazards of recent years—a downturn in the world as well as the U.S. economy, a shortage of capital, more government regulation, new occupational safety rules, new product-safety regulations, higher minimum wages—and it's no wonder the number of failures and bankruptcies is higher.

As women we have always prided ourselves on being realists, so of course we have to know these facts. And yet, and yet—as realists we must also accept (and with pleasure) the fact that, though there are failures, there are also successes. And who is to say that you—if you have the idea for going into business—aren't going to be one of the successes? Especially if, forearmed because you've been forewarned, you prepare yourself adequately, understand the risks involved, accept the drawbacks of the game, and go about the venture in the right way.

What is the right way? Good question—and though there isn't any single answer, there are some basics that go into establishing a successful business.

Small Business Prerequisites

1. *You need experience in the kind of business you have in mind.* And you need not just narrow experience—for instance, selling table linens—but also broad experience in all the aspects of a table-linen business, such as buying the merchandise, handling the financial sides of the business, keeping the books, paying the bills, getting credit, maintaining your cash flow (always having enough money on hand to meet the payroll and the company's bills), dealing with customers, suppliers, and personnel.

2. *You need capital.* And you need to be able to estimate realistically what you will need in sales volume to give you a profit sufficient to cover your expenses and provide a reasonable living. You also have to estimate how much capital you will be able (and willing) to invest in the business to see you through the difficult time of getting the business started. If you are willing to draw very little from the business, you will need less capital. If you can start in your own home, or in very unglamorous quarters—which may be a cultural shock if you've been working in a supermodern office building—your chances of success are greater.

3. *You need the right location.* "Right" has many different interpretations, depending on the kind of business you are planning. For a retail store you need high traffic—lots of people coming and going all day and able to stop into your shop, on impulse as well as actual need. A shop on a busy highway would have lots of people coming and going—but if there were no parking facilities, it would be a total loss, of course. In general experts will say "don't pay too much rent," but in the case of a retail store the amount of the rent may be almost in direct proportion to the traffic. For a manufacturing business you might need a location in a place with good transportation for your employees, and a pool of reliable employees to draw on. For some kind of service business you might need a different kind of employee: well-educated, or with office skills, or the right educational background. And so on.

4. *You need to understand the pitfalls of handling credit.* We do live in a credit economy; most of us are accustomed to charging things, and we accept

the concept that our customers also want to charge things. If extending credit is part of the price of pleasing a customer, a new business will have to comply. But the credit must be handled carefully. And carefully means that you have the capital to extend the credit without running short yourself so that you then have to rely on credit from your suppliers—which may or may not be available. You also have to estimate the cost of credit to you—how much you might have to pay in interest to be able to extend the credit, and can you afford it? Furthermore, how good are you at bill collecting? Some people find this a very onerous task—and if you think it would go against the grain and you'd hesitate to do it, you may have to try to avoid being a bill collector.

5. *You need the right lawyer.* If the business you're planning is in any way involved with leases, contracts, licenses, compliance with local, state, and/or federal regulations—in other words, if you will have to make commitments that involve knowledge of the law—you are going to need a lawyer. And a special lawyer at that. That charming lawyer in the next apartment who makes a superb martini is perfect as a dinner guest, but he won't do as your legal adviser. Neither will that dynamic feminist lawyer who spoke at the business women's lunch you went to, if she specializes in representing women who have suffered job discrimination.

Experienced lawyers say you should look for someone who specializes in corporate or business law, and it's a real boon if you find someone who is familiar with your business. He or she should have been practicing this kind of law for at least five or preferably ten years or more, so he's had time to acquire the particular background needed. If possible it should be someone from a fairly small law firm—three to five partners, so he has some diverse experience to draw on yet the firm is small enough to offer individual attention. Second choice would be a bright and ambitious junior partner in a large law firm.

Where should you look for a lawyer? Friends, relatives, and business associates are possible sources of recommendations, as long as you evaluate the recommendations carefully. It's nice to do a favor for someone's cousin Joe, but only if Joe is the right person; the success or failure of your business may depend in part on the knowledge and advice of your lawyer. Other and probably more objective sources include lawyers on the staff of corporations, your accountant or an accountant you know, your banker, if the lawyer is someone known to him personally and not just someone who brings business to the bank, professors at university law schools, or librarians of law libraries, who are usually lawyers themselves and know something about the work habits and carefulness of the lawyers who use their libraries.

Before hiring someone, you are quite right to inquire about his schooling, legal background and experience, other clients and—very important—his fee and what that fee includes. You expect him to charge for the time spent working on your problem, but you also want to know if you will be charged for phone calls, document duplication, letters, and so on. You will also want someone whose personality meshes well with yours—you'll have enough hassles without having a lawyer who irritates you. If you find the right person, he may earn his fee simply in the time he saves and the mistakes he prevents.

How can you overcome these potential problems? (There are more, but these are a good sample.) Here are some suggestions from successful businessmen who have started their own businesses.

1. *Know your limitations.* Or, as Dun & Bradstreet put it, "Recognition of limitations is important to success." Every business has limitations of some kind: Even the biggest manufacturers find themselves limited to certain areas or to certain products. It isn't modest experience or modest capital that is the pitfall so much as trying to do more than the experience or capital will carry.

2. *Plan.* Once you know your limitations, plan ahead—don't just drift. It is a good idea to write out, in advance, your policy on various questions. This serves many functions. For one thing, it forces you to focus on some aspects of the business that you either didn't have the time for or—perhaps subconsciously—put off thinking about, perhaps because you didn't know what your policy should be. For another, it takes the element of surprise out of some problems that may come up; and because you are prepared for them, you either know how to cope or you recognize that you can't make a snap decision but will have to give the question some thought.

3. *Keep good records.* Your customers may exclaim with pleasure when they come into your beautifully arranged shop. Your business may have money in the bank at the moment. But, unless you keep accurate records of where you stand, you may find that the bills due for the material so beautifully displayed in the shop far exceed the amount of money in the bank. Furthermore, your records will prove a valuable tool, in retrospect, when you are planning the future of your business. This record keeping is, unfortunately, one of the chores that you will probably have to tend to after hours, since your business day must be spent taking care of the business. But it's so vital that, according to Dun & Bradstreet, most businessmen who've succeeded say, if they had to do it over, they would learn something about bookkeeping and accounting—since the figures tell what is going on in the business. This is an area in which women have had comparatively little experience—so it brings up the next important point.

4. *Educate yourself.* Even before you start the business, and while it is going on, take the time to learn all you can. There are many courses given at local schools and colleges, at hours convenient for business people, that are

useful to beginning businesswomen—courses in bookkeeping, accounting, finance, public relations, advertising—and some of them are particularly geared to the new and small business. Some are government sponsored, particularly by the Small Business Administration. They are often at very low cost or at no charge at all. They are worth looking into: Not only will you learn the subject matter, but you will also meet people with similar problems. Sometimes the exchange of ideas alone is helpful; at other times it is possible to work out arrangements for buying some services cooperatively. A group of small businesses might get together, for instance, and hire an accountant who would service their accounts on a fee basis.

You should also go to the trade shows in your own field. Again, not only do you pick up ideas but you also meet people who can be helpful to you, particularly suppliers. Which brings up the next point.

5. *Choose your suppliers with care and deal with them fairly.* Most new businesses find that suppliers serve not only as suppliers but also as mentors, friends, sources of miscellaneous information of all types. Many businessmen who have succeeded feel they owe at least part of their success to suppliers who were extremely helpful in the beginning stages. Naturally, they have a stake in your success, since if you succeed they have a good customer. But motives aren't important; what is important is developing a good relationship with a supplier, who can be very helpful, from offering advice to extending credit and helping you build your business. A word of caution. Though you should at least listen to the advice they have to offer, you can't accept it blindly and must evaluate it in terms of your problems. What was good for customer X may not be good for you, customer Y. But it doesn't cost much to listen with an open mind—no one says you *have* to take advice.

6. *Develop a good relationship with a bank.* You already have a good relationship with a bank if you are a regular depositor in a commercial bank (the bank where you have your checking account); and when you are planning to go into business, this bank, or one in the neighborhood where you plan your business, can be of great help to you. Very often they can tell you something about the neighborhood in which you're planning to open—is it growing, remaining stable, or going downhill? They can tell you something about the creditworthiness of suppliers or customers. They can help you transfer funds quickly through interbank transfers, give you letters of credit for suppliers that need immediate payment, give you lockbox services for keeping cash, and so on. Most important of all, they can give you credit if you can prove financial stability.

How do you do that? Donna E. Young, an account officer with Chemical Bank, New York, offers the following advice. Be prepared before you go anywhere near a banker. You want to "impress hell out of her (or him)." And you do that by doing your homework. Before your first meeting, you prepare a detailed sheet telling very specifically the purpose of your business, the goals you have set for yourself, how you plan to achieve them in the short and the long run. Give facts, figures: you have so much capital available; this is the size of your market; your raw materials will cost so much; you will have to pay so much for services; your competition is such and such; you expect to be able to sell your product and service for this much; your break-even point will be thus and so, and you will be able to show a profit by . . . ; etc.

Dealing with the Bank

One of the advantages of preparing such a detailed statement for a banker is the fact that you have to sit down and analyze these figures for yourself and be sure there are no flaws. If you need to, get an accountant to advise you on the figures and perhaps on the presentation. Remember that banks are not in business to provide venture capital; their business is to lend money in order to make a profit and be able to maintain their own business. They have a responsibility to their stockholders, and risky loans violate this responsibility. They are also subject to government regulations which require that they show fiscal responsibility; poor loans don't come under this heading. All of this results in the long-standing joke in the financial community that you can't get a loan unless you can prove you don't need it. And the way you can prove you don't "need" a loan is to sustantiate, with facts and figures, that you have a viable business, show that you need a line of credit, and demonstrate how you will be able to pay back.

In the past women have often had to be more equal than men to get a loan, and have had different, more stringent, criteria used in judging their applications. It is illegal now to discriminate on the basis of sex, and the climate has changed as well. This doesn't guarantee that discrimination has ended—judging the validity of a loan application is still left to the discretion of loan officers, and their opinions may or may not be prejudiced. However, if you suspect discrimination because of sex, you can and should complain and go to a higher officer in the bank, with the law on your side. As the American Bankers Association says, you have every right to ask the officer to "Say yes . . . or say why."

Help from the SBA

What if you can't get a bank loan because you don't yet have a business history that will qualify you? Then your next source should be the Small

Business Administration—and there you will find some of the help you need, plus again, a legal guarantee against sex discrimination.

What is the SBA and how can it help you? The SBA was specifically set up to foster new companies or help struggling young companies get better established. It is the place to turn when a commercial bank will not give you a loan, though you must try the commercial banks first, since the SBA is not set up to compete with commercial banks but rather to enable a bank to take risks it would not ordinarily take, because the SBA guarantees the loan.

The interest rate the bank charges is still linked to the prime rate at the time (i.e. the rate that banks charge their most creditworthy customers), and the bank won't lend the money, despite the SBA guarantee, if the loan officer thinks the money won't be repaid. In other words, the SBA won't lend you money just because you have a great but unproven idea. The SBA too has criteria: "A loan must be of such sound value or so secured as reasonably to assure repayment." Another criterion, though not an absolute one, is whether you are able to invest some of your own funds; you have a better chance of getting a loan if you can.

For complete information (beyond the scope of this chapter) on how to get an SBA loan, consult your local office, which you will find listed in the telephone directory under United States Government. Even if you don't plan to apply for a loan, these offices have many different kinds of assistance to offer, and it's worth getting in touch with them just to see what help is available. It can range from pamphlets, to counseling, to workshop sessions, to classes, to using the services of SCORE (Service Corps of Retired Executives).

More Help Wanted? Try These Places

There are several government agencies that offer a variety of services and information, depending on your needs. The Department of Commerce has about forty field offices that work with the SBA in giving help to small businesses. The Census Bureau is part of Commerce, and for very little money it can provide all kinds of information on such questions as how many businesses of a certain type are in your neighborhood (how many boutiques?) and what the population of an area is (or even how many young children, if you're thinking of opening an after-school center for children of working mothers). Write to the Director, Bureau of the Census, Washington, D.C. 20233.

The Office of Information of the U. S. Department of Agriculture will supply you with a list of their services and publications. Some kinds of handcrafts are under their aegis, if you are considering marketing some of your handiwork. City folks who've gone back to nature and started farms have found the department's county agents very helpful with excellent advice based on the local conditions that the agents know very well.

The local offices of the United States Employment Service can help you with employment questions, such as what is the going rate on certain kinds of jobs, as well as helping you find specific workers. (However, some employers have found the service's estimates of employees' capabilities not too reliable—so you will have to do your own evaluation as well.)

Other sources are state and local agencies similar to the federal agencies I've mentioned. Your phone book is a source of information on where these are. And some major cities also have agencies that perform some of the same functions.

One person you should certainly cultivate, in your hunt for information, is your local librarian, particularly if you can get to a fairly large library system that has a branch or some librarians who specialize in business information. They can tell you what material is available, help you get it, and save you time and digging around—and time is one of your most precious assets.

Finally, some special words of advice from the long experience of Victor M. Rivera, an economist who is district director of the New York region of the SBA. Here are some do's and don'ts he stresses:

Do take advantage of counseling and courses offered, whether they're free at the local SBA office or available for a nominal charge at some local university. Women don't seem to use these as much as men do.

Don't be put off by the fact that there aren't many women counselors. Remember that women didn't have the opportunity, therefore weren't in business, so there just aren't many women who have retired and are available for counseling.

Do keep in mind the background of the men counselors when you speak to them. They are older, they grew up in different times, they may still have their biases, conscious or unconscious. They may, for instance, think that women really shouldn't be in business for themselves at all or are not really capable of running a business or can succeed only in "feminine" businesses such as boutiques, dress shops, children's clothes, or gift shops.

They may also be much more accustomed to conservative women and quite turned off by what they consider "unfeminine" or even aggressive: casual dress, informal manners, and so-called "liberated" language, which they would find offensive even if used by men outside of the locker room. Is it giving in to "sexism" if you put on a dress instead of jeans when going to the SBA and forswear your favorite four-letter words? Maybe, maybe not, says Mr. Rivera—but that's not the issue. You are "in business" the minute you start thinking about starting a business, and you have to deal with the real world as it is, not as you'd like it to be. Think of the SBA as a customer and the customer is always right.

Remember that the reverse of this may be true—and will work to your advantage. The SBA counselor may actually go very much out of his way to help you because he is chivalrous, or fatherly, or feels a special admiration for women who venture into the man's world. (Need I say that any or all of these feelings may be more pronounced if you're younger than he is and good-looking?)

Don't be put off by initial rejections. And don't have blind faith, in any person, association, source of information. Even the SBA counselors could be wrong, so don't be afraid to challenge them if you believe you're on strong ground. But of course, don't overdo it—you may be just as smart, but you should also be more tactful. (Which may prove how smart you are.) And if one person, supplier, or bank puts you off or turns you down, go to another and then another until either you are accepted or you decide you may need a different or fresh approach.

Do check all the information you get—another aspect of forgetting blind faith. If you can't check the actual information, check on or evaluate the *source* and try to arrive at a judgment that way.

Don't always think you have to go it alone. What if you have certain abilities and capabilities and sorely lack others? Maybe you're a superb buyer, able to spot trends—but very bad at dealing with people? Or you're terrific at promotion but terrible at bookkeeping. Think of a joint venture—look for someone to complement your talents; if you find the right person, the whole may be greater, and more successful, than the parts.

Do acquire as much experience as you can in the business you're interested in—even if you have to work for nothing. (That's what Mr. Rivera says—for nothing.) Expensive? In terms of time and perhaps lost earnings—yes. But it is still cheaper than investing in a business and losing your investment. You don't want to get on-the-job training on your own money; and in a new business with limited resources you can't afford to make mistakes.

And the final *don't*. Don't have an I'm-a-woman-so-what-will-you-do-for-me attitude. No one will take you by the hand and show you. Like everyone else, you will have to learn the hard way.

It's easier to start a business when times are booming and customers have lots of money left after they've provided for the necessities of life. That hasn't been the situation in much of the seventies—but despite that (and in some cases, because of that, when people couldn't find jobs and therefore had to create them) some women have succeeded. With lots of careful preparation and a little help from that feminist Lady Luck, you can too.

CHAPTER 19

You Too Can Survive Tax Preparation—or, How to Conquer the 1040

How do you rate yourself on the liberated-woman scale? Completely liberated? Very—but not quite all the way? A little bit liberated? Still deciding? Whether you're at the top, the bottom, or somewhere in the middle doesn't matter when the question is paying your income tax and filling out the 1040 form. It's a necessary skill that you too can and should acquire. Why? First, because even if you don't have to do it at this point in your life, you never can tell when you will. Second, because knowing nothing about it can cost you time, money, anguish. And this is true whether you do your own return, sign a joint return, or get some kind of outside help. Consider some of the following facts, possibilities and hazards.

1. If you want to save tax money (and who doesn't?) you will do much better if you know what kind of records to keep so that you know what is and what isn't deductible. This knowledge comes easier if you know the tax form.

2. You are ultimately liable for the statements in your tax return, no matter what kind of professional help you get in filling it out.

3. If you live in a community-property state, you may find yourself liable for some of your husband's taxes, even after he has become your ex-husband, because of the way the tax court views the ownership of property in such states.

4. You may think you will never have to fill out a tax form and that it's easier to follow the old adage and "Let George do it." Unfortunately, as I have learned from students in my Women and Money classes, and from several marriage and divorce conferences, George is not predictable. Sometimes he wants a divorce; sometimes you want a divorce from George; sometimes George saddles you with a bad divorce agreement because you always signed your joint return without looking at it. A few Georges have even been known to put their hands over the significant parts (like salary and income from

other sources) and not allow you to look at it. Other Georges happily let you look, knowing very well that since your peek was only in passing, you either didn't pay attention or knew so little about the form that even a longish look wouldn't have made any difference.

Are you reluctant? Do you hate the thought? Of course you do—everybody (well, almost everybody) does. It's a pain, a bore, a chore, and besides it reminds you how much of your money you have to part with. But it has to be done. Nobody says you have to do it the most agonizing way, however, and there are ways to ease the pain. Here are several "for instances."

For instance: If you've never done it before, don't do it under maximum pressure, which is in the last week or even the last night before filing time. Be nice to yourself and get acquainted with the problem when you can be a bit more relaxed. Go to your local Internal Revenue Service office (listed in the phone directory under United States Government) or the post office and get a copy of the government Publication 17, *Your Federal Income Tax*, which includes copies of the 1040 form. Then you can look at it and even work out a sample tax return.

You may not believe it, but the book is quite clear, especially considering the subject matter, and it is not impossible for a person of average intelligence (and of course we're better than that) with a fairly simple tax return, to understand how to fill out either the short or the long form and to complete her own tax return, especially *if she is not under deadline pressure.*

(There are even little vignettes of drama, human interest, and exciting possibilities suggested in the book, which brighten the task. Consider, for instance, Chapter 7 of the 1975 edition, which gives examples of what income is taxable. There is the story of the sly car salesman who referred his customers to an insurance broker—and then made the broker kick back part of his commission. Was the kickback income—and taxable? Yes, says the IRS.)

For instance: You think you could do it yourself with just a little bit of help. That help is available from local IRS offices—and it's free. How can you take advantage of it? Several ways. You need go no farther than your telephone, since the IRS has toll-free lines you can call and get answers to your questions. The numbers are listed in the instruction booklet you get along with your tax packet, or in your local telephone directory under United States Government—Internal Revenue Service. The IRS people who answer your questions are known as Tax Service Representatives (TSRs).

If you prefer, you can go in person (again you'll find the address in your phone book); chances are there will be an office reasonably near you with hours geared to the business hours of the area. As the deadline approaches, some of these offices will be open evenings and Saturdays, so it pays to check on the hours, not only to find out just when the office is open but also when the peak load times are, so you can avoid them. (Students and senior citizens sometimes go early in January—so if there are many of them living in your area, late January may be a better time.)

Some things you should know about this service. Unless you are really disabled, the aim of the IRS is to help you by answering specific questions, but not to fill out your form for you. However, IRS offices will review your *finished form, before you file it,* for completeness, allowable deductions, and correct computations. They may say yes, you are allowed to deduct that amount for medical expenses, and yes, you are allowed to include your new glasses in the medical deduction. They will not, however, go over your arithmetic for you. And they will not be responsible for the accuracy of any of the statements you make on your return. Instead they stamp "Reviewed but not audited" on the return, which shows you have tried to be as accurate as possible but doesn't mean that you can't be audited at some later time.

The number of income tax specialists who work in the IRS offices year-round isn't enough, very often, to take care of Ms. and Mr. Taxpayer and all their cousins and their aunts as the April 15 deadline comes closer and closer. And so other IRS employees, former employees, and sometimes even outsiders, including moonlighters from other jobs, housewives, and students are hired to help. The former IRS employees and the people borrowed from other departments are briefed on recent changes in the law; the "outsiders" are given about a week's training before they are sent out to help the troubled taxpayers. The IRS admits that a week or so of training is not enough—but says that these TSRs are used only to answer the most routine questions, asked again and again. They refer to more experienced people the questions they themselves can't answer.

If you go early in the year you will, obviously, get more personal attention, since the TSR who is helping you won't be pressured by the view of the many people waiting their turn for help. More than that, your chances are far better for getting the more experienced, more knowledgeable TSRs, which will save you time and reduce the possibilities of error. If this is the first time you are filling out a return, this can be particularly important.

But there are also things you can do to get the most out of your interview. Do your homework by taking a look at the form before you go so you know what kinds of records you are going to need to substantiate any claims you may want to make. For instance, if you are going to claim medical deductions, you might bring with you copies of canceled checks. If you are going to claim mileage expenses for your volunteer work, you could bring copies of bills for gasoline. Note that I say *copies*, not originals. The small sum you spend at your local copying center, if you can't get free time on a copying machine somewhere, will be more than paid for by the peace of mind you'll get knowing your originals are safe at home and not being accidentally left in an IRS office.

Paying for Tax Help

With this kind of free service available, why do people pay to get help? There are advantages. One is *flexibility:* You pick the time you want to go—after work, on a weekend—or perhaps even arrange for someone to come to your office or home. If you are very pressed for time, this may be worth the fee. Another is *individual attention:* This can be very helpful, particularly if you want someone to explain why and how something is done the way it is, so that you will learn for the time when you may want to do your return yourself. You are also paying for the expertise of the tax preparer. It is her/his job to ask you the questions about your expenses that will enable you to get all the deductions and exemptions you're legally entitled to.

Another advantage. The tax preparer works for you, not for the IRS. When there are several ways of interpreting a tax law—and this often happens—it's only natural that an IRS agent will know and recommend the interpretation favored by the IRS. Your preparer, on the other hand, should recommend the interpretation that favors you, or at the very least tell you what your choices are. If there is a disagreement, and you are audited, the tax preparer can argue in your favor; if you have chosen a tax service that allows someone to represent you, she or he can actually appear for you and state your case.

Which very naturally brings up the question of the kind of service you want. There are three categories:

1. *Lawyers, certified public accountants* (CPAs), *and "enrolled agents."* Enrolled agents are former IRS agents with five or more years of experience or individuals who have passed a difficult qualifying exam in tax laws, regulations, and procedures given by the U. S. Treasury Department. Note that not all lawyers and CPAs know *tax* laws; you of course want one who is knowledgeable in this specialized field. None of these can advertise, but all can represent you before the IRS in case of an audit.

2. *Tax preparation companies, both large and small.* Some specialize in preparing tax forms. Others are in business primarily to lend money, or to do tax planning for corporations or individuals, or to offer bookkeeping services; preparing taxes is just one part of their business.

3. *People who prepare taxes as a sideline* to their regular work, from keeping house to selling real estate to holding regular full-time jobs in industry that are sometimes not at all related to tax work. My friend Ruth T., for instance, has a full-time job arranging meetings for a national professional or-

ganization, and as a sideline specializes in doing tax returns for individual clients, many of them women. Neither the tax preparing companies nor the individuals who do it as a sideline can represent you, the taxpayer, before the IRS. Unlike the lawyers, CPAs, and enrolled agents, both tax preparing companies and individuals can advertise their services.

What does it take to qualify as a tax preparer? Surprisingly, nothing formal. You may or may not need a business license, depending on your local community, but you don't need a diploma or proof of any kind that you are loyal, trustworthy, honest, or *capable*. There are no standards of competence for an individual nor training requirements for people hired by companies who prepare returns. You too, if you decided that you had a natural knack for this kind of work, could set yourself up with nothing more than a discreet sign in your window or a business card passed around your office. It's true that you wouldn't undertake to do this kind of work unless you were capable —but how about all those other people? Where do you find them, and how? How do you know if they're any good?

Before you start looking, you have to know what you're looking for, i.e. how expert should your expert be? If you have a comparatively simple form and income up to $20,000 derived from your earnings, stock dividends, interest on bonds, alimony, a pension, or an annuity, the IRS believes that you can do it by yourself. If you are willing to take the standard deductions as allowed and use the 1040 short form, you can probably get all the help you need from the IRS (particularly if you get there early).

But if you earn more than this amount, or have income from other sources, or have a new situation—for example, you've recently been divorced, or changed jobs, or started a business at home, or changed your child support payments, or have moved into a new state—you may want outside help. Or perhaps you're not sure how to document your claims or you doubt your ability to understand the instructions for the tax form or even the form itself, or you're really worried about your arithmetic. Then you should have no compunction about seeking help. The question is, what level of expertise and how much will you have to pay?

Tax Service Fees

The fee is determined by two factors: the complexity of your return and the level of expertise of the person you go to for help. The most expensive help usually comes from lawyers and CPAs with large tax practices—when they are willing to take you as a client. Frequently they are not, unless you have a very large income or are a client of the firm for other business, since tax work is seasonal and they have year-round work that is more profitable.

It is much more likely that you will find the advice you need from a company that specializes in preparing tax returns, such as the H. & R. Block Company, the Tax Corporation of America, or the income tax service division of the Beneficial Finance Company. Another possibility is your bank, which may have an office set up at tax time to help you (for a fee, of course). And finally, you may decide on the individual tax preparer who does the work as a sideline.

What are the advantages and disadvantages of each? You are interested in two aspects of the problem: (1) getting the maximum legitimate deductions, and (2) having as accurate a return as possible, so that you will not be audited, or if you are, you will have a strong case and will not have to pay any additional tax. Although it doesn't always follow, it's much more likely that the more experience someone has with the tax laws, the more apt she will be to find legitimate deductions and therefore the more money she will save for you. Also, since sometimes the fee is based on time spent, the faster someone does your return—accurately of course—the more economical it will be.

But there's more to be considered than just finding the maximum deductions, filling out the form accurately, and turning it in with a sigh of relief and a tear or two. There is always the possibility that your return will be picked out by the IRS's computer and you will be called in for an audit. The difference among the various tax preparers becomes important. As I noted before, the lawyers, CPAs, and enrolled agents are allowed by law to represent you with the IRS and in the tax court. You don't even have to be present, though you are still responsible.

There are some obvious advantages to not having to be present at an audit. There is the time saved, of course, and the saving of wear and tear on your nervous system. These are important—but more important is the relationship between the IRS and a professional tax preparer, whether she is a lawyer, a CPA, or an enrolled agent. Experienced CPAs say that an IRS man is apt to be just a little more cautious in querying figures on a return with a "professional" than with the average taxpayer. More than that, however, is that taxpayers—and this could be you—don't know when to keep their mouths shut, and often volunteer information that could legitimately be kept quiet. Or, to put it another way, as one CPA said, "Truthfully most taxpayers talk too much."

Most of us, however, will be checkbook-to-checkbook with the large majority of taxpayers who can't afford and don't need expensive professionals to represent them. For us, the commercial preparer may be the answer, and the logical question is, What are the characteristics of a good tax preparation service or a good tax preparer? While keeping in mind that even going to a big, well-established company is no guarantee that *your* return will be ex-

pertly handled, here are some of the facts you should know when evaluating
a tax preparing service:

1. How long has the service been in business?
2. What kind of background and training have their employees had?
3. What kind of guarantees or references do they offer about their relia-
bility and accuracy? Can they, for example, cite clients who have come back
for several years because they were satisfied with the service? Can they name
some small or not-so-small businesses whose returns they have prepared for
several years?
4. What amends will they make if, because of their mistakes or lack of expertise, you have to redo your return, or are called in by the IRS to explain
some of the deductions you took? Although they cannot legally represent you
with the IRS, they should be willing and *available* to go with you to the audit
hearing to explain how they arrived at the tax payments they said were due.
5. If it turns out that through their mistakes or ignorance you will have to
pay interest, they should be willing to reimburse you if they were responsible
for the disallowed deduction.

Suppose you decide you don't want to go to a company but prefer to go to
an individual? Similar questions apply:

1. How long has the person been doing it?
2. What kind of training does she have that qualifies her to prepare returns?
3. Will she give you the name of satisfied repeat clients (who are not relatives).
4. What does she do the remainder of the year? Will she be available to
help you if the IRS questions your return? Or will she have taken off to a
warm climate for the winter, leaving you to face the chill of the audit all
alone?

Don't be shy—if you have any doubts, at least do some telephoning and
checking with other clients before you let someone prepare your return.

How about the fee? Whether you go to a tax-preparing firm or to an individual, this is something that should be settled in advance so that you will
not be very unpleasantly surprised afterward. Find out on what basis the
charges are computed—is it the time, the complexity of your return, or a combination of the two? If you have to file a city and state return also and you
want these done as well, get an estimate for the entire job, so that you can
judge if you want to buy the package. Surveys have shown that rates vary
depending on the preparer and the section of the country, so it pays to shop
around a bit. However, this is one instance when you are looking for quality
more than price, and it's more important to get someone reliable and recommended than someone who is less expensive.

What if this has been a year when the gods frowned on you? Your stockings got runs the minute you put them on; your hamburgers were invariably served underdone on a burnt roll; and your boss came in early the few times you were late. Then your return will be audited, right? If that happens, you will probably be notified within about five months, say by September, though the seven-year statute of limitations applies and you could be called in for any return up to this seven-year limit. What should you do?

First, go get a drink, have your hair done, practice your transcendental meditation, or do whatever you do when you feel the need to relax. Because you can relax, serene in the knowledge that the IRS is not going to collect your credit cards and haul you off to your local courthouse. An audit is not a preordained judgment that you have not paid your due share of taxes—it is an examination of your return for the tax year in question to see if you have accurately reported your financial status and paid the taxes due. As I noted before, tax laws are not absolute and there can be disagreements not only between you and the IRS but also between IRS agents and offices as to what is and what is not allowable.

Since this isn't a preordained judgment, you should be prepared, literally and psychologically, to defend your return and the deductions you made. Actually the agent will contact you in advance by mail or sometimes by phone and tell you what records to bring. You can add to his suggestions whatever you think is pertinent: canceled checks, bills marked paid, your withholding tax forms, even bills of sale from real estate transactions. This is a time when your tax preparer should be available to help and advise you, to explain how she/he decided on certain deductions. And, of course, if you've acquired a little know-how by this time, you are in a much better position.

If you can document your claims, it is entirely possible (and I know because it has happened to friends of mine) that there will be no further question and your return will be accepted. It has even happened, though rarely, that taxpayers have gotten a refund because the audit showed they had inadvertently overpaid. Remember that it is your obligation—and in your best interests—to cooperate with the agent; but remember also the CPA's comment, "Most taxpayers talk too much." *It's not your duty to volunteer disadvantageous information.*

Keep in mind always these words from the IRS:

The selection of your income tax return for examination does not necessarily mean that you owe more tax. Your return may be selected for examination if you have not furnished enough information about some item of income or deduction, if you have reported some income that is not taxable or have deducted some unallowable expense item. In such cases the Service will want to insure that the other information on the return is correct. Or you may have filed a claim for a refund, and your refund may be examined to make sure that the proper amount of tax is refunded to you.

Keep in mind also that the IRS doesn't want to clog the tax courts; in fact, they want to reach agreement on the lower levels of the service so the routine cases never get to the tax court. They recognize that there are different interpretations of the law and they are willing to listen to your arguments and to compromise if you can offer good evidence to back your claims. And, at each level of appeal—an audit by an examining officer, a conference with a District Conference Staff member, or a hearing at the IRS Appellate Division—you get a fresh look at your problem. Your appeal is judged not on what has been argued before but on how the IRS official considering your case evaluates its merits.

One final and important warning. No matter who helps you with your return, or actually prepares it, you are ultimately responsible. (Even if you are the President of the United States, as we all have learned from recent history.)

A Final Check List of Things You Might Overlook

Tax laws change all the time as taxpayers, business and private, question certain IRS rulings and the courts make decisions, or as Congress itself votes modifications and amendments. So it's not possible to make a definitive list of the tax laws, rulings, and deductions that might be of specific interest to women. Here is a check list of some things to keep in mind, however, when you are planning your budget for the year with an eye to possible tax savings, or when you are actually completing your return.

1. *Divorce settlements:* If you are planning a divorce, be sure that your attorney considers the tax implications of your agreement, not only from the standpoint of alimony versus child support but also for the benefit of the tax deduction available to working parents. Check into the possibility of taking one of your children as a dependent, increasing the tax savings available to you as a head of household and as an employer of household help. If your divorce settlement was some time ago and you have been hurt by inflation, you might be able to get an increase in alimony, since it is tax deductible for your ex-husband.

2. *Educational expenses:* If you have been taking courses required to help

you keep your job or get a promotion, and if the tuition expense is allowed, you may also be able to deduct the cost of child care while you are taking the course.

3. *Employment fees:* If you paid a fee to an employment agency to help you get a job, whether or not they succeeded, that fee may be deductible.

4. *Volunteer work:* You can't deduct for your time or your baby sitter, unfortunately (at least not as this goes to press), but you can deduct for transportation, whether you took the subway or a taxi or drove your own car.

5. *Medical expenses:* Deductible items have been updated in line with our changing attitudes. You can now take a medical deduction for birth control pills and legal abortions as well as for professional remedial sexual therapy. And don't overlook contact lenses as a medical expense.

6. *Work at home:* If you regularly bring work home from your job and have set aside part of your home as a home office, check on all the possible deductions this may entitle you to, including a portion of your rent or mortgage payments, heat, upkeep, electricity, and depreciation of your desk and other equipment, such as a typewriter and a calculator.

7. *Free-lance work* (or a moonlighting job): If you have expenses in connection with either or both of these, by all means get and keep receipts of these expenses so you can deduct them.

8. *Record-keeping:* Make the job of assembling your records easier by marking either your canceled checks or your checkbook with some kind of symbol that shows what is a sure or a possible tax-deductible expense. You could use a large M, for example, to mark medical expenses, a C for charity, and so on. If you don't want to get even that elaborate, a simple asterisk(*) will make it easier to pinpoint quickly what you need when you have to get yourself and your records together.

CHAPTER 20

She Who Pays the Piper Deserves to Call the Tune

It's great to live in an economic system based on credit, isn't it? We don't have to walk around with cash in our pocketbooks, worried about getting robbed. We can take advantage of bargains even if we don't have the money then and there, just by saying "Charge it." We can leave money in our savings accounts, collecting interest until we have to pay our bills. There's a free-to-us and too-bad-for-them time lag between the day we charge that marvelous serving tray marked down by five dollars and the day the Master Charge or BankAmericard bill arrives. If we can manage to pay the entire bill when it's due, usually not for several more weeks, we get even more free credit. No doubt about it—in general, credit is a good thing.

Notice that "in general." "In general," in the past, has had a decidedly masculine meaning. Married women's credit has been in their husbands' names, and this has meant some unpleasant surprises, to say the least, when women became either divorcées or widows. They found that the credit rating they had built up in their years as Mrs. John Dough no longer existed, and they could no longer use their charge cards. In fact, until very recently it was very difficult for a woman to re-establish credit in her own name—and sometimes she couldn't get it at all. Much of this has been changed by the new federal law, effective October 28, 1975, which guarantees women against discrimination in being granted credit, as long as they meet the other criteria for having a credit rating. Yet the question of credit is *still* more complicated for women than men, since most women adopt their husband's name when getting married, have less experience getting credit, and have shorter or nonexistent credit histories.

So let's consider the question of credit from several angles: credit in general for women who have not had much experience with it before, some special problems that women have with credit, and, finally, some things you should know about your credit rating and your rights under the Fair Credit Reporting Act.

First, the question of credit in general. How much should you use it, or what are the safe limits for acquiring debt? This will vary, depending on your personality and life style, but there are some general rules that can serve as reasonable guidelines. Bankers and credit counselors who've had experience with people who didn't handle debt well, who've watched families disintegrate or individuals get to the verge of a nervous breakdown because they've piled up too many bills, feel that about 20 per cent of net income (you know, that slim slice of what once looked like a fairly plump and respectable pie that's left after the federal, state, and local governments have taken their tax bites out of it) is all the debt that anyone can reasonably carry. If, for instance, you are earning $12,000, after taxes you may have about $9,000, or a monthly income of about $766. This means that you should not be paying various creditors more than about $153 a month. You're buying a car, perhaps, and monthly payments are about $125. You could also afford to pay out about another $25 or so on furniture, and that would be it—if you wanted to live within a reasonably sensible debt limit.

Of course, if you are someone who knows how, and is willing, to make the effort to keep a tight rein on expenditures, you can go over this limit. You may, for example, want to take an educational loan that you believe will increase your earning power—and you need that car for transportation and that furniture to eat, sleep, and relax on. You have no way of paying off the loans early and you don't want to defer the courses that are an investment in your future. You over-extend yourself, but with a good reason and on a temporary basis. But you don't do it blindly.

You sit down with a big pot of coffee, a large writing pad, and your checkbook, and see how your expenses shape up. You draw a line down the middle of the page. On one side of the line you write down all the inflexible expenses, i.e. those you can't cut easily if at all: rent, transportation, insurance, utilities, dues to unions and clubs, contributions to pension loans, etc. On the other side you write down the expenses over which you do have *some* control, the flexible outlays: food, services (laundry, dry cleaning, personal care, beauty shop bills), window washers, clothing, health care not covered by health insurance plans (doctors, dentists, opticians), medicines, daily expenses (coffee breaks, newspapers, cigarettes), recreation, gifts, donations to charities.

Then you see where you can cut the flexible expenses enough to allow for paying off another monthly bill. Can you cut the clothes budget? Will you be able to get along relaxing with the old movies on TV instead of watching the newest stars at a first-run movie house? Can you do your hair yourself for a while, though you'll miss the luxury of having someone else massage your scalp? And so on. This kind of soul-and-budget searching will tell you how much additional debt you can assume: No movies plus no hairdresser plus a careful watch over those coffee breaks and lunchtime impulse buying may add up to enough money to take on another loan. But the decision to add to your debts has to be a *conscious one*, very carefully under your control.

The Secret of Managing Credit

That, in fact, is *the secret of good management—control over your finances*. Control means making conscious choices, choices that suit your personality, your life style, your way of doing things—but choices that also leave you with some kind of financial protection, specifically, a savings account that you consider untouchable except for a real emergency. (Unfortunately, a feeling that you'll scream in the elevator if you have to go to work one more snowy morning when you long to be lolling on a beach somewhere doesn't qualify as a true emergency.)

Ah, but you say you've tried a hundred times and despite your 100 per cent pure and noble intentions you just can't put money aside. There is an answer. Don't push yourself—let someone else push you. Arrange with your employer and/or your bank to have some money skimmed right off the top of your income and deposited in a savings account before you ever get your eager hands on it. Then, you can go ahead and live as you like—or at least as you can afford—secure in the knowledge that, though you're not planning to fall, if you do you've provided your own cushion.

What if you're one of those unfortunate individuals who just can't seem to handle credit? (I say unfortunate because, *used well*, credit is really a great advantage.) If you find that (1) you never do get up the will power to tell your bank to put aside some money; (2) you are always in debt for a simple reason: you're forever paying out more than you're taking in; (3) you have skirted the edge of bankruptcy at least once; and (4) despite all of these facts you go on using your charge cards . . . then face the fact that you were never cut out to have credit.

Don't consider it a genetic defect (What's wrong with my chromosomes?); don't consider it a sign of moral deficiency (Is there something dreadful I don't know about my character?); and forget about all those noble souls you eat lunch with who seem to pay their bills almost before the mailman delivers them. You have other virtues. Cherish them. But accept the truth that credit is one of the things in life you can't handle. And don't just sit there—do something that seems absolutely rash but is, on the contrary, absolutely rational. Get up, get a pair of scissors, and cut all your credit cards into neat halves. Then, when you've paid all your current bills, sit down and write to all those nice stores and banks that gave you credit and tell them you are closing your account. Drastic? Yes. Necessary? Yes.

Of course, you don't want to walk around with lots of loose cash that can be stolen or lost, but you can carry your checkbook, a few loose checks, or traveler's checks. Admittedly, these may cost you a fee, but it may work out to be no more than the interest you have been paying on your charge accounts or loans. (In many metropolitan areas Barclays Bank International, Ltd., offers its traveler's checks to customers at no charge, and so do some savings banks and savings and loan associations. It's worth investigating.)

Let's stop at this point for just a moment and consider what banks, department stores, and other credit-grantors look for when you ask for credit. Quite logically, since in effect they are lending you money, they want your commitment to pay it back, they want to know that this commitment is guaranteed by some resources for paying it back, and they want to be sure you won't renege on this commitment. From your viewpoint, there is one hitch in this logic: How do you prove any or all of these points if you've never had credit —if you have no "credit history," to lapse into the jargon of the trade. (It's a variation of the I-can't-hire-you-because-you-don't-have-any-experience predicament, when one reason you don't have experience is that no one will give you a job so you can get some.)

This is not a new problem and not just a feminine problem, except that more of us are facing this problem as more of us become financially independent. And there is an old answer that I think is a dubious one—take out a loan that you don't really need, and pay it back, just to prove that you are responsible, thereby acquiring a credit rating (proof that you are a good risk because you've established a history of paying off a loan promptly and fully). And, since your chances of getting such a loan are best at a finance company, which is willing to take greater risks, you are advised to go to a finance company and borrow a small amount that you pay off exactly as required, proving what a real doll and good credit gamble you are.

The finance company must compensate for its willingness to take greater risks by charging higher interest rates than other lenders, sometimes two or three times as high—18 per cent or even 25 per cent, compared to a bank loan of maybe 9 per cent or less. But you are told it's worth the price because you "have to" do this to establish a credit history. I think this is expensive advice and there are better and cheaper ways to accomplish the same thing.

How to Get a Credit History

You have your first full-time job, which seems a stable one. You have committed yourself to an apartment, by signing a lease—in itself a sign of stability.

You set aside a portion of your income for savings, which you deposit faithfully, or have your employer deposit for you, in a savings account. After six months, or perhaps even less, you apply for a credit card or a charge account. If you have a secure job, you should be able to get it on the basis of proof of ability to pay and responsibility.

Another possibility, if you prefer the borrowing route, is to borrow in one of the cheapest ways possible, by using your savings account as collateral. You can borrow the entire amount by using the account itself as security. Not only are such loans offered at low rates—always considerably lower than a finance company's rate—but the amount you pay is further reduced, in effect, because you are still getting the interest on the savings account. Let's say the rate for borrowing, using your account as collateral, is 8.5 per cent, and you have your money in a day-of-deposit-to-day-of-withdrawal account earning 5 per cent. Your loan is costing you 3.5 per cent—really cheap in itself and especially cheap when compared with the rate charged by a finance company, maybe 18 to 25 per cent.

But it's not just the single woman applying for credit for the first time who has a problem—it's also the newly single woman, the divorcée or widow, who has this problem, and to her it may be more of a shock. Why? Because while she was married she had come to take her credit for granted, and never worried or even thought about the fact that the credit was issued in the name of Mrs. John Dough. It isn't so much the married name, the "Mrs.," that's important here, but what it implies. Mrs. John Dough has this credit because her husband guarantees it; the store presumes that his earning capacity insures payment. The credit rating and credit history are dependent on her husband—and when she loses her spouse, through either divorce or death, she is no longer Mrs. John Dough and therefore she no longer has Mrs. John Dough's credit rating or history.

What's the best way to handle this problem? That depends somewhat on your current status. One way is to prevent the problem by maintaining your own credit history when you get married. Let's say you decide to adopt your husband's name and therefore have to notify all the stores and banks, and anyone else who has given you a credit card, that you have changed your name. When you do this, add a note that you wish to keep your own credit rating and your own credit history.

If you are already married and have no intention of getting a divorce but still think you'd like to have your own rating, you have a way—though admittedly it's a nuisance. You can write to each of the places that has given you credit in your married name and say that now you want a separate account so that you can establish (or re-establish) your own credit history. And there the situation gets a bit tricky.

Remember that giving someone credit is not a requirement—the person has to meet the objective criteria of ability and willingness to pay. If you are a woman with an independent income, so that you meet these criteria, under the law the credit-granting institution (bank, store, gas station, whatever) cannot deny you credit unless they can prove that they would also deny credit to a man with exactly the same credentials. In other words you should be able to get credit if you're like my friend Fredda, who is a counselor in a big city school system and is married to a lawyer. The two of them jointly support their home and their two daughters, aged ten and thirteen. Although Murray, Fredda's husband, has higher earnings than she does, her job is secure, she has the professional credentials (teacher's license) to hold the job permanently, and she's been at it long enough (eighteen years) to show stability.

But suppose you're like my friend Marian, who is married to an instructor in English literature at a junior college. He does not have tenure, and his contract is renewed for one year only each spring (while they alternately hold their breath and bite their fingernails up to their elbows). Marian and Paul have two children, both under five, and she doesn't work outside their home. He has a bank credit card since there's no doubt that he has a source of income, at least as long as his job lasts. If she were to apply for a separate card, however, she probably would be turned down, according to the head of the consumer credit division of the New York State Bankers Association. (He spoke only for New York, of course, but New York is fairly typical of the country and is, if anything, more liberal.) Nor could she claim that she was being discriminated against on a sexist basis, because if the situation were reversed—if she held the teaching position and her husband stayed home with the children—he wouldn't be able to get credit either. The refusal would be on the basis of the person's current place in the social pecking order—a dependent unable really to prove the ability to meet financial obligations for a very simple and mundane reason, no independent income.

However, even in this situation there are possibilities. Instant credit is out for Marian (by instant I mean applying for and getting a credit card within the customary span of time, several weeks or a month). But, over a period of time even Marian can build up an independent credit rating. How? By following essentially the same procedure as a single person, i.e. opening a savings account in her own name and making regular deposits for a long enough period of time—say six months minimum—to establish some kind of nest egg that could be borrowed against or serve as proof of financial responsibility. (Considering the average small salary of college instructors without tenure, and the expenses of a family with two small children, the deposits would have to be *very* small—but the amount isn't as important as the regularity.)

As you may have guessed, the wives of the dean of the college, the president of the bank, and the head of the construction company that built both the bank and the college—in other words women who are married to men with substantial incomes—probably aren't going to have these problems. Not that they are any more responsible than Marian, but simply that they have more resources.

All these wives, despite any trouble they might have, would probably have an easier time getting credit than would divorcées. There is the myth, now disappearing, that women live luxuriously on alimony—but bankers know otherwise. Alimony payments are not the most reliable source of income and some divorcées have trouble establishing credit in their own name, especially if alimony is their only source of income. They too have to go the letter-writing route, asking for their own credit.

If you're thinking of a divorce, obviously you don't have to wait until the last minute, when the decree is final, to begin getting your own credit cards. If it's a mutually agreed on separation and divorce and there are still some lines of communication between you and your spouse (translation: you can still talk to each other, if not directly at least through your lawyers), it is to your spouse's advantage to help you get credit in your own name, and if he doesn't realize this, his lawyer will surely point it out to him. And certainly, the sooner you are in control of your own financial affairs, the better off you will be.

Widows have shared with divorcées the somewhat dubious distinction of having the most difficulty in establishing credit in their own name, yet it is one of the many things they have to do. If you, a widow, have not had bank credit cards in your own name, the task of getting one is easier if you apply to a bank where you are known. You too have to go through the routine of establishing credit, but a bank familiar with your previous credit history and assets should be willing to help you establish an individual credit rating.

All Is Not Roses and Readiness

We can all cheer and be cheered by the fact that it's now illegal to discriminate against us when it comes to granting credit. But there can still be many a slip between an institution's stated policies and what actually happens. Let's say you apply for credit, you believe you meet all the criteria for getting that credit—and you're refused. You don't have to just sit there, you can do something. You have several options, and you can start using them at the very moment the person interviewing you says no.

You ask the reasons, and if they don't seem justified, you say that you would like to discuss these reasons with his superior, whom you intend to see as soon as the interview is ended. And you do just that if you feel you are a good credit risk and the objections seem weak or sexist. If you have applied to a branch location of a store or a bank, where ultimate approval must come from the main office or headquarters, and are told that "headquarters" says no, find out exactly who disapproved and insist on speaking to that person. Remember that you are completely within your rights under the Fair Credit Reporting Act of 1971 when you ask to know precisely why you are being denied credit.

Credit History Drawbacks

That credit history we've been talking about is not an unmixed blessing. Once you begin to acquire such a history, you're on file in a local credit bureau. This is a private organization supported cooperatively in some cases by merchants, businesses, and banks, or run as a private enterprise selling its services to subscribers who want to know who is and who isn't a good risk. Such bureaus get their information about you partly from their subscribers or the merchants or companies that give you credit. They learn whether you pay promptly or always put it off until the third dunning letter, how much you borrowed to buy a car, what your credit limit is for your credit card.

But they also get reports from court dockets, county clerks' files, and other public records. And they have paid investigators, both full-time and part-time, who gather information for reasons you may not be aware of. The file is used for more than evaluating whether you are in good financial shape. You may be being considered for a job where you will handle large sums of cash, for instance, and your prospective employer wants to know if you can resist the temptation to tuck a few dollars into your own pocketbook. You may be applying for life insurance and the company wants to know if you're going to meet your premium payments. You may be driving your own or a company-owned car and the insurance company wants to know if you're careful or accident-prone.

But if you have a good credit history and pay your bills promptly, you have no cause to worry, right? Unfortunately, wrong. It is possible for incorrect or misleading information to get into your file. The greatest potential danger is not from the credit reports about how promptly or how slowly you pay your bills. Much more serious is the possibility that a court suit against you will be settled in your favor a year or more after it was begun; the record of the suit will remain in your file but the favorable settlement won't be entered. And equally serious is the possibility of real trouble from investigations of your character, to determine whether you are honest, stable, reliable, and able to resist temptation—whether it's an opportunity to juggle the company's books or that last drink that will make you misjudge how quickly you can jam on the brakes when you see someone crossing the street.

These evaluations are based on the work of investigators who may question your neighbors and record their not necessarily unbiased opinion of the way you live. The information gotten this way has always been open to question, but in recent years, when standards of morality and "respectable" life styles vary drastically, neighbors' judgments can be untrue, unfair, or both. (Take the question of marriage, for instance. To some people these days it's still a sacred contract, while to others it's a violation of the human spirit.)

An elderly widow and widower, each living on a small social security check, decide to pool their resources and gain companionship by moving in together. They could get married, but this would add considerably to their taxes and lower their already skimpy standard of living. So they just decide to do what might have been unthinkable to them thirty years ago, when our standards were quite different—they move in together and "live in sin."

A neighbor, reporting on this, still holds her thirty-years-ago views and tells an insurance investigator that the woman in the case is "unreliable" and "unstable." He puts this in his report and she—mother, grandmother, never sick a day in her life—either is denied automobile insurance or has to pay a higher premium for it.

Or your son, or younger brother, has shoulder-length hair, likes to go around without a shirt and barefoot, is a member of a rather noisy social and dramatic club, and is also an honor student at his high school. But your neighbors, who can't abide long hair, exposed chests and toes, and anyone with views different from theirs, tell an investigator you are not really a stable family. You're being considered for a job that gives you access to confidential files and the company feels that maybe you would talk too much, so the job goes to someone else.

But we don't have to worry only about nasty remarks from nasty people. The fact is that with so many people handling your file—clerks and typists, writers and computer programmers, new supervisors and office managers—it's just about impossible to prevent errors from getting into someone's file some time; and the unlucky person just might be you. It's important, therefore, for you to know your rights under the Credit Act, so that if you suspect you have been discriminated against or have been the victim of an unfavorable report, you will know your rights and how to proceed.

Your Rights Under the Fair Credit Reporting Act

1. You have the right to review your file. Let's say you are refused credit, or charged for some kind of insurance at a higher premium than you believe

justified, or turned down for a job—and you suspect that it's because of a bad credit rating. The law requires that, if you ask for it, you must be given the name and address of the source of the report, the credit reporting bureau which has this record of you in its files.

2. You have a right to call or go to the bureau and insist that they tell you the *substance* of the report and the sources of the information, with two exceptions. You don't have to be told the medical information in your file (this information is restricted but you can get it from your doctor of course) nor the sources of the report about your character, reputation, or personal life. Notice that I say substance, because a clerk reading this information to you either over the phone or in person is fulfilling the requirements of the law— the law doesn't say that you are entitled to an exact copy of the report on you in their files.

3. The credit bureau must also tell you the names of everyone who got an employment report about you within the prior two years plus the names of anyone else who got reports about you within the prior six months. Furthermore, the bureau has to have sufficient staff on duty to give you this information during regular business hours. And if you can't get there in person, you can write, and with proper identification, they are required to send you the information you're after. (There may be a small fee for the mail service— check on it when you look into this possibility.)

What do you do if you get the report, in person, by phone, or in the mail, and find that it has material that is outdated or untrue? You have a right to insist that the bureau go over its own records and prove that these records are accurate. If they can't prove that their information is accurate or if you can show conclusively that their information is inaccurate or no longer true, you can insist that the unfavorable information be removed from your file.

But just having the unfavorable information taken out doesn't undo the damage that's been done. You have a right to insist (and you should) that the correction on your file be sent to all employers or prospective employers if they have received the incorrect report in the prior two years. And you can also insist that the credit bureau send this information to anyone else who has gotten a report about you in the previous six months.

You should try to get to the credit bureau within thirty days after receiving a report of a credit refusal, since within that time they can't charge you for telling you what's in your file or sending out any corrections or deletions you ask for. After the thirty days, however, they can charge you for giving you the information that's in your file, but they can't charge you any more than the standard fee they charge to a merchant asking the same information, and they have to tell you the amount of the charge in advance. They cannot, however, charge you for notifying anyone that material in your report was deleted because it was inaccurate or could no longer be verified.

There is more to know—some of the specific details of the law—which you will want to look into if you believe you've been unfairly judged a credit risk. There's no need to go into them here—the important thing is for you to know that you have rights and that you should use them. How to use them is another question. The standard way is to go through regular channels. If you want to take this route and you find a credit bureau, a bank, or an insurance company uncooperative, you should write to the Federal Trade Commission, which administers the federal law. Address your letter to the FTC's Bureau of Consumer Protection, Division of Special Statutes, 6th Street and Pennsylvania Avenue, N.W., Washington, D.C. 20580. While you're at it, send a copy to the regional office of the FTC that's nearest to you (if there is one in your city, you will find it in the phone directory under United States Government), and for good measure some of the other agencies that don't administer the law but should be informed as to what's going on. (Every department loves to know what someone else is doing wrong or not enough of.) You might, for instance, send a copy to your state banking commission, department of insurance, and consumer protection agency.

The Fair Credit Billing Act

The Fair Credit Reporting Act was supplemented in November 1975 by the Fair Credit Billing Act, which gives you some added protection. Briefly, here are its main provisions:

1. Inquiries about your bills must be answered within thirty days, and the question in the inquiry resolved in no more than ninety days.

2. No dunning letters or threats to give you an adverse credit report can be sent nor other collection action taken until your inquiry is resolved.

3. A creditor cannot send an adverse report to a credit agency on an amount you are questioning or disputing unless you, the customer, also get such a report and unless the credit reporting agency is told there is a dispute on the amount of the charge.

4. Your monthly bills must have an address you can write to for handling billing disputes, and you must be reminded periodically of your rights.

5. You can withhold payment on merchandise you think was misrepresented or defective if you bought it with a bank credit card just as you might withhold payment on the same basis from a store. This protects you against buying with your credit card and then having the store go out of business, leaving you holding the bill and no one to correct what went wrong or to return your money.

The law applies to each purchase that costs more than fifty dollars and was bought in your home state or within a hundred miles of your home, whichever is the greater distance. You have to go through the regular complaint routine, i.e. try to get the "lemon" repaired or replaced, before a bank or other credit card issuer can be brought into the act and made legally liable.

CHAPTER 21

Where There's a Will There's a Way—Of Saving, Providing, and Sleeping More Easily

Do you *really* need a will?

No, not *really*—if you don't care too much who will be the guardian of your children if you are in a fatal accident.

Not really—if you don't care that part of the money you worked so hard to earn will go to pay off estate taxes, when it could have gone into a trust fund to guarantee that your grandchildren would have money to pay for their college tuition.

Not really—if you don't care that your ailing mother will have to eat peanut butter sandwiches for dinner instead of the balanced diet she needs, because she has only her social security check to live on.

Not really—if you don't mind having any or all of your assets disposed of without any consideration of your own wishes—the aunt you hate getting the jewelry you love; the books you promised to your nephew being sold at a fraction of their value to pay estate taxes, some of your stock options being allowed to lapse because the court-appointed executor of your estate doesn't handle your affairs properly.

Sure I care about these things, you say, but really they don't apply to me because:

1. I really don't own anything since I have no estate, so why should I go to the expense of writing a will.

2. My brother/sister/husband and I own everything jointly, so if I die he/she gets everything and that's that.

3. My husband has taken care of all this in his will, and we have a good lawyer, and I have nothing to worry about. (He's told me so many times.)

All of these arguments have flaws, both big and little, for big and little reasons.

1. Are you sure you don't own anything? Are you a pauper? How about

your bank account, savings account, the group life insurance your company pays for, your car, your furniture, your jewelry, your books, your record collection. How about those few shares of stock your Aunt Matilda left to you, your pension fund, your share in your house or in that place in the country. Sit down and add it all up and you may find that you are worth more than you think. But, no matter how small the total, you owe it to yourself and to the people you love to have it distributed as you want.

2. Yes, it's true that if you own things jointly, ownership is transferred to the survivor—but not before the tax man takes his share. And this share can be less, sometimes much less, if there is a carefully thought-out will.

3. There is no doubt that your husband is an ace, a wonderful guy, and has your best interest at heart—as he sees it. He doesn't want you to worry. And he has a smart lawyer who has written thousands of wills, and he knows everything about the technical and legal side of a will. Fine. But neither one of them is a fortune teller or prophet, and they can't possibly foresee what is going to happen when your husband dies. Your lawyer can't possibly foresee, for instance, changes in tax laws that might affect the status of some of the stocks and bonds you will inherit. Nor can he foretell what will happen to the neighborhood you live in, and therefore the value of your house.

Furthermore, the will is written with the assumption that your husband is going to live to a fine old age and be responsible for your finances until then. But what if he doesn't, and you are responsible? Your husband can't foresee that your lawyer may not be as good a friend to you as he was to your husband. He may raise his fee, give you bad advice, even cheat you. One of the classic examples of this was the experience of a woman in one of my Women and Money courses at the New School for Social Research. Mrs. M.'s husband adored her and didn't want her ever to have to worry about finances. He preferred that she concentrate on raising their son and daughter and taking art courses. So she never even had to write a check, let alone make any financial decisions. He didn't foresee that his business partner would bring out an old IOU with her husband's signature and present it against the estate, or that the stock they owned would plunge drastically, or that the lawyer would ask for a higher fee than Mrs. M. thought he was entitled to. And she was afraid to argue because she didn't know anything about her husband's finances.

Do I sound as if I'm making a case? I hope so, because I am, for two things: One, everyone should have a will; and, two, everyone who is a major beneficiary of a will written on her behalf should (a) know what is in the will, and (b) have some voice in the results or the decisions the will establishes.

Now, one more complicating factor. All of these premises have always been true, but in recent years they have become more important with the drastic change in the outlook and marital status of so many women. As the divorce rate has soared and as the concept of no-fault divorce has blossomed, women who thought marriage brought them financial security have found out otherwise—and sometimes it has been a bitter lesson. So, along with the other things that have to be considered at the time of separation and divorce, women also have to think about the provisions in the soon-to-be-ex-husband's will. If it is not important for them, it is important for their children. And, if new marriages take place and new families are born, women have to think of the provisions in the will that will protect their children, whether those children are from the first or a subsequent marriage.

The Consequences of Having No Will

What happens if you don't have a will? You might think—especially if there isn't much money involved—that the survivor just decides who gets what, parcels it out, and that's that. Not so. The state has a say in who gets what, and if you haven't made those decisions, the state makes them for you. They are not necessarily decisions that you would be happy about.

Let's say you are single, your parents are dead but you have a sister and a brother. Your brother is married and has no children, and he and his wife have an excellent combined income. They live in the suburbs and have two cars. Your sister is still in college, just about scraping through on a bank loan, and spends about three hours a day commuting to her school by bus. You're in a fatal accident and leave no will. Because of federal and state inheritance laws, there is an excellent chance that everything you own will have to be divided equally between your sister, who would have loved to get your car and furniture, and your brother, who would have loved her to have them. But it could turn out that, in order to satisfy the law, they will have to sell these things so that the proceeds can be divided equally. And your bank account will also be split fifty-fifty, though if you had gotten around to writing a will you would have made certain that everything went to your sister.

Or you're a divorcée and you don't have a will. You are killed in an accident and the money you leave is divided equally between your two minor children. Since you haven't appointed a guardian, the court appoints one and he decides how your children's funds are to be administered. Barbara D., a fine wills and trust lawyer, tells of one of her clients whose children's trust funds (left by her ex-husband) were administered by a court-appointed guardian. Her children had always gone to private all-day schools and summer camps since she was a working mother. But the guardian disapproved. Her children were transferred to a neighborhood school where they didn't get a particularly good education, and had to spend the summer hanging around the apartment, under the indifferent supervision of a teen-ager, being miserable.

Your Husband Doesn't Have a Will

Several years ago *Business Week* magazine interviewed more than a thousand family lawyers, accountants who did family tax work, officers of bank trust and investment advisory departments, insurance consultants, stockbrokers, independent investment counselors, and real estate brokers. On the basis of these interviews *Business Week* concluded that at least 50 per cent of all businessmen and professionals in the $30,000 and more income group had no written wills—and an estate planning adviser in the United States Trust Company of New York thinks this figure is low. In his opinion the correct statistic would be 60 per cent or more. Furthermore, even the 50 per cent who do have wills don't update them regularly, despite changes in their families, in tax laws, and in their income and property.

Let's say you haven't worked outside your home in many years. You're not rich but you have managed to accumulate some stocks, bonds, and a little cash that you assume will be your guarantee of security in your old age. Your children are grown and fairly well-to-do. Your husband dies unexpectedly in an automobile accident. You assume that everything will become yours—but, depending on your state inheritance law, that may not be so. In New York State, for instance, you would get up to $2,000 in cash and personal intangible property (such as bank accounts and stocks). In many states depending on how many children you have, you might get one half to one third. In some states you might get only one half of your husband's insurance policy although if you died your husband would get all of yours. In other words there are a mishmash of laws that mean you could be left in your fifties with an income too small to live on decently. And at that point you would have to be dependent on the good will of your children and their spouses, or have to go out and get a job, not easy for someone who's been out of the job market for so many years. Not a pleasing prospect.

O.K., you're convinced that you as an individual or you as half of a marriage partnership need a will.

Planning a Will

Now, what are the considerations in planning a good will? There are two—and sometimes they may be in conflict with each other. The first consideration is how you want your property disposed of. A will is not just a legal document providing for the disposition of property; it is in many ways an extension of your life's goals. It should provide for your dependents in ways that you would have assured had you remained alive. Therefore, these are the first things you have to decide: Who should be responsible for your dependents—children, parents, relatives—if you're not around? And, particularly in the case of children, how much responsibility can these dependents assume for their own affairs, and at what age?

This is a particularly important question when you have young adults, who may be legally old enough to handle their own affairs—but emotionally or psychologically at a particular time of their lives when getting a lump sum of money could be not a blessing but a disaster. Consider, for instance an eighteen-year-old who has led a comparatively sheltered life in a quiet home and academic community and has, since she's never really been on her own, no idea of how to manage money. Would you want her to have a large sum suddenly at her disposal, with no one to turn to for advice? Or consider, as did Jane D., an estate attorney with one of Manhattan's most prestigious law firms, the differences among her three children, all in their twenties. Each was responsible, bright, independent. The two older ones were quite indifferent to money management and material things: Her daughter was an anthropologist and her older son was studying to be a doctor. The younger son, however, was interested in money and legal affairs, and was, in fact, studying to be a lawyer. So, though custom would say that the oldest child should be executor of the estate, Jane and her husband saw that it was the younger son who would be the most knowledgeable on legal and financial questions, and he was the one they appointed as the executor.

Once you have decided who is going to be the executor of your will (and I'll talk about some other characteristics of a good executor shortly), you want to think of the other important aspect of making a will—taking maximum advantage of all possible tax savings. And at this point you are going to need legal advice, both to insure that you will be able to get all the possible tax advantages and to insure that your will is properly drawn up so that it is legal and binding. You will want a knowledgeable lawyer, a trustworthy one.

If you already have a family lawyer who is familiar with drawing up wills and she/he is someone you trust and someone who knows your family, fine. But suppose you have to find a lawyer. Where should you look or whom should you ask for recommendations? Friends and family members are always a good source, but there are other possibilities if that doesn't work out. Here are some places to go for recommendations:

1. Lawyers who don't do estate work but can recommend colleagues who do.

2. Law firms that handle only major estates (some in New York will not

consider any estate that is less than $500,000!) but that might be able to recommend someone.

3. Your company's lawyer or law firm.

4. An accounting firm or an individual accountant you know and trust.

5. An insurance company, broker, or agent you know and trust.

You can call your local bar association if all of these sources fail, but you run the risk of simply getting a list of lawyers who do estates without any kind of testimonial as to their competence. It is possible too to ask your bank, but this has its drawbacks, particularly if the estate is a sizable one. Banks are anxious for the trust business that an estate sometimes involves and may recommend a lawyer more because they know she will bring them trust business than because they are sure of her competency. Not always true, of course, but something at least to keep in mind.

Now, you've decided how you want your affairs managed, and your possessions passed on or disposed of. You've found a lawyer whom you trust, who will help you write a valid will. Before you go any further, you need to settle one thing: What will her fees be? You can get some idea of what the fee should be, *before* discussing it with the lawyer, by calling up your local bar association for its prepared list of minimum fees. These will vary from community to community. The chances are just about nonexistent that your lawyer is going to charge less than the minimum (she's no fool), but she may certainly charge more, depending on her experience and status, the size and/or complications of the estate, perhaps even her relationship with you. But she is entitled to a fair price for her work and you are entitled to a reasonable fee. You are also entitled to ask in advance before you make any kind of commitment. Armed with the schedule from the bar association, you are in a good position to judge whether you are being asked a fair price.

It is your job to say whom you want as your executor, and how you want your property disposed of. It is the lawyer's job (1) to follow your wishes, and (2) to write your will so that it takes maximum advantages of all the tax savings possibly open to you.

Here are some of the recommendations your lawyer may make:

1. The marital deduction, which allows you to leave up to half of your estate to your spouse, either outright or in the form of a trust.

2. Trust funds that enable you to postpone the final distribution of an estate, perhaps by as much as a full generation, and in this way cut out or cut down the second estate tax bill due on the property you leave at your death, if your spouse died first.

3. How to assign life insurance payment in order to minimize administrative costs, and in some states to save the state estate taxes.

4. Gifts or transfer of property while you are still living. Taxes on these

may be lower than taxes on gifts that are given after you die, because gift tax rates are lower than estate tax rates. (But this is an involved and complicated question, since there are many tax restrictions on gifts and transfers, so you and your lawyer will have to plan this in careful detail.)

Before your lawyer can begin drawing up the will, she has to know your assets and liabilities. So before you go to her, you—or you and your spouse—have to sit down and get together all the information about what you have that's to be inherited, and what you owe that will have to be paid out; in other words your assets and liabilities.

Your list should contain the following assets:

1. All your bank accounts, stocks, bonds, including of course U.S. savings bonds, and any savings certificates you bought through your bank.

2. Your most valuable personal possessions, such as jewelry, furs, paintings, silver, antiques, books.

3. Real estate—your house, cooperative apartment, or condominium—including all property you own individually or jointly (even that sixth of a beach house you own). You should list locations and exact or approximate value.

4. Insurance policies, both personal and employer-sponsored, pension plans, stock options, profit sharing, union benefits, etc. Where applicable this list should include beneficiaries, face amount of policies, loans outstanding against insurance policies, and premiums either paid for or due.

5. Any inheritances you expect to receive before your own death (since they should be considered when planning your estate).

It's at this point that you realize, when you add it all up, that you do have an estate, and that it mounts up to more sometimes than you thought it would.

But just when you're feeling rich, there comes the next step—listing your liabilities:

1. Your mortgage or lease.

2. Your outstanding debts: e.g. auto loans, payments on major appliances, vacation loans, tuition loans.

3. Taxes, and other major outstanding commitments—a loan you have cosigned, for instance.

You should then add some family information—number and ages of children, relatives you're responsible for, and something about your income and style of living. You might want your children to continue going to a special camp in the summer that encourages their interest in music, or science, or backpacking. You may want to provide for care for an aging relative. Now, as you look at *this* list it may seem very simple and straightforward, or you may foresee all kinds of complications, depending on your present marital status.

If you're single, don't own very much, and have no dependents, this can be a relatively simple task. If you're married and have acquired more possessions, it gets more complicated. If it's your second marriage or your husband's second marriage but there are no children, it may still be fairly simple. If it's the second marriage for either of you and there are children from the first marriage as well as children or plans for children in the second marriage, it can get very complicated indeed.

Some Miscellaneous Problems

Now let me add some problems that you may or may not have thought about and may or may not have control over. It will remind you again (if you need any more reminders at this point) how complicated and how important a will is.

Consider, for instance, if you are a divorcée, and your children are dependent for child support on your former husband and/or you are dependent on him for alimony: How is his will made out? What happens to these payments when he dies? If you haven't thought of this already, it's a problem you might also want to discuss with your lawyer, so that you can take some steps that will insure your future or your children's future. Even if you have thought of this already, it may be time to check into it again, or to set up a system of checking every few years to be sure the situation hasn't changed.

It's also important for your husband, either present or ex, that *you* have a will and that he know its contents. Even if he has more financial resources than you, he too has responsibilities, especially if there are young children. So a carefully thought-out and well-written will in your name is very necessary.

Machismo and Female Folly

With all logic and reason on the side of taking care of this very important part of living why don't more people have wills? An interesting question, since obviously death is one of life's few certainties. Many reasons have been advanced, each or all of them true depending on the people involved. None of us likes to think of death, and making a will is a recognition that we are going to die; putting it off is a way of putting off the inevitable. Another reason is the belief, mistaken, that since everything is held jointly—and this is particularly true where there doesn't seem to be much of an estate—a will isn't necessary.

Still another, particularly when you're young, is the belief that there is still so much time—sure it's something to be done but not until you're old, and what constitutes "old" gets older and older as *you* add on years. When you're twenty anyone in her fifties seems ancient, but when you're fifty even seventy doesn't necessarily seem *that* old. And then there are all kinds of individual psychological reasons—like my husband's uncle who had a share in a rather complicated family corporation, which included several brothers, all with wives and sons. He decided it would be too involved to say how things should be apportioned when he died, since it would involve some corporate changes that would make the other officers of the family-owned corporation angry. So he chose to die without a will, leaving the decision in the hands of the other corporate officers and the state—then no one could blame *him* if the decisions were involved, time-consuming, and costly. (He was also a man who boasted he never had a fight with his wife—since every time she argued with him, he just turned off his hearing aid and let matters ride for a while.)

So much for the masculine approach—but wouldn't you think that women, knowing that they in most cases are the ones who might pay a price both financially and in terms of things to be done, affairs to be settled, etc., would urge their husbands to have wills? Not at all. Estate lawyers say that women are notorious about not wanting to plan estates. Why? Again, no one can give a definite and unequivocal answer, but some feminist lawyers I've spoken to, who were the first to tell me about this phenomenon, think that it is most characteristic of a certain kind of woman, who, knowingly or unknowingly, clings to her dependence on her husband. She doesn't want him to make a will because she would have to face the fact that someday she is going to have to lean on herself instead of her husband.

Let's say you're not like this—you want to know where things stand and you believe in wills. Let's say even further that so does your husband. In fact, he already has a will and it's all drawn up, witnessed, even updated recently. But you've never seen it. And it doesn't occur to him that you should. He assures you that you have nothing to worry about—you are well provided for and everything is in good order. Well maybe it is—and maybe it isn't. Let's eliminate all thoughts of malice, carelessness, ill-will, greed—all evil thoughts in other words—and consider what can go wrong when there are the best of intentions.

Let's consider just the question of how much you'll have to live on. Remember, as we've noted before, men's egos are tied up with how much money they earn. They like to think they have provided well. But consider the case of Frances L., whose husband, a prosperous insurance broker, told her not to worry, she was well taken care of. And so she was *at the time* he wrote the will—she would have had a fine income from good stocks, his insurance policies, and his share of income coming into his insurance brokerage firm. But Larry had not counted on being killed in an autombile accident in Florida at a time when the stock market had hit a low point and his insurance company was hit by a lawsuit that cut into its income because of unexpected legal fees. She had to sell some of the stocks and take a loss to pay estate taxes. Her income was less than she had estimated; and in order to have a moderate standard of living, she had to take a very dull part-time clerical job, and give up her volunteer work in a Veterans Hospital—something she really enjoyed doing. If she had known what was in the will, she would have opted for fewer stocks and more bonds or savings certificates of deposit so that she could have had a guaranteed income rather than an income dependent on uncertain stock dividends.

Or take the case of Alice W., who took my Women and Money course to see if she could at least get some understanding of what the executors her husband had named to handle "their" affairs were talking about. "I learned to my surprise," she told me, "that no one is above taking advantage—if only in small ways—of a widow he thinks is ignorant." There was some question about payment for furniture and a fine law library that one of her husband's partners, who was also executor of the estate, bought from the estate. He claimed that her husband had said he could have the furniture as payment for legal fees. She claimed her husband had no such intentions and had told her the furniture and library were to be sold, though the partner had every right to make a first bid and to match any future bids. The partner simply went ahead and took over the furniture, and when she objected he said, "Sue me." She didn't of course since she was dependent on him as executor—but she never felt so frustrated at her dependency.

Admittedly, because this question is tied up with machismo on your husband's part and some fear and misgivings on your part, it's a difficult subject to broach. However, it must be broached. One of the most effective ways is to point out to your husband that if you don't know what he has planned or wishes for, his plans and wishes may not be carried out and the estate that both of you have worked so hard to build and the security you looked for may be squandered. In other words, by learning about the provisions of the will and discussing it jointly, you are simply protecting what both of you have worked for that rightfully belongs to your heirs.

One of the most telling arguments for having you understand the provisions of your husband's will is the complicated probate process. If you are executor of your husband's will, you are going to have a myriad of details to attend to, and the job is certainly not easier if you have little idea of what it is you are doing and what people are talking to you about.

Without going into all the details on a step-by-step basis, here are just a few things (which will vary somewhat depending on the size of the estate) that have to be done in the process of settling an estate: file the will, pay all taxes (the regular taxes that were due on income, real estate, school, plus federal and state inheritance taxes), settle a lease if a move is necessary, open the safe deposit box, take care of stocks if there are warrants or stock options coming due, file for social security benefits, transfer bank accounts to a single name, pay outstanding bills, check claims against the estate, make an inventory of the assets that have been left, settle any bequests that have been made.

And in the meantime of course, life goes on—and the daily chores of living go on. And there are other personal decisions to be made—and the inevitable emotional trauma that goes along with any death. Even with the best of planning it can't be an easy time. But to be faced with all these problems when you have had no idea that they were coming and don't know what to do about them makes life much more difficult than it has to be—and it will be difficult.

Choosing an Executor

The assumption, when there are two parents still married, is that each will appoint the other as executor, to safeguard their children. But parents should also name an alternate to serve in case neither one survives. Divorced parents are sometimes unwilling to name the ex-spouse as executor. (And even childless couples should name alternate executors.) Obviously, regardless of your status, you have to choose an executor very, very carefully. What are the characteristics of a good executor?

He or she should be someone you expect to survive you, who will know enough about your family to be able to make decisions from your standpoint as far as possible, who will have enough business and financial experience to be able to handle your affairs prudently, and who will have the time to handle your affairs and have the necessary concern for your survivors.

It is a big responsibility and should be given only to someone who has your complete confidence and *who is willing to assume the responsibility*. You must, of course, have the consent of someone before you name her as executor. Someone named as an executor is entitled to a fee, or commission, usually set by law and varying from state to state.

You as Executor

In the case of your family, especially if you have children, there is one person who—if adequately prepared with prior instructions—fits the description of the good executor for your husband's estate, namely *you*. Who knows better what were your aims for your children, who should get what, what is needed to live on, etc.? This does not mean, however, *that you have to do or know everything yourself.* Everyone, male or female, needs some professional advice. Your affairs should be planned so that you will get help from a coexecutor: a trusted lawyer, an astute relative, the trust department of a bank. And because you are knowledgeable, you can deal with these people intelligently, have some basis for judging whether their advice is good or not, and know when someone is trying to take advantage of you. You won't be afraid to ask questions when you have your doubts about something.

Perhaps best of all, you won't be in the position of dependency, waiting for your brother, son, lawyer, even a trust officer to *tell* you what to do, like forty-six-year-old Karen K., a stunning blond widow I know, who combined a career as a painter with that of mother, wife, manager of a lovely home, and, until her husband died, hostess for his many business friends. Karen has to gather up her bills, accounts, bank statements, get in her car and drive about fifteen miles to her brother's house at least once a month for no other purpose than to get him to straighten out her financial affairs. Her husband never explained the source of his income to her, telling her she wouldn't understand—and she was only too glad, she confesses, to let him do this. Now she is dependent on her brother's good will and must arrive at his house at his convenience. Since he is very busy, she hates to ask him to explain things, so she simply accepts what he says. Her sister-in-law considers the whole arrangement an imposition, and Karen just hates the feeling of dependency.

So does another friend of mine, Annette A., who has turned her affairs over to her son. He too is busy and she finds the role of dependent an odd role reversal for someone who prided herself on being a strong, self-reliant mother. She too hesitates to ask questions and just accepts decisions about how much she can spend and what she can and cannot afford to do, since she is unfamiliar with her own finances.

In each case the husband involved thought he was doing his wife a favor by shielding her from the realities of money management—but it has proved a real disservice. How much better it would have been if there had been some discussion, some plans, a scenario of what income there was, where it would come from, how it should be allocated, etc. And, reversing the situation, wives can discuss with husbands details of home management, so each has the feeling *in advance* that he can cope with a difficult situation. Unpreparedness is one of the greatest allies of fear.

And it's not necessary. Making these decisions in advance not only will enable you to have the best financial plan but will also give you the greatest strength and peace of mind. Keep this in mind both for yourself, and for the women in your life who need this kind of advice and perhaps even some consciousness raising from you—your aunt, your mother, your mother-in-law. Another instance where women can help themselves and each other.

CHAPTER 22

The Complicated, Dull, Confusing, Vital Question of Life Insurance

The insurance industry is a great one for giving awards, so let's turn the tables and give them an award—for dubious distinction in having insurance policies whose language is so obscure it's doubtful that agents themselves could translate the policies into English. This befuddling gobbledygook has helped make it possible for the companies and their agents to sell the wrong kind of insurance for many years. Most of it was sold to men, yet it was usually women who were affected most of all, since they were the survivors who had to hold a family together or manage alone on a sharply reduced income.

But the times are changing, women are changing—and the insurance picture is changing. One of the most important changes is that women are becoming aware of how important it is to understand insurance and buy the right kind and/or see that their husbands buy the right kind. So let's get into a discussion of what is the "right" kind.

First, what are we talking about when we talk about insurance? The word is "protection"—protection against catastrophes, both major and minor. Two main areas where you need protection are (1) the loss of income through the death of the main breadwinner, and (2) loss of earnings through illness.

As an individual or part of a family you also need protection against buying the wrong kind of insurance. And as women we all need protection against the discrimination against us in various kinds of disability insurance, which I'll point out when we get to that topic in the next chapter. But first things first, and the first thing is to get a good general approach to the whole insurance question.

Insurance is a trillion-dollar industry, not noted for leveling with consumers. So you have to know the right questions to ask, and the right person to ask them of, regardless of what kind of insurance policy you are buying. Only you know how very vulnerable you are to life's various hazards.

The Question of Life Insurance

Actually "life" is a misnomer—it's really death insurance that we are talking about, though we don't like to think about that. (In fact, we don't like to think about insurance at all, because who wants to consider all the unpleasant things that can happen? But we really must.) What would happen to your dependents if something happened to you? You don't have any dependents? No one to provide for? Then who says you need life insurance?

The fact is, you don't. And yet I have heard life insurance agents try to sell insurance to young single women on the grounds that they have to provide for their burial expenses, or they should take out a policy to make a gift to their favorite charity. (If it was a woman agent, she would invariably mention some feminist group as the recipient.) You can do either of these things if you choose to, but insurance isn't cheap and there really is no need to carry it. *A better way:* Provide in your will for necessary expenses out of your bank accounts, and make bequests to your favorite charity, if you want to.

Let's say, however, that you do have dependents. Then the right question is how much income will my dependents need to maintain the standard of living I would like them to have? You will probably feel they should have enough to maintain their present household and life style. You also have to look into the future and try to anticipate future expenses. If you are supporting or helping elderly relatives or parents, you'll consider the likelihood that their medical expenses will go up as they get older. If you are supporting young children, you'll want to provide for their support until they can be on their own, including advanced education (technical training, college, even graduate school).

Remember, however, that these are not decisions that you make entirely on your own. If you are married, these are joint decisions and they will be better decisions if you share in them. In the past women have been too prone to leave this decision to their husbands, an attitude encouraged by life insurance agents who spoke primarily to husbands, although they weren't averse to having the wives around (to listen respectfully, while the men discussed subjects which presumably were over the head of the little woman). And though I don't like to be snide, a little less machismo and a little more of women's practical questioning would have been in order—because very, very often the husbands bought the wrong kind of life insurance.

Which brings us to the next question. What is the right kind of insurance? Remember, what you are looking for is *protection* at a price. You get the maximum protection for the least money when you buy term insurance. This is not the kind of insurance that agents push, at least when they first come to call. They are much more likely to offer you a whole life (also called a straight life) policy, stressing its advantages:

1. *Level premiums*, i.e. the same premium paid for the life of the policy, so you always know what your insurance will cost. (Notice that word "premium" by the way—it's a typical example of insurance land's double talk. Anywhere else in the English language a premium is something you *get*—only in the jargon of the insurance trade is it something you have to give. I suppose the idea is to lull you into thinking that you really aren't dipping into your bank account, which is hardly the case.)

2. *Forced savings*. The whole life policy accumulates a cash value, which is a kind of automatic way of saving.

3. *Inexpensive loans*. You can borrow against this cash value at a low interest rate, always lower and sometimes considerably lower than the going interest rate.

Unless asked, however, insurance agents may neglect to point out a few *drawbacks* to whole life policies.

1. *Higher costs*. Whole life policies cost from two to three times more than term insurance policies for the same amount of protection. For instance, you might have to pay a premium of $1,009 a year for a $100,000 whole life policy covering you until you were sixty-five, compared to a premium of $352 a year for a five-year $100,000 term policy, renewable during subsequent alive-year periods at a somewhat higher rate, but still lower than the whole life rate.

2. *Slow cash value accumulation*. The forced savings, the cash-value, accumulates at a very slow pace. On a $50,000 policy, for instance, it could be only $5 per $1,000 of insurance or about $250 the first year, going up to about $137 per $1,000 or $680 plus interest by the tenth year. Suppose you bought a $50,000 term policy when you were twenty-five, deposited the difference between whole life premiums and the term policy premiums in your favorite savings bank, and let the money just sit there, accumulating interest at an average of 6 per cent a year. In ten years you would have spent about $3,600 on insurance *and* accumulated a nice little savings account nest egg of about $6,500. For the same amount of money paid in premiums for a whole life policy you would have a cash value of about $4,300. It's easy to see which is the better deal, in this case—and in most cases, I might add. (To be fair I'll mention, in a little while, when whole life has its advantages, though they are few and specialized.)

3. *Some loss of protection*. Though you can indeed borrow against that cash value at low interest rates (once enough has accumulated to make it worthwhile) the value of your insurance is *reduced by the amount of your loan*. Suppose you have a policy with a face value (to use the jargon of the

trade) of $50,000. In other words, a $50,000 whole life policy. You have accumulated a cash value of $10,000. When you borrow against that $10,000, your policy is worth only $40,000.

On the other hand, suppose you buy term insurance and cleverly put the difference in a savings account. If you need money, you borrow against this tidy little nest egg. True, depending on the interest rates at the time, you might have to borrow at a higher rate than the insurance company rate—but your insurance coverage remains the same. And interest on loans is tax-deductible, cutting the cost of the loan even more. Finally, there is the temptation not to pay back the insurance loan, which has no deadline, compared to more pressure to pay back the passbook loan, which—depending on the terms of the loan—requires some kind of regular payments.

And this brings up one of the agent's selling points for whole life—"it's forced savings," they say, "since that cash value accumulates without any action on your part." This is certainly true. Where does the cash value come from? Is it a gift from the insurance comany? Hardly. It's really *your* money. Life is paid for in equal or level premiums, i.e. the same amount every month for the duration of the policy, say twenty years. But you're not an equal risk for that whole twenty years; it costs less to insure you when you're young and healthy. The difference between what you are paying and the cost of insuring you goes into your account as the policy cash value. This is an oversimplified explanation, but you get the general idea.

There are other and better ways to have forced savings. Get your employer to deduct a set sum from your salary and put it in savings bonds or a savings account. The amount you put in could be the difference between what you would pay for straight life and what you are paying for term insurance. Or let your bank transfer money from your checking account to a savings account. This forced saving program not only pays you interest—usually compound interest at that—but it's also available should you need it. You don't have to borrow against it, as you do with the cash value on your whole life policy—it's your money.

Let's be grim and take a look at what would happen if whoever brings home the bread and bacon in your house is in a fatal accident. Suppose you've had a $50,000 straight policy for ten years and it has a cash value of $10,000. You leave a spouse and two children. What do they get? The face value of the policy, $50,000. If you had a term policy, however, your survivors would get the $50,000 plus what was in the savings account.

Some Advantages of Whole Life

Is straight life ever a good buy? Yes—if you think it would be impossible for you to save under any circumstances and/or yes, if you are in a high income bracket. Then straight life can give you savings on your taxes, since the cash value is exempt from state and federal taxes until the policy is cashed in, and sometimes not even then. (The insurance company takes the funds it doesn't need for business expenses and invests them; part of these funds are *your* cash value. And money earned from these investments is income for the company, not for you, which is why the cash value isn't taxed.)

Finally, if you or your spouse is sixty-five and prosperous, you might decide it's time to say the hell with insurance and drop your policies. If you have a straight life policy, you will get back your cash value. If you have a term policy you get nothing—unless you've been banking or investing the money you saved by buying term. In that case how much you have will depend on the return you've been getting on that money over the years.

Let's say you're not rich enough to have to worry about tax exemptions, and you are able to save—and so you have decided on term insurance. Good—I think you've made the right choice. The next question is from whom should you buy it? There are vast differences among companies, among policies, among agents. The average consumer—i.e. us, you and I—couldn't possibly take the time to learn all there is to know about insurance policies and companies in order to make the best choice. We are, therefore, partially dependent on a good insurance agent. Notice I say *partially*, because once you have some knowledge about what's available and what's best for you, you at least know some of the questions to ask, and some of the things to look for.

Types of Term Insurance

There are two types of term policies—renewable/convertible and decreasing balance. When you buy a renewable policy, you buy term insurance for a set period, usually five years, with the option to renew at the end of the five years. Let's say you buy a $100,000 policy for the five-year period, with an annual premium of $465. You're a divorcée, age thirty-five, with two children. When you reach forty, it's time to renew. You feel marvelous and your children, by now twelve and fifteen, are obviously college material. You want to keep that $100,000 insurance. But even though you feel and look marvelous, you *are* older and therefore a bit more of a risk. When you renew you find you have to pay a little more—a premium of $630—for the next five-year period in order to have the same amount of insurance. With this type of policy your insurance coverage remains the same while your premium goes up every five years until, at age fifty-five, it's $2,150.

In addition to this option to renew, you also have an option to convert to whole life. There does come a point in your life—when you are prosperous or for other reasons—such as possible retirement benefits, when it might pay you to convert to straight life. Whether you want to or not, it's important at least to have the option to do so. The big advantage of this option is that you don't have to take a physical examination or complete a medical questionnaire when you convert the policy. So, if you notice a few twinges here and a few creaks there it can remain a secret between you and your inner self.

There is another possibility—decreasing term insurance. If you have this kind of policy, you pay the same premium for the length of the policy—say twenty years—but your coverage decreases as you become more of a risk. Again let's say you're a divorcée with those two adorable children. As they get older and more self-sufficient, there is less need for you to worry about their financial future. So you might start out with a twenty-year $100,000 policy and the same payment, annually, of $425. For the first five years you have the full $100,000 coverage. Then from year five through year eight your coverage declines to $80,000; years nine through twelve, it's down to $60,000. At the end of the twenty years your children are thriving and prosperous and you have no need for this kind of insurance to protect them.

You can buy your term policy from a participating or nonparticipating company. In a participating company you "participate" in the profits of the company through dividends; this can be an advantage as long as the company earns dividends. However, the dividends are not guaranteed, so there is some element of risk involved. In a nonparticipating company the cost of the policy is somewhat less but you don't have the possibility of sharing in the company's profits if it does prosper.

Finding a Good Agent

I'm sure I don't need to convince you at this point that buying life insurance is a complicated subject—and that you don't have the time to learn all the details. What you need is a good agent; the question is how and where to find one.

Is your first thought to find a woman agent? Good—it's only recently that they've been actively recruited in the field and they need all the help they can get. Selling insurance is a very tough competitive business, and agents have to learn to survive—after the initial training period when they may be partially supported by the company—on their commissions. In the beginning many people realize they are going to almost starve to death or live on very, very short rations for a while, and unless they are very determined and very good at the business, many drop out. (Turnover among new agents, in fact, is very often more than 50 per cent.) So, in addition to the fact that insurance companies didn't actively recruit women agents, women, knowing what a tough business this was and being more security-minded than men, weren't anxious to go into the field. Those who have survived or who are now entering are proving themselves—and doing a good job. So if you'd like to give your business to a woman, and you ask for or find a woman agent, you may be doing very well for yourself as well as building her business.

Don't, however, expect more than you would expect from a man, which means that she, like her male counterparts, has a conflict of interest when it comes to giving you advice on what kind of policy you should buy. She's working on commission, right? And she is supposed to "produce" a certain amount of business for her company every month or every quarter, depending on the company. And it just happens that straight life insurance policies pay more in commissions than do term policies, since the commission is a percentage of the premium and the premium on straight life is larger than on term. The difference could be considerable: At one California company, for instance, the commission on a $100,000 straight life policy was $972.60 compared with $129.60 for a twenty-year declining term policy. It is only human for the agent to pull out the straight life policy from her portfolio first, and to explain term policies last.

And it's equally human for you to worry about your own dependents and pocketbook. So you have to make it very clear what kind of policy you are interested in. If the agent tries to put you off, or won't even discuss term insurance, you're talking to the wrong agent. Get another.

Once you've decided what kind of insurance is best for you, there are other things you should know.

1. There is a great difference in the cost of insurance depending on the company you buy it from, and when I say great I mean just that—up to 100 per cent difference. You have to do some comparison shopping. One of the best places to do this is in the report A *Guide to Life Insurance* put out by the Consumers Union, which rates various companies by the cost of their policies (a reprint of a three-part series that appeared in *Consumer Reports* in 1974; available from Consumers Union of United States, Inc., Mount Vernon, N.Y. 10550; price, $1.00). The report is worth reading.

2. How about the financial stability of the company whose insurance you are considering? No use buying a low-cost policy if the company isn't going to be able to pay, or if it's not around when it's time to collect.

3. Is the agent using the "interest-adjusted" method as a shopping guide in showing you comparisons? Don't forget that money has a time value. Money that you invest in life insurance is money that can't be invested elsewhere, and in comparing the costs of a policy this time value has to be added in. Ask your agent to compare policies using the interest-adjusted method. (Arkansas and Wisconsin have passed a law that the agent is obliged to give you these figures on request.)

4. What riders are available and which does she recommend? According to Consumers Union, one good option is the "waiver of premium," which releases you from paying your premium if you become disabled. Another is the "guaranteed insurability," which allows you to pay when you start for being guaranteed the option to buy more insurance later—a good idea for people who only need or can only afford small policies at the moment but might need larger policies later, when they have more dependents, for instance.

Insurance for Couples Who Are Splitting

Couples who are thinking of separating, are in the middle of divorce proceedings, or are already separated have to look carefully at their insurance coverage. And this is particularly true for you, the female side of the about-to-be dissolved partnership, since you are usually the more vulnerable of the partners.

The most important thing to remember is that nothing should be left to chance. If it is, the chances are that you or your children may turn out to be unprotected. Here then are the steps to follow and the vital questions that have to be answered:

1. What insurance policies are there at the moment? And this means not only policies that each of you has taken out on your own initiative and within the family budget but also any policies taken out under the auspices of the federal government (for ex-GIs), employers, unions, professional societies.

2. Whom do the policies protect? The husband, the wife, the children? Former spouses? Children of previous marriages?

3. Who can *change* the policy—either the amount or the beneficiary? *This is a very important question that should be discussed in detail.* If there is the possibility that you and/or your children may need protection against being cut out of a policy, you may want to consider or ask for an irrevocable beneficiary designation—in other words a beneficiary is decided on and there is no changing of minds. However, there are legal and administrative complications when this is done, since minor children can't receive insurance proceeds without having a guardian. Obviously this has to be carefully thought out and planned with the help of a lawyer.

4. Who can borrow against the cash value of the policy if it's a straight life policy?

5. Who is responsible for paying the premium? If your ex-spouse is responsible, the policy might lapse, either accidentally or purposefully, and you wouldn't know about it.

There are other questions of course; these five should serve to alert you to think about these things and to discuss them with your lawyer. The question you have to answer is whether your income or the support of your children is dependent in whole or in part on someone else being alive and healthy. If your answer is yes, you've got to discuss insurance policies.

One last word. When you're young it's almost inconceivable that anything could happen to you. Other people might get hit by cars, be in plane crashes, but *not you*. It's a wonderful way to feel—and the odds are in your favor. But why not increase the odds by checking your insurance coverage? You have no good reason to put off this job.

And now, with that taken care of, let's look at a subject where the odds are less in your favor—your chances of getting sick or having some kind of property loss.

CHAPTER 23

How to Have a Healthy Health and Disability Insurance Plan

Do you know what some health insurance companies call women—when no one is listening? "Clunkers," "losers," and "bad risks." Why? Because we use health care services more than men, go to the doctor more often, have more surgery, and—nuisance of nuisances!—bear children.

This is bad? Who among us doesn't know a man who should see a doctor for some ailment that needs medical treatment, but doesn't go until the pain is so severe he has to—at which point it takes him longer to recover.

Who doesn't know a mother who smiles wanly when the doctor says she has the flu and has to go to bed. She doesn't bother to ask—because she knows he has no answer—who is supposed to care for the children, who also have the flu. Who will take temperatures, give medicine, read stories, and play games to keep the feverish children quiet? Admittedly, when everyone is better, she does go see the doctor again—because by now she is so weak she can barely drag herself around.

As for having babies—even the insurance companies haven't come up with an answer to that yet.

Since the insurance industry sometimes calls us clunkers, I'm going to indulge in a bit of name-calling myself and call the insurance industry clunkers, losers, and bad risks. My *Dictionary of American Slang* defines a "clunker" as a "dilapidated, worn out car, bus, or other machine," and that might be an accurate description of the insurance industry's approach to the problems of insuring women.

As a verb "clunk" has a different meaning—"to hit or strike, especially on the head," and that's what some feminist and civil liberties groups and some government regulatory agencies have been doing to the insurance industry. As a result of law suits, unfavorable publicity, and investigations by government civil rights commissions, the industry has made changes. One leader in the field has been New York State, where disability insurance, at least, is nondiscriminatory except in the case of maternity benefits. And as we go to press a suit is pending before the U. S. Supreme Court that should settle whether or not women are discriminated against when they cannot get sick leave and disability pay while away from work because of pregnancy and childbirth.

(My friend Maureen used to say she was sometimes sorry she gave up smoking, after seeing what happens to the elderly in our society. But she didn't really mean it—all of us want to stay healthy and live long enough to be able to complain about the folly of the younger generation, one of the pleasures of getting old.)

Health insurance and its sister, disability insurance, need some special attention from us because our health problems are somewhat different from men's. First, the good news. Yes, we do live longer, on the average seven years longer, though there are no conclusive facts yet to say positively whether it's biological or environmental—whether nature just made us inherently stronger because we are the childbearers, or whether modern civilization has subjected us to less strain than men and our longer lives show it. Once we go on from this initial bonus, however, we run into problems.

Now the bad news. We are subject to "women's ailments," i.e. those illnesses that are a result of the fact that we get pregnant, carry a child, and give birth. Or, sometimes, we get pregnant and have a miscarriage or decide to get an abortion. Therefore, we have to be more concerned about health insurance and the need to pay for hospital bills. Here are some other aspects of our need for insurance:

1. Because we stay home and take care of children, we are very often cut off from the best way (in terms of cost, and often in terms of benefits as well) to buy insurance, namely a group plan.

2. Even when we can share in these benefits because we are members by proxy, i.e. because our husbands are in a group plan, this link can be broken by divorce or death—and then we either find we are not covered at all or have to settle for individual insurance that is more expensive and offers fewer benefits.

3. To add insult to injury, if we do have to get health or disability insurance on our own after a divorce or death, it's usually when we are older and more of a risk and therefore we have to pay more. In addition, as latecomers to the job market, we may find jobs only in less well established companies, which either have no health insurance plan or a plan which is not as good as those offered in better-established, more prosperous companies.

4. We are often part of the health insurance—though not on a formal basis. When someone gets sick—husband, children, relatives—we are the nurses. And this leads to a very topsy-turvy situation. Though we are around

to take care of the others, who is around to take care of us? (It's get out of bed, go make some tea and toast, wipe off the counter while waiting for the toast to pop and the water to boil—and then crawl back into bed again to be a patient.) Wouldn't you think that since we are the nurturers, we should be insured, perhaps even more than men, against disability—and should get even more benefits? But this is not the case at all—at least not as we go to press.

So, while we're all still healthy, let's take a look at the several tiers of health and disability insurance policies so we at least know what kind of coverage we should have.

The Tiers of Health Insurance

Health insurance can be thought of as a three-tier arrangement. The first tier is *basic medical,* which takes care of an initial hospitalization, surgery, and assorted services that might be needed. Usually this kind of policy puts some limit on the length of time covered and pays a specified amount for room and board and for the services required because of the hospitalization, such as X rays, laboratory tests, and drugs. If surgery is called for, there is usually a ceiling on the surgeon's fee. Once you go beyond what is specified in the policy, such as requiring special tests not in the policy, or using a surgeon whose fee is above that allowed, you must make up the difference out of your own pocket. Notice that these are costs associated with your stay in the hospital; most basic medical policies don't cover you once you are out of the hospital though you may still need some visits from the doctor, or even some rest and recuperation in a convalescent home.

The second tier is *major medical* insurance, designed to supplement your basic plan by covering more of your costs when you are out of the hospital or when you have used up your basic coverage. It may cover the cost of specialists, private nurses, long-range convalescence. Major medical usually will specify a deductible amount which must come out of your pocket before the benefits start. Frequently, major medical policies also have a copayment clause, meaning the insurance company pays 75 to 80 per cent of the expenses remaining after you pay the deductible. Some policies limit benefits for certain expenses, such as the cost of the hospital room or surgery. These two tiers are often combined into one policy which may then be called *comprehensive major medical.*

The third tier is coverage for the catastrophic illness that can absolutely bankrupt an individual or a family, such as cancer, severe and prolonged mental illness, open-heart surgery.

Obviously the best kind of health insurance policy would cover all three of these possibilities at a price we could afford. And just as obviously, considering the high cost of medical care and insurance policies, most of us aren't going to get this. And so we have to settle for what we can get for what we can pay—and this depends partly on our situation, partly on how wisely we spend our health insurance dollar, and partly on how knowledgeable we are about what we already have.

Probably the best kind of health insurance is membership in a prepaid group practice program through your employer. If you are a member of such a group, particularly a well-run group, you may have access to a whole system of health care, from regular checkups to the finest surgery. If you live or work where this kind of care is available you're lucky—but it's available to only about 20 or 25 per cent of us.

The next best thing is to be a member of a group plan which offers a comprehensive policy. Typically membership in such a group will get you greater coverage at less cost than the insurance you could buy on your own. Furthermore, group insurance plans, whether Blue Cross and Blue Shield or from a commercial insurance company, usually spend about 90 per cent or more of the premiums they receive on benefits to their subscribers, the people who paid the premiums, so they are at least getting back what they put in if they do get sick.

Buying Individual Insurance

If you are not a member of a group, you may have no alternative but to buy individual health insurance, either from Blue Cross/Blue Shield or a commercial firm. Chances are you won't do as well as if you were a member of a group, but at least you won't be without any coverage at all. If you find that you are not eligible to be a subscriber to a group plan, here, *briefly*, are some of the things to look for in an individual policy:

1. *How can it be renewed?* The best provision is "guaranteed renewability" for the rest of your life or until you reach sixty-five, as long as you pay the premium and don't get involved in fraudulent claims against the company. The *least* desirable provision is "optionally renewable," which means that a company can drop any policyholder it wants to, at any time and for any reason. Note, however, that guaranteed renewability doesn't mean guaranteed at the same cost; the company can raise its premium. It cannot, however, raise the premium for you alone—it must be a raise for a whole class of subscribers, perhaps everyone in a given age group or everyone in a certain state with the same policy.

2. *What is the maximum coverage?* The larger the maximum paid by the insurer, the better, but that's not the only criterion. Check to see on what basis the maximum is figured. Is it "per cause," i.e. per separate illness? This

can be a great advantage in an unlucky year with several serious illnesses. A per cause coverage, even though the maximum paid is only $20,000, could be better than a $40,000 lifetime maximum. Check also to see if the maximum is for the whole family or for each member separately.

3. *What is excluded?* Watch out in particular for exclusions for treatment in a mental hospital, for treatment for alcoholism, for treatment in a hospital for drug addiction, for *care* (not just rest) at home while convalescing if it's prescribed by a physician.

4. *What are the maternity benefits* and/or exclusions? Are maternity benefits excluded entirely? You may find that you have to buy a separate policy to cover these. This isn't the real hassle, because normal maternity costs can be budgeted for. *The real question and the risk comes with complications as a result of maternity and/or childbirth.* Read the fine print on this very, very carefully.

5. *What are the deductibles?* Most insurance policies don't start to pay until there's a deduction of a given minimum that *you* have to pay. It works something like this. You get pneumonia (you should have listened to your Aunt Tillie when she told you to stop working so hard and start getting more sleep), and you have a policy with a $100 deductible. You are so sick you have to be hospitalized. (Aunt Tillie comes to visit you, and when she unwraps those gorgeous red carnations, you forgive her for saying "I told you so" ten times.) You run up a hospital bill of $1,000. You pay the first $100 and your insurance policy pays the other $900. When you are checking a policy, you also want to know if the deductible is for *each* illness or if it's on a calendar year basis, allowing for only one deductible in that year, charged against all the bills. Does the company pay all the cost above the deductible or a given percentage, and if so, what percentage? As you can see, the clauses are very tricky and have to be checked very carefully.

6. *When does the coverage start?* This is particularly important when considering a family policy, which includes insuring the children. It's quite common for a policy to begin covering infants only after they are fourteen days old; yet it's within this crucial fourteen-day period that congenital birth defects often show themselves. A policy with this exclusion means that parents of children with birth defects from one cause or another will have to bear the entire burden themselves forever.

7. *Is the company licensed to do business in your state?* If it's not, and you have any trouble with a claim, your state insurance department may not be able to help you. If you have any doubts about the company's stability (and therefore its ability to pay your claims), write to your state insurance department. You could also ask them if they've had any complaints against the company.

Discrimination Against Women

Now that I've gone over the highlights of individual policies let's backtrack a bit and talk about group policies. Though everyone in a group policy is theoretically equal, some are more equal than others—at least at this writing. And guess who is discriminated against? You win the brass ring—it's women, and the question of maternity benefits.

If you're covered by a group plan through your husband and you get pregnant, you may find that the plan will pay for up to ten days of hospital care and $1,000 for medical costs. But if you're covered through your own employment you may be covered only for five days in the hospital and a maximum of $300 in cash benefits. Or even worse, you may find that you are not covered at all, while the wives of your male colleagues are. Some group plans don't provide maternity benefits for women employees unless there are more than ten in the group.

You may find, if you and your husband decide not to have children, that your group plan will pay for a vasectomy for your husband but not for a sterilization operation for you.

What should be done? The first thing, of course, is to find out the exact situation. Check with your personnel department or whoever in your company is knowledgeable about or responsible for the plan. This question of who gets maternity benefits is something that never used to be questioned—but those days have gone. If no one person is responsible, you and your colleagues will have to do the checking yourselves. A dreary task, but very important. There are few things more calculated to put you to sleep than the terms of an insurance policy, but if a few of you do it at lunch time or over a drink after work, at least you'll help each other stay awake—and it is important.

If you work in a place that has a union (whether it's called that, or an association or society of, or whatever), someone in your union should know about this already or should make it his/her business to find out. If there is discrimination, it should go on the agenda of the next meeting and should become one of the items to be negotiated when your next contract comes up.

If you are an executive in the personnel department or anywhere in your company, for that matter, this is something that *you* should have discussed at the executive level—and changed. (Interestingly enough, a bill introduced in the New York state senate, requiring insurance payments for a minimum of four days of in-hospital care for every pregnancy-related hospital admission was supported by both pro- and antiabortion women's groups. This gives you some idea of the broad backing that *prowomen* legislation has—a heartening thought!)

What if you would like to take advantage of the larger health benefits and smaller payments that group insurance offers—but you are not working outside of your home, or you are a free-lance writer or artist or run a one-woman business? Think of some of the other groups that you belong to that might be eligible for a group plan. Are you a member of a political club? A religious group? A professional society? A social club? It may be possible to form your own group and take advantage of the savings. (To find the name of your local Blue Cross/Blue Shield system and its requirements, check the directory of a major city in your area. If it's not listed, try your local hospital. They are probably affiliated and will have the phone number and address.)

If you work for a small company that can't afford a group health plan, it may still be possible to get a group plan, even if you have to pay for the coverage yourself. Of course it's better if the company pays—but if that's not possible, better to have the coverage than go without it, even if you have to take it out of your own pocket. Console yourself somewhat with the thought that the premiums are tax-deductible. As a woman, perhaps coming into the labor market later than a man, it's more likely that you will be working for a smaller, less well-financed company and this may be your only way to get the coverage you need.

It's also possible that, as a divorcée, you've lost not only your husband but also your health insurance. If you are in the process of separating from your spouse, check whether or how you and/or your children are protected by health insurance. It's very important that you get this question settled, including not only immediate coverage but also future payments, so that the coverage doesn't lapse through carelessness, malice, or new dependents.

Now let's turn to a related subject—disability insurance. Here is where women's groups have been complaining, and with good cause, because it's one area of insurance that has grossly discriminated against women in the past and still does, as of this writing. But before we get into our very legitimate complaints about disability insurance policies—and what we should do about them—let's review what disability insurance is and what makes a good disability insurance policy.

Problems of Disability Insurance

Consider one of my former students, Margo R., married for the second time (this time very happily), and responsible for a household and five children from her own and her husband's previous marriages. In addition, she is the editor of several publications put out by a major museum. Margo skis, plays tennis, and faces the hazards of living with teen-agers who leave tennis rackets where they fall out of closets on unsuspecting heads, fifth-graders who leave roller skates in the hallway, and a dog who likes to tear through the house barking furiously every time the postman comes, trusting that everyone will get out of her way—and fast. Did any of this ever bother Margo? Never.

But one day on her way to work she stepped off the curb, felt an excruciating pain, and discovered that she had broken her ankle in a particularly nasty way. She had to be out of work for three months, and then had to hobble around for another month or so on crutches. Since she worked for a nonprofit institution with a low budget, she had no company-paid-disability, and the museum could only pay her salary for two weeks. After that it was dip into the bank account, already too low, until she was able to go back to work. How she wished, during those moments, that she had had disability insurance to compensate for her lost income.

That's what disability insurance is—insurance against the time when sickness or injuries take you off the job and cut off your income, very often at a time when in addition to your ordinary bills you're getting extra ones from doctors, X-ray specialists, practical nurses, etc. Its purpose is protection against comparatively short-term injuries like Margo's plus much more serious and longer-term disabilities: serious automobile accidents, for instance, or such crippling diseases as multiple sclerosis, acute heart ailments making it impossible to work, glaucoma, etc.

Fortunately, only a small percentage of the population suffer permanent disability—a most cheering thought. Most of us don't get into accidents that result in lifetime injuries or don't become victims of the diseases that result in permanent incapacitation. Less fortunately, the figures for short-term disabilities are higher. These are the accidents and illnesses that keep people out of work for long periods of time, and affect not only the physical health of the person stricken but also her/his financial health, and the well-being of families involved.

So disability insurance is needed for financial protection against the consequences of long-run illnesses. And here are the features of a really good disability insurance policy. Not all of these features are affordable—but you should at least *know* what's best, and try to get as close to it as possible.

1. *Noncancelable*, i.e. guaranteed to be renewable at least to age sixty-five at a guaranteed premium rate. In other words, the company agrees not only to continue renewing your policy but also to renew it at the same rate. Such guarantees are *your* hedge against rising rates, and you pay for this privilege by paying a higher rate to start—so much higher in some instances that this kind of policy is known as the "Cadillac" of the disability field.

2. *Guaranteed renewable*, i.e. the company guarantees to renew, but won't guarantee at what rate and keeps the right to raise premiums. However in a

good guaranteed-renewable contract you cannot be singled out as individual and required to pay a higher premium—the rate has to be applied to large groups of individuals. Since the company isn't offering so many guarantees, they can't ask you to pay as much, and this kind of policy is cheaper. (We'll talk about comparative prices in a little while.)

3. *A definition of a covered sickness as one that "first manifests itself" while you are covered by the policy.* If a covered sickness is defined as one that "commences" or "is contracted" *after* the policy is bought, the company has the possibility of rejecting a claim on the grounds that the illness or disease existed *before* the policy was bought but had not been diagnosed.

4. *No requirement that you be homebound in order to collect.* A good policy should cover you even if you are convalescing and able to take up some of your previous chores, or even to work part time but not necessarily at your previous job.

5. *A somewhat flexible definition of disability.* Unless the definition allows for some flexibility on the kind of work you can do after the disability, and the kind of treatment you get, you could find yourself with no payments or limited payments. Consider a clause in a policy that says, "Total disability during the first *twenty-four months* means that the covered person, by reason of injury or sickness, is under the regular care and attendance of a physician and is *completely* unable to perform the duties of the full-time occupation in which he has regularly and actively engaged." That twenty-four months and the word *completely* could be open to definition by the insurance company that would either cut you off from payments altogether or limit the time in which you would be covered.

Suppose, for instance, you were an organist and you earned money playing during church services and performing at weddings, as well as by teaching a few private pupils. You injured your hands. Your doctor prescribed occupational therapy during your recovery, and as you got better you were able to teach but could no longer perform. Under the above definition you might not be able to collect, on the grounds that you were still able to carry out part of your previous occupation.

Or suppose you could never play again. Some health industry insurance specialists feel that twenty-four months is an unfair restriction—someone who has become incapacitated should be able to collect at least until age sixty-five, not just for a two-year period.

Insurance companies defend phrases such as these by saying that they don't invoke these words to deny claims, or that such phrases prevent people from never trying to return to their jobs. This is the insurance companies' problem, not yours. You have to watch out for any interpretation or any clauses that could result in less coverage for you.

Knowing some of the key features of a good disability policy (I have outlined the basics but there is more to learn) is just the start of your shopping for this kind of insurance. You also have to know some of the special features of a disability policy so you can tailor it to suit your needs. And these needs should be considered also in terms of what kind of coverage you now have, so you don't duplicate.

Remember that if you are injured on your job or get an illness that is related to your work, you would probably be entitled to some kind of benefit from workmen's compensation. Note that "probably"—eight out of ten workers are covered, but there are exceptions. Not all occupations are covered; not all states make it compulsory for employers to contribute to a worker's compensation fund; and some states exempt very small firms from making a contribution to the fund, which means their employees aren't covered.

Furthermore, there is a wide disparity in the benefits paid. To cite just one example, a U. S. Chamber of Commerce report said that loss of a fourth finger in Connecticut is "worth" $3,360, while the same injury would bring compensation of only $300 in Wyoming. And when the National Commission on State Workmen's Compensation Laws looked at these laws, they discovered that in more than half the states maximum weekly benefits for total temporary disability didn't even match the national poverty income level for a nonfarm family of four, and maximum weekly benefits for permanent total disability in most states were inadequate.

(And of course none of this applies if you are disabled or get ill while *not* on the job.)

You also have another possible source of disability income—Social Security payments. If you can offer medical proof that you won't be able to do any "substantial gainful" work *for a year*, as the result of an illness or a disability, you can collect a Social Security check after five months away from work. Disability insurance should fill in or close up the gaps from these two possible sources of income—workmen's compensation and Social Security—and they can be very very big gaps. So when you think about disability insurance, you want to plan it to mesh with other possibilities of coverage.

Now let's look at the kind of coverage you might get during the first year of the disability, starting with a waiting period, also known as the "elimination" period. This period can vary from as little as one week to as much as three months. (The longer the waiting period the less expensive the policy.) For the remainder of the first year most insurance companies usually set a ceiling of about 50 to 60 per cent of pretax earnings as the maximum amount they will give you. (They worry that you'll have so much fun sitting around the house in a cast with your crutches that you may never want to go back to work if they give you too much.) After this period, coverage is cut to allow

for payments from Social Security, if you are still disabled and meet the eligi-
bility requirements of Social Security.

Questions to Ask an Insurance Agent

O.K.—now you have some idea of where you stand, and you want to know
what questions you should ask the insurance agent who comes around to sell
you a policy. By now you know that the whole field is totally confusing—a be-
wildering variety of policies, premiums, benefits, things to be wary of—that's
the name of the health insurance game. And you *have* to shop around, because if you do you can save money, quite a bit of money, and get a better
policy. So try out these questions on your agent.

1. *If I can't do my regular job, how long will the policy pay?* The range
can be anywhere from two years to until age sixty-five.

2. *If I can go back to some kind of work, will the policy continue to pay?*
Notice that phrase "*some* kind of work"; that's very, very, *very* important.
Some policies will pay you the full benefit as long as you're not working at
your own occupation; some will pay only 50 per cent. Some have a sort of
sliding scale (downward, naturally) depending on how much you earn at a
different occupation. *Check on it.*

3. *Will the payments (also known as income benefits) always be paid in full
if I'm totally disabled?* If not, under what conditions will they be cut? Now,
sex discrimination rears its ugly head. If you were a man, your benefits might
be reduced if you were getting a pension, or if your total insurance benefits
after two years were more than your previous income. Or, you might find
that there were no conditions at all—you would just continue to get your full
benefits. But for a woman the picture is quite and unfairly different.

Consider the case of my friends Ethel and Bob C., who run a series of
workshops from their home: assertiveness training, employment counseling,
typing and secretarial services. If they are both out on their beautiful lawn
and are seriously injured—say a truck delivering office supplies runs into
them, disabling both—Bob could collect full disability payments. Ethel could
collect only half under some policies or not more than $400 a month under
others. At this writing, the only exception to this discriminatory policy is the
state of New York, whose insurance department, after a successful suit
brought by the New York Civil Liberties Union, forbids this kind of sex discrimination.

4. *What special benefits does this policy offer?* Again a wide range. Some
policies have none, some can be converted to a lifetime hospital insurance for
some given period, some will pay income for life if you're disabled before you
are forty-five. And so on. Check on it.

5. *What causes of disability are not covered?* For men, wartime injuries

and attempts at suicide are the most common exclusions. For women, in some policies, nonoccupational disabilities resulting from pregnancies—for instance a pregnancy outside the womb, or a miscarriage—are not covered.

6. *If I keep on working after sixty-five can I continue to renew my policy, and if so, for how long?* The age range here is usually to age seventy-two, but there is often a difference in whether the policy will pay for one or two years after that age, plus other differences.

Once you've got these things settled with your agent and are sure that she/he will recommend the policy that has the most favorable features for the least possible cost, you will naturally want to know what this cost will be. And here is where she is going to look very embarrassed and you are going to get very angry. Furious. Because, as of this writing, even in New York State, where discriminatory features of disability insurance coverage have been forbidden, women are still charged more than men for the same kind of insurance. And outside of New York the insult is double: fewer benefits *and* higher rates. And these are not nickel, dime, and quarter differences we're talking about. Nor even $10 or $25 differences—not that that would be acceptable. No, we're talking about major sums here—differences from about one hundred to several hundred dollars. And not even for identical policies, but for policies that may be inferior in many instances. And so far, insurance companies that offer these policies haven't come up with any conclusive proof that there are sound actuarial reasons that justify this kind of discrimination.

What's to be done about it? First you have to protect yourself by getting the best for the least. Then you have to be sure the agent knows that you find this discrimination obnoxious, to say the least, so she can report this to her company. Then you have to use your womanpower—in fact we all have to—to get the situation changed.

Complain where it will have some effect: To your employers if they are paying all or part of your disability coverage; they have a stake in this too, since they are getting less for their money than they should. To your professional society, union, or club if you've gotten a group policy that way. To government agencies—insurance departments and human rights commissions—to people who have influence on these commissions, to Congressmen, and to state representatives. To the insurance companies themselves. It's your "insurance" that you get the equal treatment you pay for and deserve. And it's our insurance, as women and also as contributing members of families and of the work force and just as people in general that we will continue to push, push, push for what should already be ours.

CHAPTER 24

Time Is Money

You may not have known for sure, though you've suspected it for a long time. You are surrounded by sly and cunning enemies. They are thieves who try, and very often succeed, in stealing from you your most precious possession: time. The one thing you can never replace, the one thing that, when gone, can never be regained. The one thing that makes other things possible —or impossible.

Women don't value their own time enough, don't put a high enough price on it, and don't insist that others pay that price if they want the time. Every minute wasted, whether you waste it yourself or allow others to waste it, is an opporunity lost—to acquire a skill, earn money, think, plan, enjoy some well-deserved leisure.

And guess who is sometimes the worst offender? You. Because unless you value your time, unless you consciously learn to control it and squeeze the most out of every minute—and I do mean minute—you are going to let a big chunk of your life go by without doing the things you want to do. You may regret it later, when your loss is irretrievable.

How do you start? By being aware of the many ways in which people steal your time, so you can put a stop to it. Some of these people are very aware of what they're doing. They carefully conserve their time by imposing on yours, and they're not bashful about it. Often it is on the advice of professional time-saving experts, the consultants who tell businessmen to "check all the tasks you perform during the working hours and see how many you can delegate—to your *wife*, office personnel, etc. . . ." Sometimes it's just the way the system has always worked: Women are supposed to adjust their schedules to the convenience of banks, utility companies, repairmen, shopkeepers, doctors, dentists, schools. Sometimes it's husbands or children who have gotten into the habit of having that superb tour-guide-concierge-personal-shopper-knowledgeable-all-around-good-kid relieve them of life's nitty-gritty little chores. (How I remember the worried mothers who came into the bookstore where I worked, with their long lists of required reading from the local high schools and colleges.)

One reason women hesitate to undertake projects, go to school, assume responsible jobs, or put in the hours required for promotion to executive-level positions is their recognition of the many demands on their time. They are afraid they can't manage without stretching their energies to the breaking point—and they may very well be right. Even in the most enlightened household women have more domestic responsibilities than men and put in longer work weeks. One study showed that the most helpful husband was the high school graduate married to another high school graduate, with both of them working full time. He "gave" her 4.6 hours per week. As for many others—according to Dr. Alice Rossi, a Goucher College sociologist well known for her work on marriage and the family—"out of the generosity of his heart he will pick up his socks."

Nor is it just a question of time; there is also the question of responsibility, another drain on your energy. If you have to worry about doing the food shopping, getting the kids to the dentist, buying a present for Aunt Rose, throwing a load of clothes in the washer while dinner is cooking, that's enough to keep all your brain cells sending out messages. Do this, remember that, make a record of this, don't forget that. Is it any wonder you are often just plain very very very tired?

Men take it for granted that they will have big uninterrupted blocks of time, whether they want to play power politics or baseball, build condominiums or sand castles. Women, for far too long, have settled for bits and pieces of time, fitted in and around other people's priorities.

I'm not going to go into the man versus woman thing at this point. It's been covered (both truly and falsely in my opinion) in many, perhaps too many, elsewheres. And it is a troublesome problem because these are confused and troubled times. I take it for granted that you are a mature adult capable of settling this question in your own fashion with another mature adult. Instead I want to offer some very practical suggestions on what you can do to find more time in your life.

Let's start where you start your day, that is, in your household itself. And let's say you are going back to work, or switching from a part-time to a full-time job, or getting a degree, or just looking for time to do something you've been postponing and postponing until you think you'll never get to it.

Before you do anything, step outside yourself for a minute and take a fresh look at the way you run your household (and I can't emphasize that "before" enough). What new time-saving methods can you introduce? What will save you the minutes that will add up to hours of time over the span of a week, and enable you to conserve your energy—energy you can then expend on things that are more important, more lucrative, more creative, or any combination thereof.

Recognize that time is limited, work is not, and you are going to have to set priorities. You cannot have new goals and stay with the same old life pattern. Something has got to go. One mistake women make when they go back to work is to try—though in their guts they know better—to do everything just as before: the same entertaining, the same gourmet meals, the same community obligations, the same errand-girl circuit. It usually takes at least one complete collapse from sheer exhaustion or one serious bout with the flu or pneumonia before women admit they are indeed mortal and can't do the work of two in the time allotted to one.

Spare yourself—why should you have to repeat the common mistake? If you have any doubts, keep a record one week, before you start your project, as to where your time goes. How many hours spent making those elegant sauces? Running to the hardware store to pick up odd electrical supplies for the home crafts*man?* Making calls for the annual community fund-raising drive? The totals will astonish you. I'm not suggesting that you give up all these pursuits, and you don't have to turn into a workaholic or a misanthrope. You just have to reassign your priorities.

Recognize also that the world is divided into A types and B types. A's are full of zip in the morning but are completely unzipped by the end of the day. They need their rest. B's drag themselves around until about midmorning, when they come alive. They can also be disgustingly cheerful and ready to hang pictures or have deep political discussions at 11:00 P.M., when A is yawning grumpily and saying, "If I don't go to bed this minute I'm going to fall asleep right here in the middle of the rug." (A's always seem to marry B's, which I used to think was a demonic plot but which I've since realized is actually Providence's way of insuring that someone is up to get the children off to school.)

If you are an A, you are better off getting up a half hour early to prepare something for the freezer for one of your not-too-frequent, as-little-work-as-possible dinner parties. If you're a B, you can stay up late and do it, because you need that extra sleep in the morning. And never mind how your boss or your next-door neighbor or your best friend runs her life—you have to follow your own internal rhythms.

Time Saving Devices

Let me list some of the possibilities for saving time and effort; pick and choose those that most nearly conform to your life style and priorities.

1. *Serving and clearing after meals:* How many trays do you own? Can you

and everyone in your household get his hands on a tray easily, quickly, and after a while automatically, for setting the table, bringing and clearing food? (Trays fit into odd spaces between refrigerator and cabinets, standing up on counters, anywhere you have a few deep but wasted inches.) At the moment I'm thinking of three of my best friends, each with several children, a full-time job or study program, a large household, and other responsibilities as faculty wives, fund raisers, community activists—the whole bit. Yet I have sat in their dining rooms or lent a hand at their parties, and watched them make twenty trips into the kitchen when one good-size tray would have done the job in two trips. Restaurants use trays because they can't afford to be inefficient. Neither can you. (After all, you don't even get a tip when you clear the table.)

2. *How about hot foods?* Do you keep jumping up to get more hot cups of coffee or tea, or have you invested in a nice big thermos bottle so you can sit at the table and have your second cup? You can be casual and buy a bright-colored inexpensive one, or you can be elegant and buy a really handsome steel, chrome, or brass one. (But find out if it has to be polished—if so, forget it!) These can be bought in the housewares department of department stores, in fancy housewares shops, or even from restaurant supply houses. They're not cheap—$35 and up, depending on how elegant you want to be—but they last almost indefinitely and pay for themselves in energy saved—on your electric or gas bills and your poor feet.

Nor are beverages the only thing to keep hot at the table. Where is the hot tray your Aunt Matilda gave you as a housewarming present? Why save it for company? Why not use it every night to keep your main dish warm so you don't have to get up? If it's not convenient to keep it plugged in on the table, how about candle power? A candle warmer uses no vital energy, is cheap, and will save steps.

3. *Easy access:* Have you ever thought of how much time you spend looking for things because they're in out-of-the-way corners in your closets? Maybe you should invest in more shelf dividers or those handy revolving trays that mean you don't have to take out the salt, pepper, and paprika every time you need the bay leaves or the tarragon. Can you hang more kitchen tools right on the wall—another restaurant trick—which not only makes them more accessible but also gives you more space inside for less-used things. Your kitchen is your workroom, your shop. Men invest in good power tools because they understand the importance of the right tool to get the job done efficiently. So should you.

I also have a few tricks for using time that would otherwise be wasted staring at the patterns in the wall paper, wondering if I should throw away that 1965 almanac, or how I would look as a blonde.

I never have enough time to read all the magazines in my field, consumer economics; so I clip the articles I particularly want to read, tuck them in my pocketbook, and read them while waiting for subways, buses, late friends, shoe salesmen who have to go into the lower depths to find my size. Not only a great time-saver—also a great temper-saver.

If I have lots of telephone calls to make, especially calls that involve hanging on the line wondering if they've dropped dead at the other end, I line up something to do with my hands while the phone—thanks to a handy little gadget—rests peacefully on my shoulder. I can polish my nails, sort bills, file odds and ends, or reorganize my pocketbook for the umpteenth time.

Hems to let down? Try keeping a sewing kit in the kitchen and just one thing that has to be lengthened. (More than one is too disheartening.) Put in a few stitches while you're waiting for the coffee to drip through the filter or the water to boil. Eventually the hem gets done.

Hard to find the time to address Christmas cards, party invitations, parent-teacher meeting notices? Pack a little kit of clipboard, pen, stamps, addresses, whatever else you need, and put it in the car when you're going some place fairly distant. Let someone else do the driving and get the nuisance job done.

Some Do Not's

So much for some of the things you can do to make your work easier. If you always have this approach, you will think of more. Now, how about some things you shouldn't do. A simple question: Do you really have to be so clean? So formal? List all the things you think you *must* do and see if they are really musts. Many working mothers have found that the sky didn't open up and a hundred thunderbolts didn't strike their roofs if they didn't change the sheets every week but only the pillow cases, if they often used paper plates for meals (not so messy if you use straw plate-holders and not so expensive if you count the cost of heating hot water, dish powder, and your time), if they had a few meals requiring absolutely no pot washing (mine is steak broiled in a foil pan, potatoes baked in foil, and canned peas in an ovenproof dish). Always, always, always keep in mind the aim of saving your time and energy.

Firing the Chauffeur

Now let's look at another time-gobbler: delivering the children to their Cub Scout, Brownie, Explorer meeting or their flute, bongo drum, ballet, figure-skating, tennis, hockey class—you name it and today's children seem to be joining it or taking lessons in it. Perhaps one of the silver linings in the dark cloud of the oil embargo and subsequent high oil prices has been the realization that more and better public transportation systems are needed if we aren't going to evolve into a new species with one foot shaped to fit a gas pedal and the other to grip the brake pedal. (I'm surprised that there isn't a woman's lobby devoted to nothing but improving suburban bus routes so children can travel more on their own.)

If you are caught in the web, you are probably already one of the chauffeurs in a car pool. But consider what some other working mothers have done: They've fired the "chauffeurs" and replaced them with one neighbor who is a careful driver and is happy to pick up extra money by delivering a few neighborhood children; with another, retired neighbor who is happy to get in a taxi with a youngster and wait through the ballet lesson; with a teen-ager who takes a boy to his hockey lesson across the city; with a regular suburban taxi driver who is glad to pick up a few fares during the off-hour afternoon lull.

If you have to deliver your preschool child to a child care center before you go to work and it's a real hassle in the morning, look into the possibility of having a regular cab service do the job for you. One of my best friends in Denver, a prominent Denver columnist, almost kissed me long-distance when I suggested this to her, based on my days as a working mother and premature women's libber. She took the precaution of checking the driver with the cab company, not only for his skills (though she had often ridden with him) but also for general character references. Her children are thriving and she no longer arrives at work feeling as if she's done half a day's work already.

Shopping by Phone: Some Tips

The reverse of the time-gobbler is the time-saver, and at this point I am usually tempted, if no one is looking, to kiss my telephone. I have learned that, with a little advance sleuthing plus a little friendly persuasion, I can do very well buying some basics by phone. Here are some of the things I do; perhaps they will give you some ideas.

Assorted underwear: I have a deal with two neighborhood storekeepers. Each will mail to me her specialty (pantyhose in one case and bras in the other, both reasonably priced) if I will call to place the order a few days in advance and mail a check for the exact amount. Macy's will do the same for my favorite panty girdle, with an indirect benefit that they wouldn't appreciate—I don't go wandering through Macy's aisles being tempted by all those goodies put out on aisle tables to make me whip out my charge account card and buy, buy, buy. The same technique can be applied to basics for husband and children, once you know the proper sizes.

Food shopping: Where I live and probably where you live, shopping for food by phone is more expensive than scooting around the supermarket by yourself, if you don't count your time. It's also more satisfactory to do the shopping yourself, since you have more choice and can pick and choose the best. Nevertheless, your time is valuable and there can be many occasions when it's either better or necessary to shop by phone. With a little advance scouting there are ways to minimize the price differential.

Go to the store that takes phone orders and scan the shelves. Note the brands they carry—which are the most expensive and which the least. Note also the canned goods. Do they have all sizes or only large? Check the paper goods—tissues, paper towels, napkins—the soap powders, bleaches, etc. In the meat department check the grade of meat and the cuts: Do they have only the rib chops or do they also have the cheaper shoulder chops? Ground sirloin, or ground chuck? After you have shopped in person once or twice, you can shop by phone, specifying you want X brand of tuna (the cheapest), the shoulder chops, the cheapest oranges for that week, the large bottle of bleach, and so on.

This is my technique when I am pressed with a very tight deadline, or I have unexpected guests. I am not voted the most popular customer of the year—in fact, I am sure that when they hear my voice on the phone they put on their Lord-help-us face and sigh several long sighs. But that's their problem, not mine. I get my money's worth.

Stopping the Time Thieves

Even when you learn to respect the value of your time, other people have to be educated. Doctors and dentists can be the worst offenders. They do it to all their patients, true, but more often to women. There is the attitude that women don't have great demands on their time and don't mind sitting around reading old magazines on uncomfortable couches with forty-watt-bulb reading lamps. You don't have to put up with this if you decide you won't.

When you make the appointment, tell the person setting the time you are very busy and you have to know about how long you will be asked to wait. She may be shocked: No one has ever challenged the appointment system like this. She may even be nasty—there are petty bureaucrats lurking everywhere. She will undoubtedly say that she can't tell you because the doctor can't tell how long he'll have to take with each patient. There is some truth in this—no one can tell precisely—but anyone can tell *generally*, or at least generally enough to allow the office staff to leave at about the same time every day, and to let the doctor keep his appointment with his tennis or golf partner.

Stand firm. Say you too are very busy and you have to have some kind of approximate time or you would like to call before you come so you don't waste too much time. To quote from *Boardroom Reports:* "Doctors tend to give priority to patients who put a premium on their own time. If you have to get back to the office, let the nurse know when you make the appointment." Again you are certainly not going to win any popularity contests, but you are going to save yourself several hours of time—and make doctors and nurses aware that they must make an effort to stagger appointments carefully and realistically.

Take the same firm stand with all the other people who automatically assume you have all day to wait for the furniture they promised to deliver, the repairman they promised to send, the telephone they promised to install. And with the people who say, "You *have* to come in"—to the bank, or the store, or the utility company office—to have this done or to straighten that out. (And when you get there wait until they dig out your file, finish their phone conversation, and straighten their desk before they can start talking.)

I have a variety of answers for this. Sometimes I say I'm too busy but I'll send my husband, which shocks the man at the other end of the line. (It would shock my husband too if he heard it; he never runs errands.) Sometimes I say I have fifteen children, all under the age of five. Sometimes I say I can't come in because I am too busy saving valuable resources: gasoline and me, a productive human being. Sometimes I just ask, "Why?"—which many people find the most baffling response of all.

There is a muffled noise at the other end of the phone, then a few moments of absolute silence, and then some standard answers. "Everybody does," or, "That's the way we've always done it," or, "It's the rule." To which I reply: "I don't," or "That's not the way I've always done it," or, "I'm sorry, I just don't think it's necessary for me to come in; I think this whole matter can be handled over the telephone or by mail. Please let me speak to your supervisor." I usually find that the whole problem *can* be handled by phone or mail or that I can at least be given an approximate time —before 11:00, or morning, or afternoon. Occasionally, when someone has been especially wasteful of my time in delivering something, I take a long time to pay the bill, after stating in a letter that I am purposely delaying as a compensation for my lost time.

Paying for Services

Which brings me to the next point: Since your time is valuable, there are occasions when the best way to use it is to pay for someone else's time. Men who work at full-time jobs wouldn't dream of spending all day Saturday cleaning their apartments or doing the laundry and the ironing. They make a point of getting a day worker and sending the dirty linens to the laundry. (In pre-women's lib days they used to count on free maid service from devoted girl friends, but I do think those days are gone forever.) Too many women, it seems to me, just don't think in these terms—and it's not just the money involved, though that's much more of a factor for them than for men, since they still earn lower salaries. Sometimes there are psychological factors involved:

1. Some women feel they don't "deserve" outside help. After years of thinking of themselves as providers of services, they find it difficult to shift mental gears and think of themselves as receivers of help. They are supposed to do "women's work" of cleaning and scrubbing, even after they've put in a hard day at the office. If this is how you look at the question, take another look. Are you, perhaps, though you can afford to pay for someone to do some of your heavy cleaning, held back by your unconscious guilt feelings—feelings fostered, unwittingly, by other women? Your grandmother, mother, or mother-in-law, for instance, who have told you how hard they worked when they started out (carrying coal in buckets up to the fourth-floor cold-water flat, scrubbing clothes on a washboard—who ever heard of wash-and-wear, Pampers, canned baby food?).

Some things to keep in mind: A study by the University of Michigan's Survey Research Center showed that women still spend about fifty-five hours a week on housework, slightly more than women spent thirty to forty years ago, probably because we have higher standards of cleanliness and nutrition now. Furthermore, unless a woman had some unusual talent or profession, she used to lose status by working, whereas today women are being pressured to look for outside jobs. The profession of wife and mother has been downgraded; many women who are or were quite contented to stay at home now feel they lose status if they don't seek outside careers.

You may also be held back by mixed signals from the women's lib movement concerning the value of housework. On the one hand women are saying that homemaking and the tasks that go with it, child care and housework, aren't sufficiently valued for the skills needed, the time spent, or the work done. On the other hand they are saying homemaking is dull, tedious, routine, demeaning—and they're putting their money where their mouth is by not paying well for household and child care help, and not offering the fringe benefits they are fighting to gain for themselves. If legislation is ever passed setting standards and pay scales for homemaking, we may all regret the low scale we have helped to establish and maintain.

You may have guilt feelings about the fact that people who do housework are generally from minority groups: Blacks, Mexicans (Chicanos), Puerto Ricans, or other Latin Americans. The fact that housework has been demeaned has meant that the people who do it are demeaned, and continuing to hire minorities is considered another way of continuing their inferior position in our society.

Finally (and this may be difficult to acknowledge) you may be dissatisfied with the way your house is organized—but so far the tomorrow when you're going to get organized hasn't dawned. You know that standard joke that shows the harassed-looking woman on the floor scrubbing, and explaining to her husband that she has to tidy up because the maid is coming in the morning and the housewife doesn't want to be thought of as a slob! Like all jokes that get a rueful laugh from us, there is an element of truth in this. You may not only feel that your house isn't well-organized—you may also feel you lack the executive ability to tell someone how to proceed.

I don't know which of these problems is yours, if any, but they are common enough among women to make me think some guidelines are in order:

Some aspects of almost any job are boring and monotonous. Doctors get to the point where they can scarcely stand to look at another sore throat; executives complain they have to sit through innumerable boring meetings; lawyers spend days poring through dull law books or listening to boring testimony. Typing can be monotonous, filing can be tedious, and routine laboratory testing can be just that—routine. There is no need to apologize for asking someone to do routine work—we all have to do it sometimes.

Guilt feelings do you no good and can be harmful to others, particularly if the others are unemployed and need and want work. No honest work is demeaning, and if you have work that needs doing and you pay a fair wage to someone for doing it, you have absolutely no reason to feel guilty. (If you *must* feel guilty about something, feel guilty about committing that common sin of working wives and mothers—working too hard, doing too much, running yourself ragged trying to be all things to all people.)

If you're dissatisfied with the way your house is organized, accept the fact that you may never get the time to clean every closet, rearrange every shelf, or whatever else you think needs doing. And you might not be able to buy those new cabinets you need right away, or that larger refrigerator. But you have to live in the meantime. Consider reorganizing one closet at a time, one shelf, even one drawer. In the meantime hire some person or some service to give you a hand. If you think you can't delegate work, give it a try—it's time you learned. Your own home, your own turf, where you know the problems, is a fine place to develop your latent executive talent and *learn* how to delegate.

Be a List-maker

One thing you can't delegate, however, is the need to keep track of all the things you have to do. And one way to do this is to have *lists*. Notice that plural; you need not one but several if you're going to make life as easy as possible. And that's what getting organized means: less work, less tension, not more. Without lists you always have that nagging feeling that there's something you should be doing, or buying or getting, and you're probably right. Without lists you have to stop cooking and run out to buy a loaf of bread. Without lists you forget to enter checks, and your bank balance gets overdrawn. Without lists you are stuck at the airport with all the stores closed, no tissues, and a terrible runny-nose head cold. Et cetera, et cetera, et cetera. So that life is a continuous nerve-racking game of steppingstones across the creek of minor crises, with the inevitable plunge into near-catastrophe now and then. It's just too hard to live that way.

The way around this is to have a few little tablets and pencils in various places around your house, so that when you get ideas or remember things, you jot them down—and your memory is never more than a notepad away. A good-size notepad hanging on the kitchen wall is a must, for "we need," and everyone in the family has to use it when consuming the last bottle of Coca-Cola or using the last package of soap powder. I keep a notepad in the bathroom, since there is something about staring at myself in the mirror, first thing in the morning, that makes me thoughtful and reminds me of all the things I should do as soon as that second cup of coffee begins to course through my veins. And I have a notepad next to my bed since, while I'm resolving the what-will-the-weather-be-and-therefore-what-should-I-wear question, I always seem to remember something I hadn't thought of while in the bathroom.

My most important list is in the little red book I carry around in my pocketbook. In it I transfer the other "to do" and "to buy" lists, jot down the checks I write that have to be entered in my checkbook, and add new things that have to be done when I get home. As you have realized by now, I am a compulsive list-maker (I'm overcompensating for a scatterbrained adolescence), and you certainly shouldn't be so compulsive. But lists are recommended to highly paid executives, by equally highly paid time-consultants, as a method for achieving an uncluttered mind that can then be devoted to thinking more creatively.

Other Women's Time

One almost last word. As we learn to appreciate our own time and to have others respect it, let's not forget to value the time of other women. Sisterhood is fine and helping each other is fine (though Oscar Wilde said, "Sister is what women call each other after they've called each other lots of other names"). But some women seem to think that a woman performing a service for another woman should charge a lower price, just because both are members of the same sex. Unfair, really. If they give their time as lawyers, doctors, secretaries, accountants, typists, whatever, they deserve to get a fair day's pay or a fair fee for the job done. It is, after all, one of the things that women's lib is all about.

The Answer to Freud

What do women want? Freud asked this question, either peevishly or plaintively, depending on whose interpretation you're reading, several decades ago. The answer is simple. We want time. Money is time, because without money we are so busy just coping we have no time to develop. Time is money, because it takes time to earn, to achieve, to learn how to manage life's complexity. We need to control both—so we can enjoy achievement in the working world and in the more important world of family and friends.

Best luck to you, and may you have a life with both time and money well spent.

Index